day by day in
Chicago Cubs history

ACKNOWLEDGEMENTS

The authors would like to express their gratitude to the following:

L. Robert Davids, Ted Ditullio, Raymond Gonzalez, Ron Liebman, Bill Loughman, Emil Rothe, John Tattersall, W. A. Wilson, Buck Peden of the Chicago Cubs, and especially...The Chicago Public Library, where we loitered for eons through rolls and rolls of microfilm.

Leisure Press
P.O. Box 3
West Point, N.Y. 10996

day by day in Chicago Cubs history

official publication of
CHICAGO NATIONAL LEAGUE BALL CLUB, INC.

by
ART AHRENS
EDDIE GOLD
Edited by
Buck Peden

A publication of Leisure Press.
P.O. Box 3, West Point, N.Y. 10996
Copyright © 1982 by
Chicago National League Ball Club, Inc.
All Rights reserved. Printed in the U.S.A.

ISBN/ 88011-048-1
Library of Congress Number: 82-81296
Text photographs: Courtesy of the Chicago Cubs
Cover design: Henry Neu

CONTENTS

Philip K. Wrigley, former owner of the Chicago Cubs.

1
THIS DATE IN CHICAGO CUBS HISTORY

JANUARY

January 10

1963 — Owner P. K. Wrigley hires retired Air Force Colonel Robert V. Whitlow as the first "athletic director" of a major league club. The experiment ends with Whitlow's departure on January 7, 1965.

January 11

1977 — Cubs trade outfielder Rick Monday and pitcher Mike Garman to the Dodgers for first baseman Bill Buckner, shortstop Ivan De Jesus, and pitcher Jeff Albert.

January 16

1916 — Chewing gum magnate William Wrigley, Jr., becomes a minority stockholder in the Cubs ($50,000) when Charles Weeghman purchases the team from Charles P. Taft at the Majestic Club dinner held at Chicago's Great Northern Hotel.

January 26

1932 — Cub owner William Wrigley, Jr., dies at age 70 in Phoenix, Arizona.

January 31

1931 — Ernie Banks is born in Dallas, Texas.

FEBRUARY

February 1

1898 — Cap Anson is fired after having played 22 years with the Cubs, the last 19 as manager.

February 2

1876 — William A. Hulbert, the Cubs first owner, organizes the National League at New York's Grand Central Hotel. Charter teams are Boston, Chicago, Cincinnati, Hartford, Louisville, New York, Philadelphia, and St. Louis.

February 11

1977 — Cubs trade two-time batting champion third baseman Bill Madlock and infielder Rob Sperring to the Giants for outfielder Bobby Murcer, third baseman Steve Ontiveros, and pitcher Andy Muhlstock.

February 14

1887 — Cubs sell Mike "King" Kelly to Boston for the then unheard of sum of $10,000.

The Cubs acquired Bobby Murcer as part of the deal that sent Bill Madlock and Rob Sperring to the Giants.

Ken Hubbs tragically died in a plane crash in the prime of his career.

February 15

1964 — Cub second baseman Ken Hubbs is killed in a plane crash near Provo, Utah, while en route to Colton, California. Hubbs had gained renown by playing 78 consecutive games at second base, handling 418 chances without error in his rookie season of 1962.

MARCH

March 7

1979 — All-time Cub great Hack Wilson is elected to Baseball's Hall of Fame.

March 27

1902 — The nickname "Cubs" is coined by the **Chicago Daily News** when an unbylined column notes that "Frank Selee will devote his strongest efforts on the team work of the new Cubs this year." It takes several years before the new nickname is fully accepted, the old name Colts being more frequently used at this time.

March 29

1954 — Cub manager Phil Cavarretta tells owner P.K. Wrigley his low esteem of the team's chances in the upcoming pennant race and is replaced by Stan Hack following an exhibition game in Dallas.

March 30

1956 — Cubs trade slugger Hank Sauer to the Cardinals for outfielder Pete Whisenant and $10,000.

APRIL

April 2

1908 — Cubs chase umpire at Birmingham, Alabama, exhibition game. Umpire sues for $5,000, having claimed Cub third baseman, Harry Steinfeldt was deliberately spiking him. The outcome of the case is at this time unknown.

April 4

1892 — Cubs trade star second baseman Fred Pfeffer to Louisville for James Canavan and an undisclosed amount of money.

1905 — Cap Anson is elected City Clerk of Chicago on the Democratic ticket.

April 5

1979 — In their earliest opening day in history, the Cubs lose to the Mets, 10-6, at Wrigley Field.

April 6

1971 — Billy Williams homers in the tenth inning for a 2-1 Cub victory as Fergie Jenkins outduels the Cardinals' Bob Gibson in the opener at Wrigley Field.

1973 — Reliever Mike Marshall walks Rick Monday with the bases loaded in the ninth inning as the Cubs beat the Expos, 3-2, in the opener at Chicago. Tony La Russa, later a White Sox manager scores the winning run — his only run in a Cub uniform.

April 7

1973 — Ron Santo's two out single in the tenth inning gives the Cubs a 3-2 victory over the Expos at Wrigley Field.

April 8

1969 — Willie Smith hits a two-run pinch homer in the 11th inning as the Cubs nip the Phillies, 7-6, in the opener at Wrigley Field. Ernie Banks had two homers for the Cubs.

April 9

1969 — Billy Williams hits four consecutive doubles as the Cubs beat the Phillies, 11-3, behind Bill Hands at Wrigley Field.

April 10

1962 — Baseball makes its major league debut in Texas as the Houston Colt .45's (Astros) gun down the Cubs, 11-2, sending the Chicagoans on a seven game losing streak.

April 11

1928 — Pat Malone is charged with six unearned runs in the eighth inning of his major league debut as the Reds trounce the Cubs, 9-3, at Cincinnati, in a game that is also Kiki Cuyler's Cub debut.

1955 — Cubs win their sixth consecutive opener as they beat the Reds, 7-5, at Cincinnati.

April 12

1932 — Stan Hack makes his major league debut in the opener at Cincinnati, getting a double and scoring a run in five at bats, but the Reds rally for four runs in the ninth inning to beat the Cubs, 5-4.

1977 — Cubs owner Philip K. Wrigley dies at age 82 in the Elkhorn, Wisconsin, hospital near his Lake Geneva estate.

April 13

1976 — Rick Monday's pop-single into short centerfield in the ninth inning gives the Cubs a 5-4 victory over the Mets before an opening day record crowd of 44,818 (broken in 1978) at Wrigley Field. Jerry Morales hit two homers earlier for the Cubs.

April 14

1899 — In their most one-sided opening day victory, the Cubs trample Louisville, 15-1, at Louisville, behind seven doubles, including two each by Bill Lange and Jimmy Ryan. Clark Griffith goes all the way for the win.

1922 — Cap Anson dies in Chicago's St. Luke's Hospital at the age of 70.

1925 — In the first regular season Cub game to be broadcast on radio, with Quin Ryan at the mike for WGN from the grandstand roof, the Cubs beat the Pirates, 8-2, before 38,000 at the season opener in Chicago. Grover Alexander goes the route for the Cubs, and hits a single, a double, and a home run.

1926 — Charlie Root makes his Cub debut, going all the way as the Cubs beat the Reds, 9-2, at Cincinnati. The Cubs score seven runs in the fifth inning and are aided by four double plays.

1936 — Billy Herman sets a major league opening day record with a single, three doubles, and a home run as the Cubs and Lon Warneke rough up Dizzy Dean and the Cardinals, 12-7, at St. Louis. Frank Demaree hits two homers, and Chuck Klein and Gabby Hartnett one each for the Cubs.

1966 — Ty Cline gets five hits and two RBI as the Cubs beat the Giants, 9-4, in San Francisco.

1978 — A record opening-day crowd of 45,777 at Wrigley Field sees the Cubs edge the Pirates, 5-4, on Larry Biittner's homer in the ninth inning. Biittner hit the first pitch leading off the inning. Arthur Food Services, Inc., begins concession operations at Wrigley Field.

April 15

1941 — Lou Stringer makes four errors in his debut at second base, but the Cubs beat the Pirates, 7-4, in their opener at Wrigley Field. Claude Passeau goes all the way and Bill Nicholson hits a two-run homer.

April 16

1906 — Johnny Evers and Frank Chance are ejected from the game as the Reds beat the Cubs, 3-0, in Cincinnati. Joe Tinker gets into a fight with a fan outside the park.

1938 — The Cubs trade pitchers Curt Davis and Clyde Shoun and outfielder Tuck Stainback, plus $185,000 to the Cardinals for Dizzy Dean.

1946 — The Cubs stun the Reds, 4-3, scoring four runs in the ninth inning in the opener at Crosley Field. Bob Scheffing, rusty from three years in the Navy, is the last available pinch-hitter, but delivers game-winning, two-run single.

1948 — In the first Chicago baseball game telecast on WGN-TV with Jack Brickhouse at the mike, the White Sox beat the Cubs, 4-1, scoring three runs off starter Hank Borowy in the first inning at Wrigley Field.

1955 — Randy Jackson, Ernie Banks and Dee Fondy hit three consecutive homers in the second inning, but the Cardinals beat the Cubs, 12-11, on Wally Moon's pop-fly single in the 11th inning in St. Louis.

1972 — Burt Hooton pitches a no-hitter in freezing weather at Wrigley Field as the Cubs beat the Phillies, 4-0.

April 17

1896 — The Cubs score 10 runs in the first inning en route to a 14-3 victory over host Louisville. Bill Dahlen had a triple and a homer in the first inning and drove in four runs.

1898 — The Cubs score 10 runs in the fourth inning, including triples by Bill Everett, Barry McCormick, Tim Donahue and Jimmy Ryan and beat St. Louis, 14-1, behind Walt Thornton, at St. Louis.

1934 — Lon Warneke strikes out 13 and pitches a one-hitter as the Cubs whip the Reds, 6-0, in the opener at Cincinnati. Adam Comorosky singles with one out in the ninth to spoil the no-hit bid as 30,247 Cincy fans boo.

This Date In Chicago Cubs History

1945 — The Cubs beat the Cardinals 3-2 on Don Johnson's ninth-inning single in the opener at Wrigley Field. Bill Nicholson beat rookie left fielder Red Schoendienst's throw to the plate. It was Schoendienst's major league debut.

1951 — Sam Snead slams a golf ball against the Wrigley Field scoreboard in pre-game ceremonies and then the Cubs win the opener at Wrigley Field, 8-3, over Cincinnati, highlighted by Dee Fondy's bases-loaded triple in the second inning. It was Fondy's first major league at bat.

1954 — The Cubs beat the Cindinals, 23-13, scoring 10 runs in the fifth inning. Randy Jackson had four hits, including a homer that bounded off an apartment building on Waveland Avenue.

1962 — Ken Hubbs gets five hits, a double and four singles and scores two runs, but the Cubs lose, 10-6, to the Pirates at Wrigley Field.

1974 — George Mitterwald hits three homers, including a grandslam, and drives in eight runs as the Cubs beat the Pirates, 18-9, at Wrigley Field.

1976 — Mike Schmidt hits four consecutive homers as the Phillies overcome a 13-2 Cub lead for an 18-16 victory in 10 innings at Wrigley Field.

April 18

1930 — Lon Warneke makes his Cub debut in the sixth inning and is charged with two hits, five walks and five runs as the Cardinals crush the Cubs, 11-1, on Wild Bill Hallahan's two-hitter at St. Louis.

1962 — Ernie Banks hits his 300th homer off Dick Farrell in the 10th inning, to beat the Astros, 3-2, behind Dick Ellsworth. It was the Cubs' first victory of the year at Wrigley Field.

April 19

1902 — Reds pitcher Bob Ewing makes a wild major league debut, walking 10 batters, seven in the fifth inning in a 9-5 loss to the Cubs in Cincinnati.

1980 — Behind 9-1 after 5-1/2 innings, the Cubs rally for four runs in the sixth inning and seven runs in the eighth to beat the Mets, 12-9, at Wrigley Field. Dave Kingman drives in six runs with a two-run homer in the sixth and a grandslammer in the eighth — after the Mets had intentionally walked Bill Buckner to get at Kingman. In the same game, Cub rightfielder Carlos Lezcano collects his second major league hit, both of which were home runs.

April 20

1888 — Jimmy Ryan hits his first leadoff homer as the Cubs beat Indianapolis, 5-4, at Indianapolis. Ryan hit 22 leadoff homers in his career, 20 with the Cubs.

Ernie Banks hit his 300th career homer off Dick Farrell of the Astros on April 18, 1962.

1916 — Cubs play their first game at Clark and Addison (now Wrigley Field) and beat the Reds, 7-6, in 11 innings on Vic Saier's RBI single. The Cubs scored two runs in the eighth inning and one in the ninth to send the game into extra innings before 20,000 fans. Cincy's Johnny Beall hit the first National League homer at the new ball park then called Weeghman Park and later Cubs Park before being officially named Wrigley Field in 1926.

1923 — The Cubs beat the Pirates, 12-11, on Gabby Hartnett's homer in the ninth inning at Wrigley Field. Hartnett and Barney Friberg hit two homers each, while Arnold Statz and Cliff Heathcote had one apiece for the Cubs. Charlie Grimm and Pie Traynor homered for the Pirates. It gave the Cubs 12 homers in two days.

1926 — Hall of Famer Hack Wilson hits his first homer as a Cub with the bases empty in the sixth inning off Wit Reinhart of the Cardinals. The Cubs won, 7-0, behind Wilbur Cooper at St. Louis.

1946 — The first Cub game is telecast over WBKB, with "Whispering" Joe Wilson at the microphone. But the Cubs lose their home opener to Harry "The Cat" Brecheen and the Cardinals, 2-0, before a crowd of 40,887.

April 21

1922 — The Cubs score seven runs in the seventh inning to beat the Reds, 8-3, at Chicago. Hack Miller goes three for four, including a two-run homer.

1964 — The Cubs score all their runs on homers by Jimmy Stewart, Ron Santo, Andre Rodgers, Billy Cowan and Billy Williams but lose, 8-5, to the Pirates at Wrigley Field. The Pirates also scored all their runs on homers, three-run blasts by Jim Pagliaroni and Gene Freese and solo shots by Roberto Clemente and Dick Schofield.

1966 — The Cubs trade pitchers Larry Jackson and Bob Buhl to the Phillies for first baseman John Herrnstein, outfielder Adolfo Phillips and an unknown pitcher named Ferguson Arthur Jenkins.

April 22

1934 — Lon Warneke pitches his second consecutive one-hitter, a fifth-inning double by Ripper Collins, as the Cubs shell the Cardinals, 15-2, in St. Louis. Chuck Klein and Gabby Hartnett led the 22-hit attack with a homer each. Victims of the assault were the Dean brothers, Dizzy and Daffy.

1980 — Ivan DeJesus hits for the cycle and Barry Foote drives in eight runs, including a game-winning grandslam homer with two out in the ninth inning to beat the Cardinals, 16-12, after spotting them a 12-6 lead at Wrigley Field. In the eighth inning, Foote's solo homer tied the score.

April 23

1914 — Gala opener at Weeghman Park (Wrigley Field) as Chicago Whales of the Federal League beat the Kansas City Packers, 9-1, Art Wilson hits two homers for the Whales, thus becoming the first player to homer at the Wrigley Field site.

1926 — Jimmy Cooney steals home on a double steal with Mike Gonzales, who takes second, as the Cubs crush the Reds, 18-1, at Chicago. Charlie Grimm collects four singles and Sparky Adams two doubles for the Cubs.

1948 — Roy Smalley makes his first error in a Cub uniform (it does not figure in the scoring) as the Cardinals beat the Cubs, 1-0, in the home opener at Wrigley Field behind Harry Brecheen. Loser Johnny Schmitz gives up only two hits.

April 24

1931 — Manager Rogers Hornsby hits three consecutive home runs, driving in eight runs as the Cubs beat the Pirates, 10-6, at Pittsburgh.

1957 — Cub pitchers walk nine Reds in the fifth inning (four by Moe Drabowsky, three by Jack Collum, and two by Jim Brosnan) as the Cubs lose, 9-5, at Cincinnati.

1958 — Lee Walls hits three home runs and drives in eight runs as the Cubs rip the Dodgers, 15-2, at the Coliseum. Cub pitcher Gene Fodge wins his first — and only — major league game.

1962 — Sandy Koufax strikes out 18 batters as the Dodgers trip the Cubs, 10-2, at Wrigley Field.

April 25

1876 — First game in Cub history! Albert Spalding pitches the first National League shutout as the Cubs win, 4-0, at Louisville, for the first of Spalding's eight shut- that season. Paul Hines scores the first Cub run in the second inning on a wild throw.

Surehanded Roy Smalley flips the ball to teammate Wayne Terwilliger for the first out of a double play.

1976 — Cub center fielder Rick Monday rescues the U.S. flag in the fourth inning from two radicals trying to set it afire in the outfield at Dodger Stadium, but the Dodgers edge the Cubs, 5-4, in ten innings.

April 26

1905 — Jack McCarthy of the Cubs becomes the only outfielder in major league history to throw out three runners at home plate, each of which became the second out in double plays. Cubs beat the Pirates, 2-1, in Pittsburgh.

1941 — The Cubs are the first team in the major leagues to install an organ. Roy Nelson plays a pre-game program of classical and soulful compositions, but the Cubs hit some sour notes by losing, 6-2, to the Cardinals' Max Lanier at Wrigley Field.

April 27

1922 — For the second straight day, Ray Grimes bats home the tying and winning runs as the Cubs beat the Cardinals, 6-4, at Wrigley Field.

1958 — Former Cub hero Hank Sauer, now with the Giants, hits into a triple play in the first inning, pitcher Dick Drott to second baseman Tony Taylor to first baseman Dale Long as the Cubs win, 5-4, at Seals Stadium, San Francisco.

Rick Monday rescues the American flag from two radicals trying to set it afire during a game against the Dodgers.

Cubs win their 11th in a row, nipping the Pirates, 1-0, behind Joe Decker at Pittsburgh. Ten of the victories came at Wrigley Field.

April 28

1906 — The Cubs beat the Reds, 1-0, when manager Frank Chance steals home in the ninth inning at West Side Grounds in Chicago.

1972 — Jim Hickman hits two homers and drives in six runs as the Cubs outlast the Reds, 10-8, at Wrigley Field.

April 29

1898 — Frank Chance makes his debut in a Cub uniform as the Cubs beat Louisville, 16-2, at West Side Grounds. Chance, who replaced Tim Donahue behind the plate in the eighth inning, was allegedly ordered by pitcher Clark Griffith to drop a pop-up, allowing a run to score, because he had a superstition against shutouts.

1913 — The Cincinnati Reds appear at West Side Grounds **wearing the uniforms of the White Sox**, losing to the Cubs, 7-2. The Reds' trainer had inadvertently left the uniforms behind when the team left St. Louis.

1935 — Cubs score ten runs in the eighth inning to edge the Pirates, 12-11, at Pittsburgh. Kiki Cuyler gets two hits in the inning, including the game winner, while Phil Cavarretta drives in four runs with a double and a homer. In the fifth inning there was a free-for-all in which Billy Jurges and Pop Joiner of the Cubs, and Cookie Lavagetto and Guy Bush of the Pirates are ejected.

1979 — Behind 5-0 with two out in the ninth and two on, the Cubs rally to beat the Braves, 6-5, at Atlanta, capped by Bobby Murcer's three-run home run.

April 30

1899 — A paid crowd of 27,489 — the largest in baseball history up to that time — jams the West Side Grounds to watch the Cubs beat the Cardinals, 4-0, behind Jimmy Callahan's 12-hit shutout.

1946 — Pitcher Hugh Casey walks pinch-hitter Dom Dallesandro on four pitches with the bases loaded in the 11th inning as the Cubs beat the Dodgers, 2-1, at Wrigley Field.

1949 — Rocky Nelson of the Cardinals gets a game-winning inside-the-park home run in the ninth inning when Andy Pafko's catch — ? — is ruled a trap by umpire Al Barlick. Pafko, believing he caught it cleanly, races in with the ball while Nelson circles the bases, turning a 3-2 Cub victory into a 4-3 Cub loss at Wrigley Field.

1970 — Billy Williams plays his 1,000th consecutive game but the Braves beat the Cubs, 9-2, at Atlanta Stadium.

MAY

May 1

1879 — In his debut as Cub manager, Cap Anson helps the team to a 4-3 victory over Syracuse with two singles and a run batted in at the season opener in Chicago's Lakefront Park.

1914 — Cubs complete a triple play in the second inning against the Cardinals at Chicago, centerfielder Jim Johnston to third baseman Tommy Leach to shortstop Heinie Zimmerman to catcher Roger Bresnahan. Cardinals win, 2-0, on Hank Robinson's two-hitter.

1927 — Chuck Tolson becomes the first Cub to hit a pinch-hit, grandslam homer when he connects off Remy Kremer of the Pirates in the seventh inning at Forbes Field. But the Cubs lose, 7-6, in the bottom of the ninth when Charlie Root walks the bases full and Paul Waner singles home the winning runs.

1964 — The Cubs score 10 runs in the first inning, with Billy Williams driving in a club record five runs on a grandslam homer and a single. Williams drives in another run with an eighth-inning double as the Cubs kick the Colt .45's, 11-3, at Houston.

1973 — Billy Williams, Ron Santo and Jose Cardenal homer in the fourth inning as the Cubs beat the Dodgers, 9-5, at Dodger Stadium behind Burt Hooton.

May 2

1876 — Ross Barnes hits the first home run in National League history, an inside-the-park smash off Bill Cherokee in Cincinnati, as the Cubs crush the Reds, 15-9.

1910 — President William Howard Taft watches the Cubs lose, 5-2, to the Pirates at Pittsburgh.

1917 — Fred Toney of Cincinnati and Jim "Hippo" Vaughn of the Cubs pitch a double no-hitter for the first nine innings at Wrigley Field. The Reds win, 1-0, on two hits in the 10th inning, Jim Thorpe driving in the only run.

1948 — Rookie Cub outfielder Hal Jeffcoat hits two doubles in the eighth inning and the Cubs score seven runs en route to a 13-4 romp over the Cardinals at St. Louis. Peanuts Lowrey goes four-for-five and Bob Chipman picks up the win in relief.

1956 — Cub third baseman Don Hoak strikes out six times as the Giants beat the Cubs, 6-5, in 17 innings at Wrigley Field. The teams used 48 players — 25 by the Giants, 23 by the Cubs.

1958 — Behind 7-0 after six innings, the Cubs rally to beat the Braves, 8-7, on two Moose Moryn homers, the clincher coming in the ninth inning off Dick Littlefield, at Wrigley Field.

1976 — Jose Cardenal gets six hits (four singles, a double, and a home run) and drives in four runs, including the game winner, as the Cubs edge the Giants, 6-5, in 14 innings, at San Francisco.

May 3

1896 — Cubs hit nine triples in one game, including three by Bill Dahlen, in a 16-7 romp over St. Louis. An overflow crowd of 17,231 at West Side Grounds caused the umpire to rule any ball hit into the crowd a ground-rule triple.

1931 — Billy Jurges makes his big league debut, subbing for third baseman Les Bell late in the game, and flying out in his lone at bat. Cubs beat the Reds, 13-1, at Chicago, behind homers by Bell and Hack Wilson. Kiki Cuyler and Rogers Hornsby get three hits apiece.

May 4

1897 — Cap Anson Day at West Side Grounds as the long-time Cub player-manager is given a silver dining service and numerous other testimonials. Anson goes one-for-three as the Cubs beat St. Louis, 5-2, in the home opener.

1923 — Cub utility man Marty Callaghan steals home in the tenth inning to beat the Cardinals, 2-1, at St. Louis. In the eighth inning, Hack Miller ties it up with a pinch hit homer.

1929 — Pitcher Pat Malone gets three singles and two RBI's, Hack Wilson and Kiki Cuyler get two doubles each, and Rogers Hornsby homers as the Cubs beat the Phillies, 16-0, at Baker Bowl. Cubs then win second game, 9-7.

1937 — Rip Collins, Joe Marty, and John Bottarini homer in the eighth inning as the Cubs crush the Phillies, 14-7, at Philadelphia, scoring six runs in the seventh inning and five in the eighth.

1960 — Lou Boudreau is summoned from the radio booth to succeed Charlie Grimm as Cub manager. Grimm, in turn, replaces Boudreau at the mike as the Cubs beat the Pirates, 5-1, behind Dick Ellsworth at Wrigley Field.

1963 — Braves pitchers commit six balks, including three by Bob Shaw in the third inning, issue eight walks and a wild pitch as the Cubs win, 7-5, at Milwaukee. In the meantime, Lou Brock steals two bases for the Cubs.

May 5

1876 — In the National League's first 1-0 game, George Bradley of St. Louis beats Al Spalding of the Cubs at the river city.

1900 — Jimmy Ryan hits the 20th leadoff homer of his career, and his last as a Cub, as Chicago beats Noodles Hahn and the Reds, 4-3, at West Side Grounds.

1938 — Cubs score 12 runs in the eighth inning to beat the Phillies, 21-2, at Wrigley Field, behind Al Epperly. Joe Marty collects four hits, scores four runs, and drives in four, while Augie Galan gets three hits, three runs, and drives in four runs with a triple and a homer.

1946 — Cubs score 11 runs in the seventh inning as pitcher Hank Borowy drives in four of them with two doubles, and breeze to a 13-1 win over the Phillies before 45,505 at Wrigley Field.

May 6

1922 — Cubs pitcher Vic Aldridge gets five hits (most by a Cub pitcher) in five trips, scoring once and driving in a run as the Cubs beat the Pirates, 11-7, at Pittsburgh.

1941 — Cubs trade second baseman Billy Herman to the Dodgers for infielder Johnny Hudson, outfielder Charlie Gilbert and $40,000.

May 7

1880 — Cub outfielder George Gore goes six-for-six (all singles) as the Cubs beat Providence, 20-7, at Lakefront Park, behind Larry Corcoran.

1934 — Bill Lee blanks the Phillies, 2-0, in his first major league start at Wrigley Field.

1944 — Charlie Grimm begins his second term as Cub manager, replacing Jimmy Wilson after Roy Johnson served as interim field boss for one day following a 13-game losing streak. This is the longest in Cub history to date.

May 8

1877 — The defending champion Cubs open their second season with a 6-5 victory over Hartford at Chicago. Cap Anson and John Glenn (not the astronaut) collect three hits each, and winning pitcher George Bradley contributes a two run single in the second inning.

1890 — Cubs score 12 runs in the sixth inning in an 18-9 victory over the Reds at West Side Park, after being behind, 9-4, in the bottom of the sixth. Cub pitcher Bill Hutchison's home run in the fourth inning bounces off a horse and carriage in centerfield, while Howard Earl's grandslammer in the sixth lands on Congress Street.

1925 — Cubs play the Braves in Boston, in a game that National League president John Heydler declares a golden jubilee contest, Chicago and Boston being the only charter members left as the league begins its 50th season. Braves win, 5-2.

May 9

1963 — Ernie Banks makes 22 putouts at first base as the Cubs beat the Pirates, 3-1, on Dick Ellsworth's two-hitter at Chicago.

1967 — Ron Santo gets five hits in five at bats as the Cubs clip the Giants, 10-2, at Wrigley Field.

May 10

1876 — In the first home game in Cub history, played at 23rd and State Streets, Albert Spalding shuts out the Cincinnati Reds, 6-0.

The great Stan Musial on his last trip to Chicago as an active player receives a gift from The Cubs.

May 11

1934 — Cubs complete a triple play in the eighth inning against the Dodgers at Wrigley Field, first baseman Dolph Camilli to shortstop Billy Jurges. Former Cub Hack Wilson hits into the triple play, but the Bums pound the Cubs, 13-1.

1955 — Ernie Banks hits his first grandslam homer in the first inning and Dee Fondy clouts a three-run homer in the fifth as the Cubs beat the Dodgers, 10-8, at Wrigley Field, halting the Brooklyn winning streak at 11 games.

May 12

1930 — Cliff Heathcote, Hack Wilson, Clyde Beck and Charlie Grimm hit home runs in the seventh inning but the Cubs lose to the Giants, 14-12, after spotting them a 14-0 lead. Heathcote and Clyde Beck each have two homers in the game, while Mel Ott, Larry Benton, and Fred Leach homer for the Giants, at Wrigley Field.

1955 — Sam Jones pitches a no-hitter against the Pirates at Wrigley Field, walking the bases loaded in the ninth, then striking out the side for a 4-0 victory. It is the first no-hitter at Wrigley Field in 38 years.

1959 — Earl Averill hits a pinch-hit, grandslam homer off Lew Burdette in the bottom of the ninth to give the Cubs a 7-3 win over the Braves at Wrigley Field. Earlier in the inning, Moose Moryn's home run had tied the game for the Cubs.

1970 — Ernie Banks hits his 500th career home run and produces his 1,600th RBI in the second inning off Atlanta Braves pitcher Pat Jarvis at Wrigley Field. Cubs win, 4-3, in eleven innings on Ron Santo's infield single.

May 13

1942 — Boston Braves pitcher Jim Tobin hits three home runs to beat the Cubs, 6-5, in Wrigley Field.

1958 — Stan Musial, pinch-hitting for the Cardinals, gets his 3,000th hit, a double off Moe Drabowsky in the sixth inning as St. Louis beats the Cubs, 5-3, at Wrigley Field.

1962 — Barney Schultz (who later becomes a Cub pitching coach) wins both ends of a doubleheader in relief against the Phillies, 8-7 and 8-5, at Wrigley Field. The second game marks Schultz's ninth consecutive appearance in as many games, a record for a relief pitcher. George Altman hits two homers for the Cubs while Ernie Banks, Billy Williams, Ken Hubbs and Lou Brock collect one apiece.

1969 — Ernie Banks drives in seven runs, posting RBI number 1,500, as the Cubs beat San Diego, 19-0, at Wrigley Field, behind Dick Selma.

May 14

1878 — Cubs play their first game at Lakefront Park (Michigan and Randolph), losing 5-3 to Indianapolis in the home opener.

1893 — Cubs play their first Sunday home game, losing to the Reds, 13-12, at West Side Grounds before 13,233 paid. This was also the first game played at the Taylor and Wolcott (then Lincoln) location, their home base through 1915.

1912 — Heinie Zimmerman extends his hitting streak to 23 straight games with a single and a double as the Cubs beat the Phillies, 2-0, at West Side Grounds. Zimmerman was stopped in his next game.

1927 — Pitcher Guy Bush goes the distance as the Cubs beat the Braves, 7-2, in 18 innings, at Boston. Sparky Adams collects four hits, Jimmy Cooney drives in the winning run, and Charlie Robertson — who five years earlier pitched a perfect game for the White Sox — goes 17-1/3 innings for the Braves.

1967 — Billy Williams gets five hits as the Cubs beat the Dodgers, 6-3, in 11 innings, in the second game of a doubleheader, with Ken Holtzman the winner, at Los Angeles. Dodgers won first game, 2-1.

1978 — Dave Kingman smashes three home runs and a single, driving in eight runs as the Cubs beat the Dodgers, 10-7, in 15 innings at Los Angeles. Dave's three-run blast in the top of the 15th provides the margin.

May 15

1960 — In his Cub debut, Don Cardwell pitches a no-hit game, beating the Cardinals, 4-0, in the second game of a doubleheader, at Wrigley Field. Cub leftfielder Moose Moryn makes a running, shoe-string catch of Joe Cunningham's sinking liner for the final out.

1971 — Billy Williams powers his 300th career home run as hosting Cubs down San Diego, 6-4.

May 16

1972 — Rick Monday hits three home runs in one game as the Cubs beat the Phillies, 8-1, behind Burt Hooton at Philadelphia.

May 17

1923 — Cubs score seven runs in the seventh inning to beat the Phillies, 7-4, at Philadelphia. All seven runs score after two are out, and Gabby Hartnett drives across runs number five and six with a two-run double. Winning pitcher Grover Alexander walks Curt Walker in the first inning to end his streak of 51 consecutive innings without issuing a free pass.

1927 — Cubs beat the Braves, 4-3, in 22 innings, as Charlie Grimm's single drives in Hack Wilson with the winning run, at Boston. Wilson goes four-for-eight as the Cubs collect 20 hits to the Braves' 15. Winning pitcher Bob Osborn pitches the last 14 innings for the Cubs while loser Bob Smith goes all the way for the Braves. This is the longest game, inning-wise, in Cub history. Time of the game is four hours, thirteen minutes.

1939 — Cubs play a 19-inning, 9-9 tie with the Dodgers at Wrigley Field. Dodger Pete Coscarart's double with two out in the ninth ties up the game.

1977 — Cubs annihilate the Padres, 23-6, at Wrigley Field. Larry Biittner, Steve Ontiveros, and Gene Clines homer in the third inning, while Biittner, Jerry Morales, and Bobby Murcer hit consecutive homers in the fifth. Davey Rosello hits the seventh Cub homer in the eighth inning to tie the club record for most home runs in one game.

1979 — Dave Kingman smashes three home runs and drives in six runs as the Phillies beat the Cubs, 23-22, in ten innings, at Chicago, having earlier led by a 21-9 margin. Bill Buckner hits a grandslammer for the Cubs and drives in seven runs for the game. Mike Schmidt hits two homers for the Phillies, including the game winner in the tenth. Bob Boone drives in five runs for the Phils and Larry Bowa collects five hits. It is the largest scoring game since the Cubs beat the Phillies, 26-23, on August 25, 1922.

May 18

1898 — Cub pitcher Walt Thornton hits three consecutive batters in the fourth inning as St. Louis beats the Cubs, 11-4, at West Side Grounds. Former Cub George Decker gets four hits for the Cardinals.

1947 — A paid crowd of 46,572 jams its way into Wrigley Field to see Jackie Robinson of the Dodgers make his Chicago debut. Robinson goes hitless, but Brooklyn wins, 4-2.

1950 — Al Walker of the Cubs and Monte Irvin of the Giants each hit grandslam homers in the sixth inning as the Giants beat the Cubs, 10-4, in a game called after six innings because of rain, at the Polo Grounds. This is the only time in major league history that both teams hit grandslammers in the same inning.

1973 — Glenn Beckert hits safely in his 26th straight game as the Cubs beat the Phillies, 9-2, at Philadelphia. Beckert's streak is broken the next day.

May 19

1887 — Jimmy Ryan, normally stationed in the outfield, pitches a 9-6 complete game victory over Washington at the Capitol, helping his own cause with a single and a triple.

1895 — Cub pitcher Bill "Adonis" Terry doubles and homers in the third inning as the Cubs score eight runs that inning en route to a 14-9 win over Brooklyn at West Side Grounds. Terry's home run is a fluke, coming when the ball rolls into a hole near the outfield fence, enabling him to circle the bases.

1928 — Cubs win their 13th consecutive game as they edge the Braves, 3-2, at Wrigley Field on pitcher Charlie Root's sacrifice fly. Hack Wilson homers for the Cubs. Streak ended next day.

1941 — Cub pitcher Claude Passeau hits a grandslam home run off Hugh Casey in the second inning and the Cubs score nine runs that frame, in coasting to a 14-1 victory over the Dodgers at Wrigley Field. Brooklyn manager Leo Durocher protests the game, but to no avail, claiming the Cubs were over the 25-man player limit.

May 20

1895 — Cubs slaughter the Phillies, 24-6, at West Side Grounds, sparked by a 25-hit attack. Cub second baseman Asa Stewart hits an inside-the-park grandslam homer, and Cub pitcher Clark Griffith collects five hits in as many at bats, all of them singles. Phillies make 13 errors.

1927 — At the Cub-Dodger game in Brooklyn, Ebbets Field fans shower umpire Pete McLaughlin with hundreds of pop bottles and one whiskey bottle. McLaughlin picks up the whiskey bottle but discards it when he finds the contents are empty. In the meantime, Tony Kaufman and the Cubs tip the Dodgers, 7-5.

1962 — Rookie Cub second baseman Ken Hubbs collects eight singles in a doubleheader with the Phillies at Philadelphia, going three-for-three in the opener, and five-for-five in the nightcap. Lou Brock hits a grandslam homer in the second inning of game one, and the Cubs win both games, 6-4 and 11-2, Cal Koonce and Bob Buhl being the winning pitchers.

1967 — Cubs beat the Dodgers, 20-3, at Wrigley Field, as Adolfo Phillips drives in six runs, Randy Hundley hits a grandslam homer, Ted Savage steals home, and Glenn Beckert hits an inside-the-park homer. From the Dodger dugout, Don Drysdale waves a white flag of surrender in the seventh inning, and winning Cub pitcher Ken Holtzman leaves for the Army the next day.

May 21

1892 — Cubs win their 13th straight game as Bill Hutchison shuts out the Pirates, 1-0, on three hits at West Side Park, while the Cubs make only two safeties. Pittsburgh pitcher Jim Galvin has a no-hitter for 7-2/3 innings before Bill Dahlen singles home Malachi Kittredge (who had reached on an error) for the only run. Streak ended the following day.

1907 — A riot erupts at the Polo Grounds after the Cubs beat Christy Mathewson and the Giants, 3-2. The police fire their revolvers into the air to prevent the frenzied New York mob from hanging the Cubs to lampposts. Joe Tinker, one of the few batters who solved Matty's fadeaway pitch, gets two hits.

1927 — Lindbergh lands in Paris and the Cubs celebrate by sweeping the Dodgers at Brooklyn, 6-4, and 11-6, scoring nine runs in the ninth inning of game two. In that ninth inning, the Cubs send up five pinch-hitters, three of whom collect hits (Pete Scott, Chuck Tolson, and Gabby Hartnett), while the other two (Cliff Heathcote and Howie Freigau) draw walks. At the end of the game, Dodger coach Otto Miller leads an angry Ebbets Field mob after umpire Frank Wilson, but a policeman escorts him to safety.

1936 — Cubs trade outfielder Chuck Klein and pitcher Fabian Kowalik plus $50,000 to the Phillies for outfielder Ethan Allen and pitcher Curt Davis.

1955 — George Crowe's homer, the lone hit of the game, with one out in the ninth spoils Warren Hacker's no-hit bid, but the Cubs beat the Braves, 2-1, at Milwaukee's County Stadium.

May 22

1883 — Billy Sunday, who went on to become a famed evangelist, makes a swinging debut as a Cub, striking out four times in four trips against Boston's Jim Whitney, but the Cubs win, 4-3, behind Larry Corcoran, at Lakefront Park.

1946 — Cub shortstop Lennie Merullo and Ed Stanky of the Dodgers brawl, and Claude Passeau rips off Leo Durocher's jersey in a massive 10th inning rhubarb at Ebbets Field. Dodgers win, 2-1, in 13 innings. The next day, Merullo and Dixie Walker fight during batting practice, and the Dodgers win again, 2-1, in 11 innings.

May 23

1925 — Cubs trade catcher Bob O'Farrell to the Cardinals for catcher Mike Gonzales and third baseman Howie Freigau.

1926 — Hack Wilson becomes the first player to hit a home run off the Wrigley Field scoreboard in centerfield (then situated at ground level) in the fifth inning as the Cubs scalp the Braves, 14-8, thanks to a seven-run, eighth inning rally. Sparky Adams collects four hits for the Cubs, and the fans throw pop bottles at umpire Jim Sweeney for kicking Cub third baseman Howie Freigau out of the game. That night, Hack and several companions are arrested at a friend's apartment for drinking beer in violation of the Prohibition Act.

1961 — Ernie Banks makes his debut in leftfield as the Phillies edge the Cubs, 2-1, in 10 innings at Chicago. Ernie has one single in four at bats.

May 24

1920 — At the request of the Cub management, policemen disguised as sailors, teamsters, soldiers, ice wagon drivers, sewing machine agents, bootblacks and farmers raid the Wrigley Field bleachers and arrest 24 fans, making and taking bets. Sergeant George Cudmore hauls away the gamblers as Grover Alexander blanks the Phillies, 6-0.

1957 — In his first two major league at bats, Cub Frank Ernaga hits a solo homer in the second inning and a run-scoring triple in the fourth as Moe Drabowsky beats Warren Spahn and the Braves, 5-1, at Wrigley Field.

1963 — Cub catcher Dick Bertell gets five hits but the Colt .45's (Astros) beat the Cubs, 6-5, in 13 innings at Wrigley Field.

1969 — Ernie Banks hits the 12th and final grandslam home run of his career, off Jack Baldschun, as the Cubs beat the Padres, 7-5, at San Diego.

May 25

1898 — Bill Everett collects four singles and Sam Mertes gets two singles and three walks as the Cubs crush Baltimore, 20-4, at West Side Grounds.

1908 — Joe Tinker clouts one out of the park in the bottom of the ninth but is only credited with a double under ground rules of that time (the winning run was on first base; as the Cubs beat the Giants, 8-7, at West Side Grounds.

1981 — Behind 8-0 in the middle of the fourth inning, the Cubs rally to edge the Pirates, 10-9, in 11 innings at Wrigley Field.

May 26

1957 — Rookie Cub pitcher Dick Drott strikes out 15 batters (Hank Aaron four times) as the Cubs beat the Braves, 7-5, at Wrigley Field.

May 27

1884 — Fred Goldsmith becomes the first Cub pitcher to hit two home runs in one game as he leads the team to a 14-6 romp over Buffalo on their turf.

1956 — Thanks to Hobie Landrith's dropped third strike on batter Lindy McDaniel, Cub pitcher Jim Davis has four strikeouts in the sixth inning of the first game of a doubleheader, but the Cardinals beat the Cubs, 11-9, at St. Louis. Cardinals also win second game, 12-2.

May 28

1886 — Cubs beat Washington, 20-0, in their most lopsided shut-out victory in history, at the Capitol, with only two of their runs being earned. After the third inning, Cub pitcher Jim McCormick switches positions with rightfielder John Flynn.

1914 — Larry Cheney goes 13 innings as the Cubs beat the Cardinals, 4-3, in 16 innings, at Chicago. George Pearce is the winning pitcher in relief.

1925 — Cubs score 12 runs in the seventh inning on 11 hits en route to a 13-3 win over the Reds at Cincinnati. In the big inning, Barney Friberg doubles and triples, Charlie Grimm singles and doubles, and Arnold Statz and Wilbur Cooper, the Cub pitcher, gets two singles apiece.

May 29

1962 — Ernie Banks hits three home runs in one game, and Billy Williams, Bob Will, and George Altman hit one each but the Braves beat the Cubs, 11-9, in ten innings at Wrigley Field.

1966 — Ron Santo homers to beat the Braves, 3-2, connecting in the tenth inning at Wrigley Field. On the previous day, Ron's three-run homer in the 12th had also given the Cubs an 8-5 win over the visiting Braves.

May 30

1883 — Cubs take two from the Phillies, 15-8 in the opener and 22-4 in the second game, at Philadelphia. In the second game, Cubs score seven runs in the first inning and nine runs in the fifth, as Mike Kelly, Fred Pfeffer, and Tommy Burns get three hits apiece in the game.

1884 — Cub third baseman Ed Williamson becomes the first player in major league history to hit three home runs in one game, as the Cubs beat Buffalo, 12-2, in the second game of a doubleheader at Lakefront Park. Cubs also win first game, 11-10.

1890 — Bill Hutchison pitches and wins both ends of a doubleheader at Brooklyn, 6-4 in the morning and 11-7 in the afternoon. Hutchison goes the distance both times, and only three of the runs off him are earned.

1904 — Cub first baseman Frank Chance is hit by pitched balls three times in the first game and twice in the second contest, suffering a black eye and a cut forehead, as the Cubs split with the Reds at Cincinnati, losing the first one, 7-1, and winning the second, 5-2.

1906 — Cub pitcher Jack Pfiester fans 17 batters but the Cardinals beat the Cubs, 4-2, in 15 innings, at St. Louis.

1910 — Cubs win their 11th straight by beating St. Louis, 6-1, in the morning game, at West Side Grounds, behind Mordecai Brown. Cardinals win nightcap, 3-1.

1922 — Between the morning and afternoon games of a doubleheader, the Cubs trade Max Flack to the Cardinals for Cliff Heathcote. Cubs win both games, 4-1, and 3-1, at Wrigley Field. Flack goes zero-for-four in the opener as a Cub and one-for-four as a Card in game two, while Heathcote is zero-for-three as a Card in game one, and two-for-four as a Cub in the second game.

1927 — Cub shortstop Jimmy Cooney performs an unassisted triple play — the last in the National League to date — in the fourth inning of the morning game against the Pirates at Pittsburgh. Cooney snags Paul Waner's liner, steps on second to double Lloyd Waner, then tags Clyde Barnhart coming down from first. Cubs go on to win, 7-6, in 10 innings, but lose second game, 6-5, also in 10 innings. The Cub victory in game one halts the Pirate winning streak at 11 games.

1958 — Moose Moryn hits three home runs in the second game as the Cubs take a doubleheader from the Dodgers, 3-2 and 10-8, at Wrigley Field.

1963 — Ron Santo collects five hits in six trips, including a double, and scores twice as the Cubs whitewash the Mets, 12-0, in the first game of a doubleheader, behind the pitching of Larry Jackson. Cubs score ten runs in the fourth inning, high-lighted by a double steal by Santo and Billy Williams. Mets win second game, 2-1, at New York.

May 31

1903 — Cubs collect 17 hits — all of them singles — to beat the Cardinals, 17-4, at West Side Grounds, behind Jake Weimer. The Cardinals issue three walks and commit six errors.

1920 — Cub pitcher Grover Alexander homers in the bottom of the tenth inning to win his own game, 3-2, over the Reds at Wrigley Field. It is Alex's 11th straight win.

1948 — A record paid crowd of 46,965 at Wrigley Field sees the Cubs split a doubleheader with the Pirates, winning the opener 4-3, and dropping the second game, 4-2.

1954 — Pitcher Paul Minner, Randy Jackson, and Bill Serena homer in the fourth inning as the Cubs trounce the Cardinals, 14-4, at Wrigley Field. Minner was also the winning pitcher while going the distance.

1973 — Cubs score 10 runs, all unearned, in the first inning as they beat Houston, 16-8, at Wrigley Field. Doug Rader's muff with two out and nobody on in the bottom of the first opens up the floodgate.

JUNE

June 1

1919 — Pitcher Hippo Vaughn goes three-for-three and drives in the winning run in the seventh inning en route to a 3-1 victory over the Cardinals in St. Louis.

June 2

1908 — A bottle of ammonia explodes in Cub outfielder Jimmy Sheckard's eyes. Prompt remedies save his eyesight, but Pirates beat Cubs, 6-2, at Chicago.

1928 — Trailing 6-2 in the top of the eighth inning at Pittsburgh, the Cubs rally for eight runs to beat the Pirates, 10-6. Riggs Stephenson drives in the tying run with a two-run single, and Woody English scores the lead run when outfielder Paul Waner's overthrow goes into the Cub dugout.

1949 — Dutch Leonard, at 40, becomes the oldest Cub pitcher to hurl a complete game shutout as he blanks the Giants, 3-0, on three hits at the Polo Grounds. The Cubs scored their runs in the sixth inning on Harry Walker's fly and Hank Edwards' two-run homer.

1964 — Billy Williams, Ron Santo, and Billy Cowan homer in the fourth inning as Cubs beat Cardinals, 6-2, at Wrigley Field.

June 3

1971 — Ken Holtzman pitches his second no-hitter as the Cubs nip the Reds, 1-0, at Riverfront Stadium. He also scores the only run of the game.

June 4

1929 — Rogers Hornsby, Hack Wilson and Charlie Grimm hit homers in the fifth inning and Wilson and Earl Grace add homers as the Cubs tip the Giants, 10-9, at Wrigley Field.

1953 — The Cubs trade pitcher Bob Schultz, catcher Toby Atwell, first baseman Preston Ward, third baseman George Freese, outfielders Bob Addis and Gene Hermanski, and an estimated $100,000 to Pittsburgh for pitcher Howie Pollet, catcher Joe Garagiola and outfielders Catfish Metkovich and Ralph Kiner.

June 5

1885 — Cub second baseman Fred Pfeffer pitches a 7-4 complete-game victory over hosting Detroit. Pfeffer strikes out six and only two of Detroit's runs are earned.

1899 — Bill Everett goes five-for-five, including a double and triple, scores four runs and drives in three as the Cubs beat the Orioles, 9-4, at Baltimore. Orioles manager John McGraw almost incites a riot with his verbal attacks on umpire Nat Swartwood.

1916— Heinie Zimmerman steals home in the fourth inning as the Cubs beat the Braves, 1-0, at Boston.

1925— The Cubs complete a triple play in the seventh inning against the Dodgers, first baseman Barney Friberg to shortstop Rabbit Maranville at Wrigley Field. But Zack Wheat, who lined into the triple play hits two homers and the Dogers win, 7-5.

June 6

1885— The Cubs play their first game at West Side Park (Congress and Throop), beating St. Louis, 7-2. George Gore hit two homers and a triple and pitcher Johnny Clarkson went the route.

1898— Three Cubs have five hits each in a 15-2 romp over the Dodgers in Brooklyn. Bill Dahlen has three triples and two singles, while Frank Isbell and Bill Everett have five singles each.

1946— Frank Secory hits a grandslam homer off Dave Koslo as the Cubs beat the Giants, 10-6, in 12 innings at Wrigley Field.

1962— With Jim Davenport on second and Tom Haller on first for the Giants, and the hit-and-run on, Cub shortstop Andre Rodgers muffs a chance for an unassisted triple play when he drops Jose Pagan's line drive. The Giants went on to crush the Cubs, 11-4, at Wrigley Field.

1963— With the bases loaded and one out in the top of the 12th inning, Cub relief pitcher Lindy McDaniel picks Willie Mays off second and then strikes out Ed Bailey. McDaniel follows with a homer in the bottom of the inning and the Cubs win, 3-2, at Wrigley Field.

1981— Rookie sensation Fernando Valenzuela is knocked out in fourth inning, highlighted by Mike Tyson's three-run pinch homer as the Cubs beat the Dodgers, 11-5, before 30,556 at Wrigley Field.

June 7

1906— The Cubs score 11 runs in the first inning off aces Christy Mathewson and "Iron Man" McGinnity, beating the Giants, 19-0, at the Polo Grounds. Jack "Giant Killer" Pfiester hurls a three-hitter for the Cubs.

1926— The Cubs trade outfielder Joe Munson, infielder Maurice Shannon and cash to Indianapolis for infielder Henry Schreiber and outfielder Riggs Stephenson. Stephenson became the Cubs top batsman when he retired eight years later with a .336 average.

June 8

1900— Sam Mertes leads off with a homer, but the Cubs lose, 6-5, to the Braves in Boston. The following day Mertes again hits a leadoff homer and the Cubs beat the Braves, 6-2.

June 9

1954 — Ralph Kiner hits two homers and drives in three runs and Hank Sauer hits one homer and drives in three runs as the Cubs nip the Phillies, 6-5, at Wrigley Field, beating Robin Roberts.

1957 — Ernie Banks hits his 100th career homer with two on in the eighth inning off Robin Roberts and the Cubs beat the Phillies, 7-3, behind Dick Drott at Connie Mack Stadium.

1963 — Ernie Banks hits three homers, two off Sandy Koufax, but the Cubs lose, 11-8, to the Dodgers at Wrigley Field.

1978 — Rookie pitcher Dennis Lamp tosses a one-hitter as the Cubs down the Padres, 5-0, at Wrigley Field. Gene Richards spoils the no-hit effort with a single with two out in the sixth. Dave Kingman has a two-run homer, a bunt single and two spectacular catches in left field.

June 10

1973 — Rick Monday, Pat Bourque and Ron Santo homer in the first inning and the Cubs hang on for a 9-7 victory over the Reds at Wrigley Field.

June 11

1904 — Bob Wicker hurls a nine-inning no-hitter, allows a hit in the 10th inning and the Cubs tip the Giants, 1-0, when Frank Chance doubles and Johnny Evers singles him home in the 12th inning at the Polo Grounds. The loss snapped "Iron Man" McGinnity's 12-game winning streak.

1911 — Heinie Zimmerman hits two homers, a triple and two singles, and drives in nine runs (a Cub record) in a 20-2 romp over the Braves behind King Cole at West Side Grounds.

1952 — Hank Sauer hits three homers off Curt Simmons for all the Cub runs in a 3-0 victory over the Phillies at Wrigley Field.

1966 — Ernie Banks ties a modern major league record with three triples as the Cubs rout the Astros, 8-2, at the Astrodome.

1967 — Ted Savage steals home as the Cubs edge the Mets, 5-3, in the opener at Wrigley Field. In the second game, the Cubs sweep, 18-10, with Adolfo Phillips hitting three homers. The Cubs hit four more homers and the Mets add four to tie a major league record of 11 in a game. For the doubleheader, Phillips had four homers and two singles for eight RBI.

1981 — Cubs beat Giants, 2-1, in suspended game and 7-4 in regular game as Dick Tidrow gets saves in both games at Wrigley Field. They were the final games before the baseball strike.

June 12

1923 — Hack Miller drives in seven runs with two homers and a single as the Cubs edge the Braves, 12-11, at Wrigley Field. Miller's grandslam in the fifth ties the score, 7-7, and his two-run homer in the sixth gives the Cubs a temporary two-run lead. It was the Cubs' seventh straight win, and the Braves' eighth consecutive loss.

1935 — After getting a clubhouse tongue-lashing from manager Charlie Grimm (who imposed a ban on poker games), the Cubs beat the Phillies, 15-0, behind Larry French at Philadelphia. Phil Cavarretta gets a single, double, homer and four RBI's, and Chuck Klein hits a three-run home run.

1949 — Frankie Frisch is named Cub manager, replacing Charlie Grimm.

1955 — Harry Chiti, Randy Jackson and Dee Fondy homer as the Cubs beat Don Newcombe and the Dodgers, 9-5, in the opener at Ebbets Field. The Cubs pull a triple play in the seventh inning of the second game, third baseman Jackson to catcher Chiti to first baseman Fondy and back to Chiti, but the Cubs lose, 6-2.

June 13

1893 — Cub pitcher Sam Shaw hits five batters as the Cubs lose to Washington, 10-6, at the Capitol.

1904 — Frank Chance hits for the cycle as the Cubs and Mordecai Brown beat Christy Mathewson and the Giants, 3-2, at New York.

1905 — Christy Mathewson pitches a no-hitter and edges Mordecai Brown and the Cubs, 1-0, at West Side Grounds.

1925 — The Cubs beat the Braves, 2-0, on Charlie Grimm's two home runs at Wrigley Field.

1937 — The Cubs score 10 runs in the fifth inning en route to a 16-8 win over the Phillies at Philadelphia. Billy Herman and Rip Collins each collect four hits and three runs.

1950 — Bob Ramazzotti, Phil Cavarretta and Bob Borkowski homer in the sixth inning, and Roy Smalley hits a two-run homer in the 11th inning as the Cubs beat the Dodgers, 6-3, at Brooklyn.

June 14

1886 — Jocko Flynn strikes out 13 batters as the Cubs bounce Kansas City, 6-1, at West Side Park.

1901 — Cubs execute a triple play off Al "Kip" Selbach in the fourth inning, third baseman Fred Raymer to catcher Mike Kahoe to second baseman Clarence Childs to first baseman Charlie Dexter back to Childs and back to Kahoe, but the Giants win, 4-1, at West Side Grounds.

1949 — Ex-Cub first baseman Eddie Waitkus (then with the Phillies) is shot by 19-year-old Ruth Steinhagen (who claimed she was in love with him) at Chicago's Edgewater Beach Hotel. Waitkus battled for his life and came back to play the following season.

As a Cub, Lou Brock became only the third hitter in history to hit a home run into the centerfield bleachers at the Polo Grounds.

1959— Ernie Banks hits his 200th career home run off Carlton Willey in the seventh inning as the Cubs beat the Braves, 6-0, behind Dick Drott at Wrigley Field.

1980— In an Old-Timers Day reunion, the Tigers of 1945 beat the Cubs of '45, 4-1, in a two inning "replay" of the Cubs' last World Series. Cubs beat the Braves, 10-5, in the regular game, at Wrigley Field.

June 15

1949— Cubs trade outfielders P-Nuts Lowrey and Harry Walker to the Reds for outfielders Hank Sauer and Frankie Baumholtz.

1951— Cubs trade outfielder Andy Pafko, pitcher Johnny Schmitz, infielder Wayne Terwilliger and catcher Rube Walker to the Dodgers for outfielder Gene Hermanski, pitcher Joe Hatten, infielder Eddie Miksis, and catcher Bruce Edwards.

1964— Cubs trade outfielder Lou Brock, and pitchers Jack Spring and Paul Toth to the Cardinals for pitchers Ernie Broglio and Bobby Shantz, and outfielder Doug Clemens.

June 16

1927— Cubs win their 12th consecutive game, beating the Phillies, 7-2, behind Hal Carlson at Wrigley Field. The Phillies had traded Carlson to the Cubs nine days earlier for infielder Jimmy Cooney.

1958— Dick Ellsworth makes his Cub debut by pitching the Cubs to a 1-0 win over the White Sox at the Boys Benefit game at Comiskey Park.

1981— The Cubs announce the sale of the franchise to the Tribune Company for $20.5 million, ending 66-year ownership by Wrigley clan.

June 17

1913— Heinie Zimmerman is ejected from his third game in five days, but the Cubs beat the Phillies, 4-0, at West Side Grounds.

1915— Zip Zabel relieves Bert Humpheries with two out in the first inning and pitches the longest relief stint in major league history (18-1/3 innings) as the Cubs beat the Dodgers, 4-3, in 19 innings on Vic Saier's home run at West Side Grounds. Loser Jeff Pfeffer goes the route for Brooklyn.

1962— In the first inning of game one, Cub outfielder Lou Brock becomes only the third hitter in history to hit a home run into the centerfield bleachers at the Polo Grounds, a distance of 475 feet, as the Cubs beat the Mets, 8-7. Cubs also win second game, 4-3, on Ron Santo's ninth inning homer. The other two players who homered into the Polo Grounds' centerfield were Babe Ruth and Joe Adcock.

1971— Don Kessinger has six hits in six at bats as the Cubs edge the Cardinals, 7-6, in 10 innings, at Wrigley Field.

June 18

1929 — Hack Wilson drives in six runs with a grandslam home run and a two-run homer as the Cubs beat the Cardinals, 13-6, behind Guy Bush, at Wrigley Field.

June 19

1900 — Pitcher Clark Griffith drives in the winning run and goes the route as the Cubs tip Rube Waddell and the Pirates, 1-0, in 14 innings at West Side Grounds. This was the longest shutout win, inning-wise, in Cub history at that date, with Waddell fanning 12 Cubs in the process.

1913 — Wilbur Good hits the first pinch-hit home run in Cub history in the eighth inning but the Cubs lose to Grover Alexander and the Phillies, 2-1, at West Side Grounds.

1952 — Carl Erskine pitches a no-hitter as the Dodgers beat the Cubs, 5-0, at Ebbets Field, in a rain-delayed game.

June 20

1882 — Pitcher Larry Corcoran hits two singles, a double, and the first grandslam homer in Cub history, in a 13-3 romp over Worcester at Lakefront Park.

1974 — Rick Reuschel pitches a 12-hit shutout as the Cubs blank the Pirates, 3-0, at Wrigley Field. There were Pittsburgh runners on base in every inning.

June 21

1888 — George Van Haltren pitches a six-inning no-hitter as the Cubs beat the Pirates, 2-0, at West Side Park. Van Haltren actually pitched seven hitless innings but the game was called because of rain with the Cubs batting in the bottom of the seventh, so the top half did not count.

1907 — Mordecai Brown wins his 10th consecutive game as the Cubs beat the Cardinals, 2-0, at West Side Grounds. Cub catcher Johnny Kling nails four runners attempting to steal second base.

1928 — Milkman rattles Wilson! The Cubs split a doubleheader with the Cardinals at Wrigley Field, winning the first game, 2-1, and losing the nightcap, 4-1. After grounding out in the bottom of the ninth in the second game, Hack Wilson climbed into the stands and attacked Edward Young, a milkman who had been drinking something other than milk, and was insulting Wilson. Teammates Gabby Hartnett and Joe Kelly broke up the fight, after which Riggs Stephenson popped up for the final out. National League President John Heydler fined Wilson $100 and Judge Francis P. Allgretti fined Young $1.

1936 — The Cubs win their 15th consecutive game, beating the Dodgers, 7-2, in the first game of a doubleheader at Ebbets Field, behind the five-hit pitching of Curt Davis, who singles, doubles and scores twice. The Bums win the second game, 6-4, to end the streak.

1942 — Dom Dallessandro's pinch-hit grandslam homer with two outs in the ninth inning helps the Cubs to a 7-2 victory over the Giants at the Polo Grounds.

June 22

1888 — The Cubs score 11 runs in the sixth inning and beat the Pirates, 12-6, at West Side Park. Fred Pfeffer drives in four runs with a single and a three-run inside-the-park homer. Obviously riled, Pirate pitcher Pud Galvin is fined $10 by umpire Tommy Lynch in the eighth inning for disputing a called "ball" on one of his pitches.

1902 — Jack Taylor goes the route as the Cubs beat the Pirates, 3-2, in 19 innings at West Side Grounds on Bobby Lowe's run-scoring single. Loser Deacon Phillipe also goes the route for Pittsburgh.

June 23

1895 — A pressure group called the "Sunday Observance League" led by Rev. W.W. Clark, holds up play in the third inning and the entire Cub team is arrested for "aiding and abetting the forming of a noisy crowd on a Sunday." Cub owner Jim Hart posts bond, securing a warrant from Justice Cleveland of Norwood Park, and the game is resumed. Hart invites Rev. Clark to stay for the game, but he declines. The Cubs go on to trounce Cleveland, 13-4, behind Clark Griffith before 10,000 fans at West Side Grounds.

1930 — Hack Wilson hits for the cycle with two singles, a double, a triple and a homer, scores five runs and drives in six as the Cubs rip the Phillies, 21-8, at Wrigley Field. Pitcher Guy Busy chips in with a triple and two singles.

1946 — Eddie Waitkus and Marv Rickert hit back-to-back inside-the-park homers in the fourth inning, the first in major league history and the only time in the National League as the Cubs lose to Giants, 15-10, at the Polo Grounds. Cubs win second game, 9-4.

1961 — Ernie Banks' consecutive playing streak ends at 717 games when he is sidelined with a knee injury. His streak began on August 26, 1956. But the Cubs go on to beat the Braves, 5-3, behind Jack Curtis at County Stadium.

June 24

1885 — John Clarkson wins his 13th in a row and the Cubs win their 18th straight, beating the Phillies, 12-2, at West Side Park.

1905 — Ed Reulbach goes the route as the Cubs nip the Cardinals and Jack Taylor, 2-1, in 18 innings. First baseman Frank Chance had 27 putouts and two assists for the Cubs at St. Louis.

1915 — Heinie Zimmerman steals home with two out in the bottom of the ninth as the Cubs beat the Cards, 14-13, at West Side Grounds. The Cubs trailed, 13-10, going into the inning. Zimmerman drove in the tying runs with a two-run pinch-double. Jimmy Archer went four-for-five, including two doubles at West Side Grounds.

June 25

1881 — George "Piano Legs" Gore steals seven bases, second five times and third twice, leading the Cubs to a 12-8 victory over Providence at Lakefront Park. Gore also has three hits and scores five times.

1909 — Auto way to go! Joe Tinker's foul ball in the second inning sails over the grandstand and bounces through an auto windshield parked outside West Side Grounds. This is probably a first, as there are only 300 autos registered in Chicago at this time. The Cubs motored past the Reds, 7-0, with Mordecai Brown at the steering wheel during the rest of the game.

1930 — Gabby Hartnett drives in seven runs, including the game winner in the ninth inning, hitting two singles and two homers as the Cubs tip the Phillies, 13-12, at Wrigley Field.

1937 — Augie Galan becomes the first switch-hitter in major league history to hit a homer left-handed and right-handed in the same game. The Cubs beat the Dodgers, 11-2, on Tex Carleton's five-hitter at Wrigley Field.

1949 — Hank Sauer hits a second-inning homer for his fourth in as many days and his fifth in the last six in leading the Cubs to a 4-1 victory over the Giants at Wrigley Field. Bob Rush is the winning pitcher. Hank's brother Eddie Sauer appears in game for Boston.

1950 — Hank Sauer drives in four runs with two homers and two doubles and Roy Smalley and Phil Cavarretta add homers as the Cubs check the Phillies, 11-8, at Shibe Park. Johnny Schmitz is the winner over Jim Konstanty.

1977 — Old Timers game at Wrigley Field. The Cub Old Timers beat the Hall of Famers, 4-1. In the regular game, the Cubs score three unearned runs in the ninth inning and beat the Mets, 5-4.

June 26

1960 — Ron Santo makes his major league debut, goes three-for-seven and drives in five runs as the Cubs sweep the pennant-bound Pirates, 7-6, and 7-5, at Forbes Field.

1972 — Rick Reuschel makes his first major league start as the Cubs rip the Phillies, 11-1, at Wrigley Field.

1978 — Dave Rader hits a pinch-hit grandslam homer and Rodney Scott steals home as the Cubs edge the Mets, 10-9, at Wrigley Field.

June 27

1884 — Larry Corcoran pitches his third no-hitter as the Cubs beat Providence, 6-0, at Lakefront Park.

1887 — Rookie Cub pitcher George Van Haltren walks 16 batters, hits two batsman and heaves a wild pitch as Boston beat the Cubs, 17-11, at West Side Park. Former Cub King Kelly walks five times.

1930 — The largest crowd in Wrigley Field history (51,556) sees the Cubs top the

Dodgers, 7-5, on Kiki Cuyler's 10th-inning homer. There is 30,476 Ladies Day guests and 1,332 passholders, so the paid attendance is only 19,748. Guy Bush went the route.

1947 — Dom Dallessandro, Bill Nicholson and Don Johnson homer in the sixth inning, but the Pirates whip the Cubs, 12-8, at Wrigley Field.

June 28

1910 — Joe Tinker steals home twice as the Cubs bomb the Reds, 11-1, behind Mordecai Brown at West Side Grounds.

1929 — The Cubs hit five homers, three in the second inning by Hack Wilson, Pat Malone and Rogers Hornsby to take over first place, beating the Cardinals, 9-5, at Sportsman's Park. Wilson added another homer and Earl Grace the fifth. Malone goes the route.

1933 — Billy Herman gets five hits and sets major league record with 16 put-outs at second base in a doubleheader, 11 in the first game. The Cubs sweep the Phillies, 9-5 and 8-3, at Baker Bowl.

1950 — Roy Smalley hits for the cycle and Phil Cavarretta and Andy Pafko had homers and Doyle Lade goes the route in a 15-3 victory over the Cardinals at Wrigley Field.

1963 — A crowd of 40,226, the largest at Wrigley Field since 1952, sees the Cubs roll past the Cardinals, 5-2 and 16-11.

June 29

1897 — The Cubs score in every inning en route to a 36-7 triumph over Louisville at West Side Grounds. The Cubs had 30 hits, including six by Barry McCormick and five by winning pitcher Jimmy Callahan.

1952 — Trailing the Reds, 8-2, with two out in the ninth and nobody on base, the Cubs rally for seven runs and a 9-8 victory at Crosley Field. Ex-Red Johnny Pramesa drives in the winning rin.

1969 — It's Billy Williams Day at Wrigley Field before 41,060 paid. Billy responds with five hits as the Cubs sweep the Cardinals, 3-1 and 12-1. Williams passes Stan Musial as the National League's all-time "Iron Man" by playing in his 895th and 896th consecutive games.

June 30

1892 — Addison Gumbert pitches the entire 20 innings as the Cubs tie the Reds, 7-7, at West Side Park. Time of the game was only two hours and 30 minutes.

1909 — The Cubs beat the Pirates, 3-2, in the first game played at Pittsburgh's Forbes Field before a crowd of 30,338.

1920 — Jim Vaughn pitches a one-hitter as the Cubs tip the Pirates, 1-0, at Wrigley Field. Fred Merkle drives in Charlie Hollocher with the lone run in the first inning.

1959 — Two balls are in play in bizarre fourth inning against the Cardinals at Wrigley Field. On a three-and-two count, Cub pitcher Bob Anderson delivers the pitch that sets off the confusion. Anderson's pitch either ticked Stan Musial's bat or was a wild pitch. The ball bounces toward the screen and Cub catcher Sammy Taylor ignores it, thinking it hit Musial's bat for a foul ball. Cub third baseman Alvin Dark rushes in to retrieve the ball, but the bat boy picks it up and flips it to field announcer Pat Pieper. Musial, meanwhile, thinks it is ball four and goes to first base. Umpire Vic Delmore pulls out another ball and hands it to Anderson. Pieper gives the original ball to Dark. Musial streaks for second as Dark and Anderson fire in that direction. Anderson's throw was wild and sails into center field, while Dark's toss goes to shortstop Ernie Banks, who tags the sliding Musial. Stan ignores Banks' tag, gets up and tries for third base. Centerfielder Bobby Thomson retrieves the other ball and casually lobs it into the Cub dugout. Play is stopped. Umpire Delmore rules Musial out at second base. Umpire Al Barlick rules Musial safe at first base. They huddle and Musial is called out. (They don't mention which base). Cardinal manager Solly Hemus announces he's playing the game under protest, claiming the bat boy interferred with the ball. Cub manager Bob Scheffing protests that the ball ticked Musial's bat and should be ruled a foul ball. The end result? The Cardinals drop their protest after winning the contest, 4-1. The National League dropped Delmore from its umpiring crew at the end of the season.

JULY

July 1

1885 — Fred Pfeffer, Abner Dalrymple, Tommy Burns and John Clarkson homer as the Cubs bounce Boston, 24-10, at West Side Park. Pitcher Clarkson makes eight putouts.

1886 — Jim McCormick wins his 16th straight game as the Cubs beat New York, 7-3, at West Side Park.

1891 — Jimmy Ryan hits for the cycle as the Cubs dump Cleveland, 9-3, behind Bill Hutchison at West Side Park.

1892 — The first sports writer is assaulted. George Bechel of the Chicago Evening News criticizes the play of Cub outfielder Jimmy Ryan, who quarrels with Bechel after the game. Ryan then pounds lumps on Bechel.

1912 — Frank Schulte's homer in the 12th inning beats Marty O'Toole and the Pirates, 1-0, at Pittsburgh. Jimmy Lavender goes the route for the Cubs.

1935 — The Cubs play their first night game (on the road, naturally), beating the Reds, 8-4, at Crosley Field behind Roy Henshaw. Billy Herman leads the Cubs with two triples, two doubles and a single.

1955 — Hank Sauer, Randy Jackson and Gene Baker homer in the second inning as the Cubs beat the Cardinals, 11-7, at Wrigley Field. Ernie Banks also homers for the Cubs.

1958 — Tony Taylor gets an inside-the-park homer when Giants' leftfielder Leon Wagner is confused while getting instructions from the Cubs' bullpen as to the whereabouts of the ball, which rolled into the gutter drain. The Cubs beat the Giants, 9-5, at Wrigley Field.

1973 — Ron Santo gets five hits in five at bats and Randy Hundley hits a three-run homer in the ninth inning as the Cubs edge the Mets, 6-5, in the second game before 43,105 at Wrigley Field. Santo had two hits in the first game, but the Cubs lose, 6-5.

July 2

1891 — The Cubs score 11 runs in the third inning and whip Cleveland, 20-5, at West Side Park. Every Cub gets a hit and scored a run. Jimmy Ryan raps four hits for the Cubs.

1937 — Gabby Hartnett slams the 200th homer of his Cub career, a two-run blast off the Pirates' Red Lucas in the eighth inning at Wrigley Field. The Cubs win, 8-7, on Augie Galan's two-run homer in the ninth inning.

1950 — Andy Pafko drives in five runs with a double, triple and a homer; Bill Serena hits a three-run homer and Hank Edwards collects four hits and three RBI as the Cubs rout the Reds, 16-0, at Crosley Field on Monk Dubiel's four-hitter.

1957 — Lee Walls hits for the cycle, but the Reds stun the Cubs, 8-6, on Wally Post's grandslam homer in the 10th inning at Wrigley Field.

1972 — The Cubs complete a triple play in the seventh inning at Three Rivers Stadium, third baseman Ron Santo to second baseman Glenn Beckert to first baseman Jim Hickman, but the Pirates win, 7-4.

July 3

1883 — The Cubs annihilate Buffalo, 31-7, on 32 hits at Lakefront Park. The Cubs hit 14 doubles, four each by Cap Anson and Abner Dalrymple. Anson, Dalrymple and King Kelly had five hits each, while Ed Williamson had a single, two doubles and a triple. Larry Corcoran was the winning pitcher.

1945 — Phil Cavarretta, Don Johnson and Stan Hack score five runs each as the Cubs collect eight doubles and clobber the Braves, 24-2, behind Claude Passeau at Braves Field. Cavy also stopped five hits and drove in five runs and Mickey Livingston homered. Johnson drills five hits also.

1967 — Billy Williams, Ron Santo and Randy Hundley homer for the Cubs and Rico Carty and Felipe Alou for the Braves — all in the first inning — to tie a major league record (five in one inning). Carty later homered but Glenn Beckert's three-run homer helps the Cubs and Ray Culp to a 12-6 victory at Atlanta Stadium.

1971 — Don Kessinger hits an inside-the-park homer and Cub outfielder Brock Davis makes a diving catch of pinch-hitter Charlie Sands' sinking liner with two on and two out in the ninth inning to preserve a 3-1 victory for Milt Pappas over the Pirates at Wrigley Field.

July 4

1882— The Cubs beat Troy, 9-5, behind Larry Corcoran in 14 innings at Lakefront Park. The 14 innings marked the longest game in Chicago history up to that time.

1884— Tommy Burns hits two homers as the Cubs pound Philadelphia, 22-3, behind Fred Andrus in the second game of a doubleheader at Lakefront Park. The Cubs won the opener, 3-1, with Larry Corcoran pitching.

1895— The Cubs edge Cincinnati, 8-7, in the morning game and, 9-5, in the mid-afternoon game at West Side Grounds. The second game attracted a record 22,913, the first 20,000-plus crowd in Chicago baseball history.

1900— Approximately 1,000 fans (out of a total attendance of 10,000) appear at West Side Grounds armed with revolvers, and fire them constantly in celebration of the holiday. Some of them shot holes in the roof. The Cubs, meanwhile, shot holes in the Phillies, sweeping a doubleheader, 10-4 and 5-4, in 12 innings.

1906— The Cubs sweep the Pirates by identical 1-0 scores at West Side Grounds. Mordecai Brown hurls a one-hitter in the opener and Carl Lundgren a five-hitter in the nightcap.

1908— Mordecai Brown pitches his fourth consecutive shutout (his second in three days), setting a Cub record (later tied by Ed Reulbach, 1908 and Bill Lee, 1938) as the Cubs horse-collared the Pirates, 2-0, in the opener at Pittsburgh. The Cubs win the second game, 8-3, behind Reulbach, with "Circus" Solly Hofman driving in four runs on two singles and a double.

1929— Hit by train? Hack Wilson jumps into the Reds dugout to battle pitcher Ray Kolp, who had been needling him. Wilson never reached Kolp, but was ejected by umpire Cy Rigler. The Cubs went on to win, 10-5. That evening, Wilson floors Red pitcher Pete Donahue at Union Station, where both teams were waiting for trains.

1934— Kiki Cuyler hits three doubles and a triple and scores three runs as the Cubs beat the Cardinals, 6-2, behind Jim Weaver at Sportsman's Park.

1939— Hank Leiber hits three consecutive homers, but the Cubs lose, 6-4, to the Cardinals in the opener at Wrigley Field. The Cubs win the second game, 3-2, on Gus Mancuso's run-scoring single in the 10th inning.

1942— Stan Hack sets a National League record (since broken) of 54 games without an error at third base as the Cubs beat the Cardinals, 6-5, on Lou Novikoff's bases loaded double off Mort Cooper. But Hack's streak ended when he fumbled Stan Musial's grounder with the bases loaded in the third inning of the second game. The Cardinals went on to win, 9-3, at Sportsman's Park.

1966— Ron Santo sets a modern-day Cub record by hitting in his 28th straight game. The Santo streak started May 31. The Cubs split a doubleheader, losing, 7-5, to the Pirates and winning, 6-4, at Wrigley Field. Santo is held hitless in the second game.

July 5

1937 — Frank Demaree gets eight hits as the Cubs sweep a doubleheader, beating the Cardinals, 13-12, in 14 innings on Billy Jurges' bases loaded single, and 9-7. The games took 6-1/2 hours before a crowd of 39,240 at Wrigley Field. Demaree has three doubles among his six hits in the opener.

July 6

1925 — Rabbit Maranville replaces Bill Killefer as Cub manager and leads team to a 10-5 victory over the Dodgers at Ebbets Field. Maranville celebrated that evening and is arrested for getting into a fight with a taxi driver.

1932 — Cub shortstop Billy Jurges is shot in the left side and left hand by a 21-year-old dancer named Violet Popovich Valli, who also shot herself. The incident occurred at the Carlos Hotel. The wounds are superficial and Jurges returns to the lineup several weeks later. Violet later appears on the stage of a local theatre as Violet "I Did It For Love" Popovich.

1970 — Ron Santo drives in 10 runs as the Cubs sweep the Expos, 3-2, and, 14-2, at Wrigley Field. Santo powers a two-run homer in the opener, and a two-run homer and a grandslam homer in the nightcap.

1980 — Cubs play the longest game in their history, 5 hours, 31 minutes, but lose, 5-4, in 20 innings to the Pittsburgh Pirates at Three Rivers Stadium. Cub relievers pitch 12-1/3 hitless innings (from the eighth to the 20th). Cub slugger Dave Kingman goes 0-for-9.

July 7

1886 — Cap Anson belts a double and a homer and Ed Williamson a triple and a homer as the Cubs rattle the Giants, 21-9, at West Side Park. The game is called because of darkness after eight innings.

1936 — Augie Galan, Billy Herman, Gabby Hartnett and Frank Demaree collect five of the National League's nine hits in their first All-Star victory, 4-3, over the American League at Graves Field. Hartnett drives in one run with a triple and Galan hit a foul-pole homer.

July 8

1880 — The Cubs beat Providence, 5-4, behind Larry Corcoran at Lakefront Park for their 21st straight victory. Streak ends the next day.

1907 — Cub first baseman-manager Frank Chance, angered at Brooklyn fans throwing pop bottles at his team, starts heaving them back, lacerating one fan in the leg. The Cubs won, 5-0, behind Mordecai Brown, and Chance left the park in an armored auto accompanied by three policemen to escape the mob.

1912 — The Cubs snap Rube Marquard's 19-game winning streak, beating the Giants, 7-2, behind Jimmy Lavender at West Side Grounds. Marquard's winning streak is still the longest in major league history along with Giant Tim Keefe's 19 straight in 1888.

1952 — Hank Sauer's two-run homer off Bob Lemon in the fourth inning gives the National League a 3-2 victory over the American League in a rain-shortened All-Star game at Shibe Park. Cub Bob Rush is the winning pitcher.

1956 — Monte Irvin's ninth-inning grandslam homer gives the Cubs a 10-6 victory over the Braves at County Stadium.

July 9

1885 — Cub outfielder George Gore sets a major league record (tied by several players) by getting five extra base hits in one game with three doubles and two triples as the Cubs beat Providence, 8-5, at West Side Park.

1887 — John Clarkson wins his 11th consecutive game as the Cubs defeat the Phillies, 5-3, at Philadelphia.

1969 — Rookie Jimmy Qualls one-out single in the ninth inning spoils Tom Seaver's no-hit bid, but the Mets beat the Cubs, 4-0, at Shea Stadium.

July 10

1886 — A crowd of 14,000, the largest in Chicago up to that time, watches the Cubs beat Detroit, 3-1, on John Clarkson's five-hitter at West Side Park.

July 11

1918 — Phil Douglas beats the Braves twice, getting a relief win in game one and a distance job in the second game, by scores of 4-3 (10 innings) and 3-2 at Wrigley Field.

1944 — Phil Cavarretta gets a triple, a single and three walks, and Bill Nicholson a pinch-RBI double as the National League rips the American League, 7-1, in the All-Star Game at Forbes Field.

1949 — The Cubs beat the White Sox, 4-2, in the first Boys' Benefit Game at Comiskey Park, Johnny Schmitz over Bob Kuzava.

1960 — Ernie Banks doubles and homers, driving in two runs in the National League's 5-3 victory over the American League in that season's first All-Star Game at Kansas City's Municipal Stadium.

1972 — Billy Williams is three-for-three in the opener (a home run and two singles) and five-for-five in the nightcap (home run, a double and three singles) as the Cubs and Astros split at Chicago. The Astros win the first, 6-5, while the Cubs take the second, 9-5.

1978 — Cub fireman Bruce Sutter retires all five batters he faces, striking out AL home run king Jim Rice, and gains credit for the victory, 7-3, in the All-Star game at San Diego Stadium.

July 12

1931 — The Cubs and Cardinals combine for 23 doubles and 43 extra base hits as the Cards win, 17-13, in the second game of a doubleheader. There were 13 doubles by the Cardinals and 10 by the Cubs, including three each by Gabby Hartnett, Woody English, Rip Collins, and Gus Mancuso. In the first game, the Cardinals had five doubles and the Cubs four as the Cubs won, 7-5. An overflow crowd of 45,715 at St. Louis caused the umpires to rule any ball going into the crowd a ground rule double.

1945 — The Cubs win their 11th in a row, stopping Tommy Holmes' hitting streak at 37 games. Hank Wyse stops Holmes and the Braves, 6-1, but the Braves snap the Cubs streak, 3-1, in the nightcap, at Wrigley Field.

1946 — P-Nuts Lowrey hits two singles and a home run, driving in seven runs as the Cubs rout the Dodgers, 13-2, behind Hank Wyse at Wrigley Field.

1965 — Ron Santo's seventh inning single drives in Willie Mays with the winning run as the National League beats the American League, 6-5, in the All-Star game at Metropolitan Stadium in Bloomington, Minnesota.

July 13

1896 — Ed Delehanty of the Phillies hits four inside-the-park home runs and a single, driving in seven runs, but the Cubs win, 9-8, at West Side Grounds.

1977 — A blackout engulfs the New York area with the Cubs leading the Mets, 2-1, in the sixth inning at Shea Stadium. The game is finished September 16, with the Cubs winning, 4-3, behind Ray Burris, who waited patiently for the win.

July 14

1882 — Cubs beat Detroit, 23-4, behind Larry Corcoran at Lakefront Park. George Gore, Mike Kelly and Ed Williamson each drive in three runs and score three runs.

1965 — In the second game of a doubleheader at Wrigley Field, the Cubs execute a triple play in the second inning on a bunt by Woody Woodward of the Braves, the play going from catcher Ed Bailey to shortstop Don Kessinger to pitcher Bill Faul to second baseman Glenn Beckert. This is the only time the Cubs have turned a triple play on a bunt. Braves won, 6-3, after the Cubs won the opener, 5-2.

1970 — Jim Hickman of the Cubs drives home Pete Rose with a 12th inning single as the National League nips the American League, 5-4, in the All-Star game at Cincinnati's Riverfront Stadium.

July 15

1884 — Mike Corcoran (Larry's brother) throws five wild pitches in his first and only major league game as the Cubs lose, 14-0, in Detroit.

1923 — Barney Friberg's grandslam homer in the 10th inning beat the Giants, 9-5. The victory gave Grover Alexander a 29-28 record against the Giants, in a game played at New York.

1942— Cubs reliefer Hi Bithorn whirls toward the Dodger dugout and fires a ball at manager Leo Durocher's head in the fifth inning at Wrigley Field. Lou Novikoff and Jimmy Foxx homer for the Cubs, but the Dodgers win, 10-5, with ex-Cub Billy Herman hitting a homer and ex-Cub Kirby Higbe getting the victory, with relief help from Hugh Casey, another former Cub.

1945— Cubs sweep the Giants, 5-3 and 7-2, behind Hank Wyse and Hy Vandenberg before 43,803 fans at Wrigley Field.

1975— Cub Bill Madlock's bases-loaded single in the ninth inning gives the National League a 6-3 victory over the American League in the All-Star Game at Milwaukee's County Stadium.

July 16

1885— Bill Kennedy wins both ends of a doubleheader as the Cubs dump Buffalo, 9-3 and 13-9, with relief help from Ed Williamson in the sixth inning of the nightcap at Buffalo. They were Kennedy's last major league victories.

1905— Charles W. Murphy purchases an interest and is made vice president of the Cubs. He soon becomes president and remains until 1913.

1922— Hack Miller hits a home run in the fourth inning, his fourth in three days, but the Phillies overpower the Cubs, 10-7, at Wrigley Field.

July 17

1895— The Cubs score 12 runs in the fourth inning and beat the Phillies, 12-7, at West Side Grounds. The Cubs scored five more runs in the seventh inning, but the Phillies concede defeat in order to catch a train, so the runs didn't count. Walt Wilmot, Bill Everett and Asa Stewart had two hits each in the fourth, while winning pitcher Walt Thornton had a double and a walk.

1908— Joe Tinker hits an inside-the-park homer in the fifth inning as the Cubs and Mordecai Brown edge the Giants and Christy Mathewson, 1-0, at West Side Grounds.

1918— Lefty Tyler goes the route as the Cubs nip the Phillies, 2-1, in 21 innings at Philadelphia. Max Flack, who had five hits, singled home the winning run. Loser Milt Watson went the route for the Phillies.

1964— Major league baseball makes its debut on pay TV when Subscription television screens the Cub-Dodger night game at Los Angeles. Don Drysdale fans 10 batters as the Dodgers whiff the Cubs, 3-2.

1966— Billy Williams hits for the cycle as the Cubs bounce the Cardinals, 7-2, behind Ken Holtzman at St. Louis.

July 18

1897 — Cap Anson gets his 3,000th hit (this total includes 59 bases on balls officially counted as hits in 1887), a fourth inning single to ignite a three-run Cub rally, as the Cubs beat Baltimore, 6-3, at West Side Grounds. In the eighth inning, the Orioles' John McGraw purposely steps in front of Clark Griffith's pitches twice to get hit, but umpire Jim McDonald refuses to award him first base. Joe Kelley and Jake Stenzel of Baltimore are both fined for swearing at the ump.

1912 — Gavvy Cravath steals home in the 11th inning as the Phillies beat the Cubs, 9-8, in the opener at Chicago. Cubs win second game, 4-2, on back-to-back homers by Johnny Evers and Vic Saier.

1979 — For the second straight year, Cub fireman Bruce Sutter is the winner in the All-Star game as the National League edges the American, 7-6, at Seattle, with Sutter fanning three.

July 19

1940 — Hank Leiber hits a grandslam homer in the first inning and Bill Nicholson hits a two-run homer in the eighth as the Cubs rip the Dodgers, 11-4, at Wrigley Field. A free-for-all erupts in the eighth inning when Cub pitcher Claude Passeau throws his bat at Dodger pitcher Hugh Casey after a Casey pitch plunks him between the shoulder blades. Passeau and Dodger bench jockey Joe Gallagher are tossed out of the game, but Passeau gets his 11th win of the year.

July 20

1886 — Mike Kelly gets four singles and scores four runs, and Cap Anson, Jimmy Ryan and Abner Dalrymple homer in the third inning as the Cubs wallop St. Louis, 20-4, at West Side Park.

1911 — Frank Schulte hits for the cycle as the Cubs edge the Phillies, 4-3, at Philadelphia.

1929 — Hack Wilson hits safely in his 26th consecutive game as the Cubs beat the Dodgers, 5-1, at Brooklyn, behind Sheriff Blake. Wilson is halted the next day.

1933 — Babe Herman hits three homers, including a grandslam, and a single, driving in eight runs as the Cubs trounce the Phillies, 10-1, behind Bud Tinning, at Wrigley Field.

1938 — Gabby Hartnett replaces Charlie Grimm as Cub manager.

1966 — Ernie Banks collects his 2,000th hit but the Reds clip the Cubs, 5-4, at Wrigley Field.

July 21

1951 — Phil Cavarretta replaces Frankie Frisch as Cub manager.

1963 — Cubs execute a triple play against the Pirates at Pittsburgh off Bob Clemente in the third inning, catcher Merritt Ranew to shortstop Andre Rodgers, Cubs lose, 6-5, in 14 innings after winning the opener, 5-1.

1971 — Ernie Banks hits his 511th home run, tying Mel Ott, as the Cubs beat the Mets, 11-7, at Wrigley Field.

July 22

1876 — Louisville pitcher John Ryan uncorks ten wild pitches and the Cubs add 31 hits en route to a 30-7 victory at 23rd Street Grounds. Cal McVey gets six hits for the Cubs, who score in every inning but the second, including a 10-run fourth.

1965 — Ed Bailey hits a grandslam homer and drives in eight runs as the Cubs beat the Phillies, 10-6, at Wrigley Field.

1968 — Glenn Beckert hits safely in his 27th consecutive game, going two-for-five as the Cubs beat the Giants, 7-2, at San Francisco.

July 23

1923 — Cubs explode for nine runs in the top of the 12th, capped by Otto Vogel's three-run triple, to beat the Pirates, 12-3, at Pittsburgh. This is a Cub record for most runs scored in an extra inning.

1944 — After having hit one home run in the first game and three in the second, Bill Nicholson is walked intentionally by Giant manager Mel Ott in game number two with the bags loaded in the seventh inning, at New York. Giants win, 12-10, after having dropped the opener to the Cubs, 7-4.

1957 — Dick Drott strikes out 14 batters, Bob Speake homers, and Moose Moryn hits a two-run double as the Cubs beat the Giants, 4-0, at Wrigley Field.

1979 — Cubs beat the Reds, 9-8, in 18 innings at Wrigley Field. The first nine innings were actually played May 10, with the game having been suspended because the Cubs had to catch a plane. Steve Ontiveros drives in the tying run with two out in the eleventh inning, and the winning run in the 18th. In the regularly scheduled game, the Cubs win, 2-1, on Dave Kingman's two run home run in the bottom of the ninth.

July 24

1882 — Seven Cubs get four hits apiece (Abner Dalrymple, Mike Kelly, George Gore, Ed Williamson, Tommy Burns, Frank Flint, Hugh Nicol) en route to a 35-4 rout of Cleveland, at Lakefront Park. Cubs collect 29 hits, including 10 doubles, a triple, and three home runs.

1972 — Whitey Lockman replaces Leo Durocher as Cub manager.

1974 — Jim Marshall replaces Whitey Lockman as Cub manager.

July 25

1876 — Cubs collect 26 hits, six by Cal McVey, as they trounce the Reds, 23-3, behind Al Spalding at 23rd Street Grounds.

1894 — George Decker hits a 520-foot home run and Jimmy Ryan scores six runs as the Cubs beat the Pirates, 24-6, at West Side Grounds.

1948 — Bill Nicholson smashes his 200th home run in the seventh inning, and Eddie Waitkus hits a three-run inside-the-park homer in the fourth as the Cubs top the Giants, 6-3, at Wrigley Field.

1965 — In the fourth inning of game two of a twin bill at Wrigley Field, the Cubs execute a triple play off Bob Clemente of the Pirates — second baseman Glenn Beckert to shortstop Don Kessinger to first baseman Ernie Banks. Cubs win, 5-0, behind Bill Faul, after having lost the opener, 3-2.

1980 — Joe Amalfitano replaces Preston Gomez as Cub manager.

July 26

1930 — Hack Wilson hits three homers while Gabby Hartnett and Pat Malone hit one apiece as the Cubs rip the Phillies, 16-2, at Philadelphia. Malone goes the distance.

1942 — Clyde McCullough knocks three consecutive home runs, but the Phillies edge the Cubs, 4-3, at Philadelphia.

1970 — Glenn Beckert gets five hits in five trips as the Cubs nip the Braves, 4-3, before 39,189 fans at Wrigley Field in the second game of a doubleheader. The Braves won the first game, 4-3.

1975 — Bill Madlock has six hits, five singles and a triple, but the Mets beat the Cubs, 9-8, in ten innings, at Wrigley Field.

July 27

1876 — The Cubs get 23 hits, six by Ross Barnes, and crush the Reds, 17-3, behind Al Spalding at 23rd Street Grounds. The Cubs thus scored 88 runs in the last four games for a major league record.

1885 — John Clarkson pitches a no-hit game as the Cubs beat Providence, 4-0, at Providence.

1930 — Reds pitcher Ken Ash delivers one pitch that accounts for three outs, is lifted for a pinch-hitter, and gains a 6-5 victory over the Cubs at Cincinnati. Charlie Grimm hit the pitch and lined into a triple play in the fifth inning.

1945 — Pitcher Hank Borowy is acquired for $97,500 via the waivers from the Yankees. Borowy helps the Cubs win the pennant with an 11-2 record and wins two World Series games.

1969 — Cub manager Leo Durocher goes AWOL, visiting his stepson at Camp Objiwa at Eagle River, Wisconsin, creating a furor that simmers all summer.

Dizzy Dean, a member of the famous St. Louis Cardinal's "Gashouse Gang," used his blazing fastball with much success against the Cubs. Dean was traded to the Cubs in 1938 and helped them win a pennant as a spot pitcher, but he had to depend on his new "dipsey doodle" pitch and sheer cunning after a toe injury altered his throwing motion.

July 28

1888 — Jimmy Ryan hits for the cycle, with his homer landing in a vacant lot on Harrison Street. Cap Anson adds two homers, and Hugh Duffy and Tommy Burns one each as the Cubs collect 30 hits for a 21-17 victory over Detroit before 10,000 at West Side Park.

1968 — A crowd of 42,261, the largest at Wrigley Field in 20 years, sees the Cubs pull over the .500 mark (52-51) with 8-3 and 1-0 victories over the Dodgers behind Joe Niekro and Ken Holtzman.

1977 — Cubs beat the Reds, 16-15, in a wild 13 inning game lasting four hours and 50 minutes. The Cubs overcame Cincy leads of 6-0, 10-8, 13-11 and 15-14, winning on Dave Rosello's RBI single. Rosello's error in the 12th gave the Reds the lead. Davey thus went from goat to hero. There were 11 home runs, six by the Cubs.

1979 — Dave Kingman hits three home runs but the Mets beat the Cubs, 6-4, at New York. Kingman had two homers the night before in a 4-2 Cub victory, giving him five in two days to tie a major league record first set by Cub star Cap Anson in 1884, and tied by several other players, including Billy Williams of the Cubs in 1968.

July 29

1947 — Cubs score five runs in the seventh inning, highlighted by walks to pinch-hitters Bill Nicholson, Dom Dallessandro and Marv Rickert, and top the Phillies, 5-4, at Chicago.

1951 — Manager Phil Cavarretta hits a pinch grandslam homer off Robin Roberts in the seventh inning of the second game as the Cubs sweep the Phillies, 5-4 and 8-6, at Chicago. Cavarretta had three RBI's in the opener and seven altogether.

July 30

1933 — St. Louis' Dizzy Dean strikes out 17 Cubs, most by a pitcher to date in a nine inning game, during an 8-2 win before Card home fans.

1943 — Phil Cavarretta has a homer, double, two walks, and scores three runs while Bill Nicholson has a homer, a double, a single and a walk and drives in five runs as the Cubs maul the Dodgers, 13-2 behind Hi Bithorn at Wrigley Field.

July 31

1901 — "Long Tom" Hughes fans 15 in 14 innings but the Cubs lose to the Reds, 5-4, at Cincinnati. Noodles Hahn fanned 11 Cubs for Cincy.

1910 — Len Cole pitches a seven inning no-hitter as the Cubs beat the Cardinals, 4-0, at St. Louis. The game was abbreviated because both teams had to catch a train.

1968 — Billy Williams, Ernie Banks and Jim Hickman homer in the fourth inning as the Cubs roll the Astros, 6-1, behind Fergie Jenkins at Wrigley Field.

1974 — Bill Bonham strikes out four Expos in the second inning (Mike Torrez reaches base on catcher Dick Stelmaszek's passed ball) but Montreal wins, 7-4, at Wrigley Field.

AUGUST

August 1

1894 — Cubs crush St. Louis, 26-8, at West Side Grounds. Bill Dahlen collects three hits, three runs, and three RBI's, hitting safely in his 38th consecutive game. The streak extended to 42 games before it ended August 7.

1896 — George Decker hits safely in his 26th consecutive game with a seventh inning triple as the Cubs beat Louisville, 8-3, at West Side Grounds. The streak was ended the next game.

1905 — Frank Chance is appointed Cub manager. They go on to win four pennants and two world series under his leadership — after they blow a 5-0 lead and lose to the Phillies, 7-6, in 11 innings at West Side Grounds.

1927 — Hack Wilson hits safely in his 26th consecutive game with a single and a triple as the Cubs beat the Phillies, 6-5, at Wrigley Field. He went hitless the next game to end the streak.

1939 — In his Cub debut, Bill Nicholson hits a home run off Kirby Higbe in the fifth inning as the Cubs beat the Phillies, 6-2, behind Larry French at Wrigley Field.

1963 — Ellis Burton hits home runs batting left-handed and right-handed as the Cubs beat the Giants, 12-11, in 10 innings, at Wrigley Field. Cubs get six runs in the eighth to tie, and win in the tenth on Ron Santo's double and Jimmy Schaffer's single.

August 2

1911 — Jimmy Archer's home run in the bottom of the tenth inning gives the Cubs a 1-0 victory over Nap Rucker and the Dodgers at West Side Grounds. King Cole pitches a two-hitter for the Cubs.

1950 — Andy Pafko hits three home runs in the second game, driving in five runs, but the Cubs lose two to the Giants at the Polo Grounds, 11-1 and 8-6.

1955 — Ernie Banks hits his fourth grandslam homer of the year as the Cubs beat the Pirates behind Bob Rush, 12-4, at Wrigley Field.

August 3

1929 — Cubs complain that Brooklyn pitcher Dazzy Vance is wearing a ragged shirt sleeve to distract the vision of the batters, but they pound the Dodgers, 12-2, at Wrigley Field behind Hal Carlson.

1972 — Bill Hands pitches a one-hitter as the Cubs whitewash the Expos, 3-0, in the second game of a doubleheader at Montreal. Expos take first game, 2-1, in 13 innings.

August 4

1932 — Charlie Grimm replaces Rogers Hornsby as Cub manager and the Cubs crush the hosting Philadelphia Phillies, 12-1, on an eight-run second inning and a four-run fourth. Grimm celebrates with a single and two doubles, driving in three runs. Kiki Cuyler adds a homer and two RBI's.

1937 — Gabby Hartnett hits safely in his 24th straight game as the Phillies beat the Cubs, 2-1, at Chicago. Gabby has two singles in three at bats.

1955 — Ernie Banks slams three home runs off Pittsburgh pitchers (Lino Donoso, Max Surkont and Dick Littlefield) at Wrigley Field during an 11-10 victory by Cubs.

1960 — Billy Martin of the Reds breaks Cub pitcher Jim Brewer's cheekbone after throwing his bat toward the mound, claiming that Brewer was throwing at his head. But the Cubs go on to win, 5-3, on Ernie Banks' homer at Wrigley Field.

1968 — Pinch hitter Lee Elia singles home the winning run as the Cubs beat the Cardinals, 6-5 in 13 innings at Busch Memorial Stadium. A crowd of 47,443 was on hand in 93° heat to see the unveiling of the Stan Musial statue.

1969 — Glenn Beckert drills five hits in six trips to the plate and Fergie Jenkins fans 12 as the Cubs dump the Astros, 9-3, at Houston.

August 5

1894 — With Cap Anson at bat in the sixth inning, a fire breaks out in the grandstand at West Side Grounds. With 10,000 fans in a wild stampede, hundreds are injured as the crowd tears through the barbed wire fence which had been put up to prevent the 25-cent bleacher fans from mobbing the umpire. In spite of it all, the Cubs win, 8-1, behind Clark Griffith in a game that is called after six innings.

1944 — Bill Nicholson hits three singles and a triple as the Cubs beat the Pirates, 7-2, at Pittsburgh for their 11th consecutive win. Bill Fleming is the winning pitcher with relief help from Claude Passeau. Streak ends the following day when the Pirates make the Cubs walk the plank with a doubleheader sweep, 13-5 and 5-4.

August 6

1884 — Cap Anson hits three home runs in a 13-4 victory over Cleveland at Lakefront Park, giving him five homers in two days to establish a record tied by Cubs Billy Williams in 1968 and Dave Kingman in 1979. Larry Corcoran goes the route for the win.

1894 — Bill Dahlen gets two hits and scores twice, extending his hitting streak to 42 games as the Cubs beat Cincinnati, 12-9, at West Side Grounds, with the burnt out section sealed off. Dahlen goes hitless in six trips the next day to end the streak, even though the Cubs beat the visiting Reds again, 13-11, in ten innings.

1919 — Braves beat the Cubs, 2-0, when Boston pitcher Ray Keating's fly ball bounces through a hole in the wire fence in centerfield for a home run, at Chicago. Grover Alexander is the loser as the Cubs collect only three hits.

1922 — Cubs score six runs in the top of the ninth to beat the Giants, 10-3, at New York.

1959 — Billy Williams makes his Cub debut and goes zero-for-four but drives in a run as the Cubs beat the Phillies, 4-2, at Wrigley Field.

August 7

1877 — Cubs score 13 runs in the second inning en route to a 21-7, 24-hit win over the Reds at 23rd Street Grounds in Chicago. Dave Eggler, John Peters, Jimmy Hallinan, and Cal McVey each get two hits in the big inning, and Peters collects five hits in seven trips for the game, scoring twice.

1906 — Under Giant manager John McGraw's orders, umpire James Johnston is refused admittance at the Polo Grounds, and the scheduled game is forfeited to the Cubs, 9-0. Giant owner John Brush allows Johnston to enter the following day and the Cubs win, 3-2, behind Mordecai Brown and Ed Reulbach.

1911 — Joe Tinker, one of the few batters to hit well off Christy Mathewson, has his greatest day off Matty, going four-for-four with two singles, a double, and a triple. Tinker scores three runs, steals home, and executes two double plays as Mordecai Brown beats the Giants, 8-6, at West Side Grounds.

August 8

1947 — Shortstop Lennie Merullo and first baseman Eddie Waitkus combine on a triple play in the seventh inning and Bill Nicholson hits a home run in the 11th inning as the Cubs nip the Reds, 2-1, at Wrigley Field.

1965 — Pinch-hitter Ed Bailey is walked twice as the Cubs rally for six runs in the ninth inning to beat the Mets, 14-10, in game two of a twin bill at Shea Stadium. Cubs also won first game, 7-6.

August 9

1906 — Cub pitcher Jack Taylor beats the Dodgers in Brooklyn, 5-3, for his 187th consecutive complete game, a major league record. The streak began June 20, 1901, and during the span Taylor also made 15 relief appearances. His streak ends August 13 when he is relieved in the third inning of a game against Brooklyn.

1919 — Jim Vaughn steals home in the eighth inning as the Cubs beat the Giants, 3-1, at Wrigley Field. This was the last time a Cub pitcher stole home.

1929 — Guy Bush wins his 11th consecutive game as the Cubs beat the Phillies, 12-6, at Philadelphia.

1942 — Cubs beat the Reds, 10-8, in 18 innings at Cincinnati, the Reds having tied the score in the ninth, tenth, and twelfth innings before the Cubs finally hang on. Stan Hack collects five hits and three runs, while Hi Bithorn picks up the win in relief.

August 10

1909 — Cub pitcher Ed Reulbach wins his 14th consecutive game as he holds the Dodgers to six hits en route to an 8-1 victory, at West Side Grounds.

August 11

1941 — Phil Cavarretta, Stan Hack, and Bill Nicholson hit consecutive homers in the fifth inning, but the Cardinals beat the Cubs, 7-5, at Sportsman's Park.

1961 — Warren Spahn wins his 300th game as the Braves beat the Cubs, 3-1, at Milwaukee.

1966 — Randy Hundley hits for the cycle, driving in three runs, as the Cubs beat the Astros, 9-8, at Wrigley Field, in 11 innings.

1968 — Don Kessinger gets five hits in seven trips as the Cubs beat the Reds, 8-5, in 15 innings, on Billy Williams' three-run, inside-the-park home run in the top of the 15th at Cincinnati. Williams also had a two-run homer in the sixth.

1972 — Milt Pappas drives in five runs with a single, a double, and a home run to lead the Cubs to a 7-2 victory over the Mets at Wrigley Field.

August 12

1890 — In a wild, see-saw game, the Cubs outlast the Pirates, 13-12, in 12 innings at Pittsburgh. Jimmy Cooney collects four hits for the Cubs, walks, is hit by a pitch, and steals a base.

August 13

1897 — Clark Griffith, who considered it bad luck to pitch a shutout, hurls the first one of his career (in his seventh season in the majors), as the Cubs trip the Reds, 2-0, at Cincinnati.

1913 — Cubs trade pitcher Lew Richie to Kansas City of the American Association for pitcher Jim "Hippo" Vaughn.

1922 — Charlie Hollocher hits three triples as the Cubs clip the Cardinals' wings, 16-5, at Wrigley Field.

1937 — Cubs trounce the Reds, 22-6, at Wrigley Field, helped along by eight Cincinnati errors and a nine-run third inning. Ken O'Dea collects four hits, four runs and four RBI's, while Frank Demaree gets four hits and four runs.

1959 — Rookie Cub outfielder George Altman gets five hits in six at bats as the Cubs beat the Giants, 20-9, at Wrigley Field. Altman hits two home runs, Al Dark has a grandslam homer, Dale Long a pinch-hit home run, and Tony Taylor homers also. Time of the game was three hours, 50 minutes, for the longest nine-inning game in major league history up to that time.

1979 — Former Cub Lou Brock collects his 3,000th hit as the Cardinals beat the Cubs, 3-2, in 10 innings at St. Louis.

August 14

1888 — Cubs halt New York pitcher Tim Keefe's major league record winning streak at 19 straight as they clip the Giants, 4-2, at New York, behind the five-hit pitching of Gus Krock.

1889 — Hugh Duffy hits two home runs and Duke Farrell one as the Cubs beat the Phillies, 19-7, aided by a ten-run eighth inning, at West Side Park.

1959 — For the second consecutive day, Dale Long hits a pinch-hit home run as the Cubs beat the Giants, 7-5, at Wrigley Field. Ernie Banks and Moose Moryn also homer, and winning pitcher Glen Hobbie fans ten batters.

1972 — In the last Boys Benefit game played, the Cubs beat the White Sox, 3-1, at Comiskey Park. Ernie Banks, brought out of retirement for the evening, gets a standing ovation when he appears as a pinch-hitter.

August 15

1945 — Catcher Paul Gillespie — the first Cub player to wear a crewcut — drives in six runs with two homers and a single as the Cubs maul the Dodgers 20-6, at Ebbets Field. Andy Pafko and Heinz Becker also homer, and Hank Borowy goes the route for the win.

1964 — It's Ernie Banks day at Wrigley Field, but Ernie fails to hit the ball out of the infield as the Pirates beat the Cubs, 5-4.

August 16

1890 — Cubs score 13 runs in the fifth inning, en route to an 18-5 victory over Pittsburgh at West Side Park. Tommy Burns and Malachi Kittredge each hit a grandslam home run in the big inning.

1911 — Frank Schulte hits his fourth grandslam homer of the season to set a record (broken by Ernie Banks in 1955) as the Cubs beat the Braves, 13-6, at Boston.

1932 — It's Charlie Grimm day at Wrigley Field before 32,000, and the Cubs rally for four runs in the bottom of the ninth to beat the Braves, 4-3, highlighted by Billy Jurges' bases-loaded single.

1956 — Dee Fondy homers and "Sam Sam" Jones strikes out 13 batters as the Cubs beat the Braves, 4-2, at Wrigley Field.

August 17

1932 — Cubs beat the Braves, 3-2, in 19 innings on Frank Demaree's long fly with the bags loaded at Wrigley Field. Reliever Bud Tinning pitches 12-2/3 shutout innings.

August 18

1886 — John Clarkson strikes out 16 batters — a Cub record — as he beats Kansas City, 7-2, at West Side Park.

1907 — Grandstand catches fire during the Cub exhibition game at Bridgeport, Connecticut. Cubs help put out the fire and then beat Bridgeport, 3-1.

1930 — Woody English scores five runs and Hack Wilson hits his 42nd home run of the year as the Cubs crush the Phillies, 17-3, at Wrigley Field. Pitcher Pat Malone also homers and goes the distance for the win.

1952 — With two out in the bottom of the ninth, Phil Cavarretta hits a pinch-hit home run with a man on to give the Cubs a last-minute 4-3 victory over Murry Dickson and the Pirates, at Wrigley Field. It is Cavarretta's last home run as a Cub.

August 19

1880 — Larry Corcoran pitches the first no-hitter in Cub history as he blanks Boston, 6-0, at Lakefront Park. Cap Anson has 21 putouts at first base for the Cubs.

1913 — Cubs get nine straight hits off Grover Alexander in the ninth inning, scoring six runs for a 10-4 victory over the Phillies at Philadelphia.

1965 — Jim Maloney throws a 10-inning no-hitter, striking out 12 and walking 10 as he beats the Cubs and Larry Jackson, 1-0, at Wrigley Field. Cubs beat the Reds, 5-4, in the second game, on homers by Billy Williams and Don Landrum in the eighth and ninth innings, respectively.

1969 — Ken Holtzman throws a no-hitter as the Cubs beat the Braves, 3-0, before 41,033 at Wrigley Field. In the seventh inning Billy Williams backs into the left field vines to catch Hank Aaron's deep fly, thereby preserving the no-hitter.

1970 — Cubs hit seven home runs as they beat the Padres, 12-2, at Wrigley Field, behind Fergie Jenkins. Jim Hickman hits two homers, and Glenn Beckert, Joe Pepitone, Johnny Callison, Fergie Jenkins, and Billy Williams hit one each, with Callison, Beckert, and Pepitone all connecting in the eighth inning.

August 20

1958 — With Sammy Taylor out for a pinch-hitter, Moe Thacker in the hospital, and Cal Neeman having been ejected, Dale Long becomes the first and only left-handed catcher in Cub history, wearing his first baseman's mitt behind the plate in the first game of a doubleheader with the Pirates. Cub split, losing the first game, 4-2, but winning the second, 5-1, at Wrigley Field.

August 21

1876 — Behind 7-6, the Cubs walk off the field in the ninth inning at St. Louis, protesting an umpire's call, becoming the first team to forfeit a game, 9-0.

1898 — Cub pitcher Walter Thornton hurls a no-hitter, beating the Dodgers, 2-0, in the second game of a doubleheader at West Side Grounds.

1905 — Cubs complete a triple play in the first inning against the Dodgers in Brooklyn, the play going from pitcher Jake Weimer to shortstop Joe Tinker. Cubs win, 12-2, aided by a seven-run eighth inning.

1935 — After losing the first game of a doubleheader, 13-12, the Cubs score twelve runs in the sixth inning of game number two to pulverize the Phillies, 19-5, at Philadelphia. Frank Demaree and Phil Cavarretta each collect five hits in the second game (Demaree has three in the first game, Cavarretta two), while Chuck Klein scores eight runs in the doubleheader, three in the first game and five in the second.

1975 — Rick and Paul Reuschel combine for baseball's first all-brother shutout as the Cubs beat the Dodgers, 7-0, at Wrigley Field.

August 22

1891 — Cub outfielder Walt Wilmot receives six straight bases on balls, a major league record, a the Cubs beat Cleveland, 11-9, at West Side Park.

1908 — Not a single ball is hit to Cub third baseman Harry Steinfeldt as the Braves beat the Cubs, 3-1, in 15 innings at West Side Grounds on ex-Cub Bill Dahlen's single.

1942 — Catcher Clyde McCullough, shortstop Lennie Merullo, and first baseman Phil Cavarretta combine on a triple play in the top of the 11th inning, and Bill Nicholson homers in the bottom of the 11th as the Cubs beat the Reds, 5-4, at Wrigley Field.

1954 — It's Hank Sauer Day at Wrigley Field as 30,093 patrons shower the big leftfielder with packets of tobacco and other gifts. But Sauer muffs a fly ball and gets only one hit in five trips as the Braves beat the Cubs, 12-6. Rookie Ernie Banks hits two homers for the Cubs.

1970 — Ken Holtzman allows only one hit, a single by Hal Lanier with one out in the eighth, as the Cubs pummel the Giants, 15-0, at San Francisco.

August 23

1924 — Cubs complete a triple play against the Dodgers in the second inning at Wrigley Field, third baseman Bob Barrett to second baseman George Grantham to first baseman Harvey Cotter. But Brooklyn wins, 6-5, behind Dazzy Vance.

August 24

1886 — Cap Anson hits two home runs, singles, and scores six times as the Cubs maul Boston, 18-6, at West Side Park.

1905 — Ed Reulbach goes all the way as the Cubs nip the Phillies, 2-1, in 20 innings, at Philadelphia. Frank Chance's single drives in Jack McCarthy with the winning run, and loser Tully Sparks also goes the distance for the Phillies.

1927 — Hack Wilson goes four-for-five, hits two home runs, steals a base, scores five runs and drives in four as the Cubs beat the Phillies, 13-1, in the second game at Philadelphia. Sparky Adams goes five-for-six with three doubles, including two in the first inning. Wilson also homered in the first game, but the Phillies won, 7-6.

1971 — Ernie Banks hits his 512th and final home run as the Cubs beat the Reds, 5-4, at Wrigley Field. Homer comes off Jim McGlothin in the first inning.

Chuck Connors gave up his baseball career with the Cubs for an acting career. He is best known for his leading role in the TV series "The Rifleman."

August 25

1891 — Pitcher Jack Luby hits two home runs and Cap Anson hits two triples as the Cubs make bums out of Brooklyn, 28-5, at West Side Park. Luby, Anson, Jimmy Ryan, and Walt Wilmot collect four hits apiece in the slaughter.

1922 — In the highest scoring game ever played, the Cubs beat the Phillies, 26-23, at Wrigley Field, scoring 10 runs in the second inning and 14 in the fourth. Cubs lead 25-6 after four innings but barely hold on as the Phillies leave the bases loaded when the final out is made in the ninth inning. Cliff Heathcote collects five hits for the Cubs, and Hack Miller hits two home runs, driving in six runs.

August 26

1876 — Cap Anson collects two singles, a triple, and a home run, and commits five errors at third base as the Cubs beat St. Louis, 23-3, at 23rd Street Grounds.

1894 — Cub catcher Billy Schriver, on the first try, catches a ball dropped 500 feet from atop the Washington Monument.

1948 — A near-riot erupts at Wrigley Field when umpire Jocko Conlan credits Phil Cavarretta with a ground-rule double instead of an inside-the-park homer in the third inning in the second game of a doubleheader. (Braves leftfielder Jeff Heath allegedly pretended to lose the ball in the vines when it was actually down by his foot.) Play is held up 20 minutes as the field is showered with straw hats and beer bottles, and Conlan chews out a Chicago policeman for not taking action. But Cubs win, 5-2, when Andy Pafko is walked and "P-Nuts" Lowrey hits a three-run triple, in the same inning. Cubs also won first game, 5-1.

1951 — Chuck Connors (the "Rifleman" of TV several years later) hits his second and last major league home run, a three-run blast off Sal Maglie in the top of the ninth, to tie up the Cub-Giant game at four apiece. Giants win in the bottom of the inning when Wes Westrum knocks a homer off Cub reliever Walt Dubiel, at New York. Giants also win second game, 5-1, to extend their winning streak to 14 games.

1966 — Leo Durocher rips the phone out of the Cub dugout at Houston and throws it onto the field after the Astrodome Message Board begins harassing him in the ninth inning with various cartoons. Cubs lose, 7-4, on Bob Aspromonte's grandslam homer off Cal Koonce, and Leo later receives a bill for the damage.

1972 — Ron Santo collects his 2,000th career hit, a three-run home run, as the Cubs edge the Giants, 10-9, at Wrigley Field, in ten innings. In the same game, Billy Williams gets five hits in six trips, including two homers, driving in four runs.

August 27

1895 — Bill Lange knocks one out of the park in the bottom of the 11th inning but is only credited with a single under rules of that time because the winning run was already on second base. Cubs beat Washington at the Capitol, 5-4.

1910 — Cubs complete a triple play against the Giants in the third inning at West Side

Grounds, second baseman Johnny Evers to third baseman Heinie Zimmerman. However, Giants clobber Cubs, 18-9.

1941 — Charlie Root becomes the first and only pitcher to win 200 games in a Cub uniform. Root delivers a clutch single in the ninth inning as the Cubs score three runs to beat the Boston Braves at Braves Field, 6-4.

August 28

1931 — Billy Herman makes his major league debut at second base and singles in his first at bat. In his second time up, Herman is struck over the right ear by a foul tip and is carried off the field. Cubs go on to beat the Reds, 14-5, at Wrigley Field on homers by Hack Wilson, Charlie Grimm, Clarence Blair, and Vince Barton. Going the route for his 15th win, Charlie Root gets two doubles and a single.

1937 — Clay Bryant, pitching in relief of Charlie Root, hits a grandslam homer in the 10th inning as the Cubs beat the Braves, 10-7, in Boston. Root had homered earlier in the game.

1950 — Hank Sauer hits three home runs as the Cubs beat the Phillies, 7-5, at Wrigley Field. Dutch Leonard makes his only start of the year and wins.

August 29

1918 — In a war-shortened season, Cubs clinch the pennant as George "Lefty" Tyler beats the Reds, 1-0, at Wrigley Field.

1955 — Harry Chiti, Dee Fondy and Gene Baker homer in the fourth inning as the Cubs beat the Giants, 6-3, at the Polo Grounds with Warren Hacker going the route.

August 30

1921 — Cubs complete a triple play in the third inning against the Giants at New York, second baseman Zeb Terry to shortstop Charlie Hollocher to first baseman Ray Grimes, but the Giants win, 5-3. On the same day, the Boston Braves pulled a triple killing against Cincinnati, but the Reds won, 6-4. It was the only time in major league history in which two triple plays were executed on the same day.

1945 — Stan Hack collects his 2,000th hit, a single off the Pirates' Preacher Roe to open the first inning at Pittsburgh. Hack scores later that inning but the Pirates come back to win, 6-4.

August 31

1896 — In the bottom of the 10th inning at Washington, Cub centerfielder Bill Lange makes a diving, somersault catch off the bat of Gene DeMontreville. During the same inning, Cub first baseman George Decker broke his wrist. Since there was a hospital adjacent to the ball park, Kip Selbach of Washington battered down several boards of the outfield fence to give Decker a convenient exit. This incident evolved into a popular legend which claimed that Lange had crashed through the fence making a catch off Selbach. Washington won the game, 1-0, in eleven innings.

1915 — Cub pitcher Jimmy Lavender pitches a no-hit game as the Cubs beat the Giants, 2-0, in the first game of a doubleheader at the Polo Grounds.

1932 — With the Cubs trailing, 9-7, with two out in the bottom of the 10th at Wrigley Field, Kiki Cuyler hits a three-run home run to give the Cubs a 10-9 victory over the Giants, extending their winning streak to twelve games. It was Cuyler's fifth hit of the game and his fourth homer in five games. His streak was halted the next day.

1971 — Don Kessinger raps five hits in six at bats, including a game-winning single in the 10th inning as the Cubs beat the Expos, 7-6, in the first game of a doubleheader at Wrigley Field. Don adds two hits in game number two, but the Cubs lose, 11-2, in a game completed the following day after it was suspended because of darkness.

SEPTEMBER

September 1

1883 — The Cubs score 11 runs in the third inning on four singles, two doubles, a triple, two errors and two passed balls and beat Cleveland, 21-7, at Cleveland. The Cubs drill nine doubles, with Abner Dalrymple and Fred Pfeffer getting four hits each.

1906 — The regularly assigned umpires are ill (food poisoning was suspected) and Cub pitcher Carl Lundgren and Cardinal catcher Peter Noonan are selected as umpires. The Cubs, with Mordecai Brown pitching a five-hitter, beat the Cardinals, 8-1, for their 14th victory in a row at West Side Grounds.

1947 — The Cubs pull a triple play in the fourth inning against the Reds at Wrigley Field, shortstop Bobby Sturgeon spearing a liner, stepping on second and firing to third baseman "P-Nuts" Lowrey but Cubs lose nightcap, 13-2, at Wrigley Field. after having won the opener, 1-0, on four-hitter by Bob Chipman.

1961 — Catcher Cuno Barragan hits a homer in his first major league at bat as the Cubs lose, 4-3, in 14 innings to the Giants at Wrigley Field. Barragan hit no more homers in his abbreviated career.

September 2

1929 — Cubs beat the Cardinals, 11-7 and 12-10, before 81,000 at Wrigley Field. There were 38,000 at morning game and 43,000 at afternoon game. Rogers Hornsby hit two homers and Hack Wilson hit one.

1932 — Kiki Cuyler hits his fifth homer in six games as the Cubs stop the Cardinals, 8-5, for their 13th in a row behind Burleigh Grimes and Charlie Root. Mark Koenig also homered for the Cubs. The streak hit 14 the next day, but Dizzy Dean stopped them, 3-0, in the second game before a crowd of 45,000, at Wrigley Field.

1955 — Ernie Banks hits his 40th homer of the season as the Cubs rout the Cardinals, 12-2, at Wrigley Field. The homer set a record for shortstops, topping Vern Stephens' 39 with the 1949 Red Sox.

1965 — Ernie Banks hits the 400th homer of his career off Curt Simmons with two on in the third inning as the Cubs top the Cardinals, 5-3, behind Bob Hendley at Wrigley Field.

1970 — Billy Williams plays his 1,117th consecutive game, a National League record, as the Cubs rip the Phillies, 17-2, at Wrigley Field. Williams was rested the following day, ending his streak. Lou Gehrig of the Yankees holds the Major League record with 2,130.

1972 — Milt Pappas pitches a no-hitter as the Cubs trounce the Padres, 8-0, at Wrigley Field. Pappas just missed a perfect game when he walked Larry Stahl on a full count with two out in the ninth inning.

September 3

1908 — The Cubs lose to the Pirates, 1-0, in 10 innings at Pittsburgh. Cub second baseman argues that Pirates' Warren Gill failed to touch second base on the game-winning hit, but his plea is ignored by umpire Hank O'Day. This game was a forerunner to the Fred Merkle incident of September 23 and O'Day and Evers are again involved.

1925 — Rabbit Maranville is replaced by George Gibson as Cubs' manager after president Bill Veeck Sr. learns the Rabbit raced through the Pullman, anointing players with water from a spittoon.

1944 — The Cubs complete a triple play in the first inning of the first game against the Reds at Crosley Field, shortstop Lenny Merullo to second baseman Don Johnson to first baseman Stan Hack. Cubs win, 5-1 and 6-2, behind Hank Wyse and Claude Passeau and Bill Nicholson hits his 30th homer of the season.

1971 — Owner Philip K. Wrigley takes out advertisements in the newspapers, criticizing the players in the "dump Durocher clique", and praising Durocher. Wrigley added a P.S. — If only we could find more team players like Ernie Banks.

September 4

1885 — Jim McCormick wins his 14th consecutive game as the Cubs defeat Buffalo, 12-4, at West Side Park.

1891 — In mockery of sportswriters suggesting he is too old to play, 40-year-old Cap Anson plays the entire game wearing a false white beard. Cap goes 0-for-3, with a walk, but the Cubs beat Boston, 5-3, at West Side Park.

1929 — The Cubs collect 10 straight hits in the fourth inning and rip the Braves, 13-6, at Wrigley Field.

September 5

1890 — Cub pitcher John Luby hits three batters in the sixth inning and wound up with four hit batsman and seven walks, but he also homered as Cubs beat Cincinnati, 12-8, at West Side Park.

1918 — Babe Ruth outduels Hippo Vaughn as the Red Sox edge the Cubs, 1-0, in the opener of the World Series at Comiskey Park. The Cubs used the White Sox park because of its larger seating capacity.

1962 — Ken Hubbs breaks Bobby Doerr's major league record by handling 418 chances in 78 games without an error at second base before he makes a wild throw in Cincinnati in the fourth inning as the Reds beat the Cubs, 7-5.

September 6

1883 — The Cubs score a record 18 runs in the seventh inning to maul Detroit, 26-6, at Lakefront Park. Tommy Burns sets a major league record with two doubles and a single in the big inning.

1918 — The Cubs beat the Red Sox, 3-1, in the second game of the World Series behind Lefty Tyler at Comiskey Park.

1939 — Bill Nicholson, Rip Russell, and Larry French homer in the third inning as the Cubs wallop the Cardinals, 11-3, at Wrigley Field.

September 7

1913 — Vic Saier has 21 putouts at first base as the Cubs sweep the Cardinals, 4-1 and 7-1, at West Side Grounds. Frank Schulte hits two home runs.

1964 — Ellis Burton hits two home runs — one righty, one lefty — for the second time in his career but the Braves beat the Cubs, 10-9, at Wrigley Field.

1973 — Billy Williams gets five hits, including one double, and drives in three runs as the Cubs beat the Cardinals, 8-2, at Wrigley Field.

September 8

1953 — The Cubs purchase the contract of pitcher Bill Dickey and a skinny shortstop named Ernie Banks for $10,000 from the Kansas City Monarchs of the Negro American League.

1972 — Fergie Jenkins wins his 20th game by beating the Phillies, 4-3, at Philadelphia, becoming the first Cub pitcher to win 20 games six years in a row since Mordecai Brown (1906-11).

1977 — Bruce Sutter ties a National League record for relief pitchers by striking out six consecutive batters as the Cubs edge the Expos, 3-2, at Wrigley Field.

September 9

1882 — George Gore, Cap Anson, Mike Kelly, Tommy Burns and Frank Flint get four hits each and Larry Corcoran hurls a three-hitter as the Cubs trounce Troy, 24-1, in a game called after eight innings because of darkness, at Lakefront Park.

1894 — Bill Dahlen extends his second hitting streak to 28 games, but Cleveland wins, 9-5, at Chicago.

1955 — Dee Fondy, Ernie Banks and Eddie Miksis homer in the first inning of the first game and Fondy, Gene Baker and Banks homer in the eighth inning of the second game as the Cubs beat the Dodgers, 11-4, in the opener but lose the nightcap, 16-9. There were 13 homers hit in the doubleheader at Wrigley Field.

1965 — Sandy Koufax fans 14 and pitches a perfect game, beating the Cubs, 1-0, at Dodger Stadium. Cub pitcher Bob Hendley allows only one hit, a double by Lou Johnson, and the one run is unearned.

September 10

1915 — Cub pioneer Albert Spalding dies at Point Loma, California.

1918 — The Cubs beat the Red Sox, 3-0, behind Jim Vaughn in the fifth game of the World Series at Fenway Park.

1968 — Billy Williams hits three homers as the Cubs trip the Mets, 3-1, at Chicago, behind Bill Hands. Williams had two homers the previous day, giving him five for two days, to tie Cap Anson's record.

1980 — Bill Gullickson strikes out 18 Cubs as the Expos win 4-2 in Montreal. It was the most strikeouts by a rookie pitcher in major league history.

September 11

1918 — The Red Sox beat the Cubs, 2-1, behind Carl Mays to win the World Series in six games at Fenway Park.

1968 — Cub pitcher Fergie Jenkins loses, 1-0, at Jim McAndrew of the Mets at Wrigley Field. It was Jenkins' fifth 1-0 loss of the year, tying a major league record.

September 12

1919 — Cubs complete a triple play in the sixth inning of the first game against the Dodgers at Wrigley Field, shortstop Charlie Hollocher to first baseman Fred Merkle. Cubs win, 3-1, on Merkle's seventh inning home run **through** the fence in the left field corner. Cubs lose second game, 5-4.

1980 — Cubs explode for five runs in the top of the 14th inning to stun the Mets, 10-5, at New York.

September 13

1906 — Mordecai Brown wins his 11th straight game as the Cubs beat the Cardinals, 6-2, at St. Louis.

1913 — Jim Vaughn blanks the Dodgers, 4-0, on two hits at West Side Grounds. On the same day Heinie Zimmerman, who less than three months earlier was awarded $100 by a generous fan for his "reformed" behavior, is suspended by National

League President Thomas Lynch for having sworn at umpire Bill Byron on September 11.

1927 — Cubs acquire pitcher Pat Malone from Minneapolis of the American Association. However, he does not pitch until the following April.

1931 — Cub manager Rogers Hornsby hits a pinch grandslam homer in the 11th inning as the Cubs beat the Braves, 11-7, at Chicago. Cubs also win second game, 8-1, on Guy Bush's one-hitter.

1942 — Cub shortstop Lennie Merullo makes four errors in the second inning of the second game against Boston. His son is born that day and is named "Boots." Cubs win, 12-8, after losing the opener, 11-6, at Braves Field.

1960 — Danny Murphy, at 18 years and 20 days, is the youngest Cub to hit a homer as the Reds beat the Cubs, 8-6, at Cincinnati.

1970 — With the Pirates leading, 2-1, outfielder Matty Alou drops a fly ball with two out in the ninth inning, enabling the Cubs to rally for a 3-2 victory on Billy Williams' single at Wrigley Field.

September 14

1905 — Joe Tinker and Johnny Evers, previously on good terms, engage in a fist fight on the field during an exhibition game at Washington, Ind., after arguing over Evers' taking a taxi to the park while leaving the other players in the hotel lobby. The two remain on non-speaking terms for the rest of their Cub careers, although they co-operate brilliantly on the field. The Cubs beat the locals, 7-3, in the exhibition game.

1907 — Solly Hofman gets five hits as the Cubs rip the Reds' Andy Coakley for 19 hits and 12 runs as the Cubs win, 12-5, at West Side Grounds.

1913 — Larry Cheney allows 14 hits, the most ever allowed in a shutout, but the Cubs blank the Giants, 7-0, at West Side Grounds.

1953 — Ernie Banks and Gene Baker join the Cubs and watch them win their 10th in a row beating the Dodgers, 3-1, at Wrigley Field. During batting practice Banks hit the first pitch into the left field bleachers.

1957 — Ernie Banks hits three consecutive solo homers as the Cubs beat the Pirates, 7-3, in the nightcap at Wrigley Field. Pittsburgh won the opener, 3-1.

1965 — Bob Hendley gains revenge on the Dodgers' Sandy Koufax, pitching a four-hitter as the Cubs win, 2-1, on Billy Wiliams homer at Wrigley Field.

September 15

1880 — Pitcher Larry Corcoran's clutch double sparks the Cubs to a pennant-clinching 5-2 victory over the Reds at Cincinnati.

1902 — Only 260 fans witness the first Tinker-to-Evers-to-Chance double play as the Cubs beat the Reds, 6-3, behind Carl Lundgren at West Side Grounds.

1968 — Ernie Banks plays in his 2,254th game in a Cub uniform — surpassing Cap Anson's record — as the Cubs blank the Phillies, 4-0, behind Fergie Jenkins at Philadelphia.

1971 — Burt Hooton strikes out 15 Mets in his second major league start as the Cubs win, 3-2, to sweep a doubleheader at Shea Stadium. They also won the opener, 6-2, behind Bill Hands.

September 16

1884 — Fred Pfeffer collects five hits in six trips, including a home run, and George Gore smashes two homers as the Cubs pummel Boston, 17-0, behind Larry Corcoran at Lakefront Park.

1894 — George Decker rockets two home runs and hits for the cycle as the Cubs outslug the Dodgers, 13-10, at West Side Grounds.

1909 — President William Howard Taft is among the crowd of 27,000 at West Side Grounds, as Christy Mathewson and the Giants edge Mordecai Brown and the Cubs, 2-1. This was the only time in history that a Chief Executive attended a baseball game in Chicago while in office.

1923 — Hack Miller goes four-for-four with three doubles and a triple, scoring twice, but the Giants beat the Cubs, 10-6, at Wrigley Field. In the eighth inning, hundreds of fans start throwing pop bottles at umpire Charlie Moran when he calls Sparky Adams out at second base on a force. Baseball Commissioner Kenesaw Mountain Landis shakes his cane at the angry mob and play is held up for fifteen minutes. At the game's conclusion, Giant manager John McGraw and the umpiring crew need a police escort to get out of the park.

1972 — Ellie Hendricks draws five of 15 Cub walks and pitcher Burt Hooton hits a grandslam home run off Tom Seaver as the Cubs blast the New York Mets, 18-5, at Wrigley Field.

1975 — Rennie Stennett collects seven hits as the Pirates scuttle the Cubs, 22-0, at Wrigley Field. It was the most lop-sided shutout in modern baseball.

September 17

1928 — Gabby Hartnett hits a two-run homer and Kiki Cuyler, Hack Wilson and Charlie Grimm collect two doubles each as the Cubs bounce the Braves, 15-5, at Boston. In the ninth inning, pitcher Ray Boggs hits three batters (Woody English, Cuyler and Riggs Stephenson) and throws two wild pitches.

1938 — Bill Lee allows 13 hits, but pitches his third straight shutout as the Cubs beat the Giants, 4-0, in the Polo Grounds.

1945 — Bill Nicholson makes 10 putouts, setting a record for rightfielders, but the Dodgers blank the Cubs, 4-0, at Wrigley Field.

1953 — Ernie Banks plays his first major league game and goes 0-for-3, scores once, and makes an error as the Phillies beat the Cubs, 16-4, at Wrigley Field. Banks goes on to set an all-time record of most consecutive games from the start of a career, 424.

September 18

1903 — Charlie Fraser of the Philadelphia Phillies pitches a no-hitter, beating the Cubs, 10-0, in the second game at West Side Grounds.

1904 — Jack McCarthy drives in both runs and pitcher Buttons Briggs goes the route as the Cubs beat the Reds, 2-1, in 17 innings at West Side Grounds.

1929 — Carl Hubbell and the New York Giants beat the Cubs, 7-3, at Wrigley Field, but Chicago clinches the pennant when the Pirates lose, 5-4, to the Braves in the first game of a doubleheader.

1950 — Ron Northey hits a pinch grandslam homer to lead the Cubs to a 9-7 victory over the Dodgers at Ebbets Field. It was Northey's third pinch slam, setting a major league record. Northey's other two came while he was a Cardinal.

1960 — Don Zimmer, Ron Santo and George Altman homer in the sixth inning and Ernie Banks receives a record 27th intentional pass as the Cubs beat the Dodgers, 5-2, at Wrigley Field.

September 19

1881 — Although the Cubs do not play, they clinch the pennant as Troy defeats second place Buffalo, 7-5.

1885 — John Clarkson pitches a two-hitter for his 50th victory of the season as the Cubs beat Boston, 10-3, at West Side Park.

1906 — The Cubs clinch the pennant, beating the Braves, 3-1, behind Ed Reulbach at Boston.

1955 — Ernie Banks sets a major league record with his fifth grandslam homer of the season, but the Cardinals nip the Cubs, 6-5, on "Rip" Repulski's 12th-inning homer off Jim Davis.

September 20

1882 — Larry Corcoran pitches his second no-hitter as the Cubs whip Worcester, 5-0, at Lakefront Park.

1894 — The hosting Cubs score 10 runs in the first inning to wallop the Phillies, 20-4. Bill Lange, Walt Wilmot and Bill Dahlen get three hits each and Dahlen scores five runs at West Side Grounds.

1924 — Grover Alexander wins his 300th game as the Cubs beat the Giants, 7-3, in 12 innings at New York.

1932 — The Cubs clinch the pennant, beating the Pirates, 5-2, on Kiki Cuyler's bases-loaded triple in the seventh inning at Wrigley Field. Guy Bush went the route for his 19th victory.

1941 — Bob Scheffing hits a pinch grandslam homer in the ninth inning as the Cubs beat the Cardinals, 7-3, at Sportsman's Park.

1953 — Ernie Banks hits his first career homer off Gerry Staley with none on in the eighth inning, but the Cubs lose, 11-6, to the Cardinals at Busch Stadium.

September 21

1901 — Clarence Childs singles home the winning run in the 17th inning as the Cubs edge Boston, 1-0. "Long Tom" Hughes strikes out 13 while going the route for the Cubs. It was the longest stint — by innings — since Clark Griffith's 14 on June 19, 1900. There were no extra base hits in the contest played at West Side Grounds. This is still the longest shutout by a cub pitcher.

1919 — Short and sweet! In the final home game of the year, the Cubs beat the Braves, 3-0, behind Grover Alexander's five-hitter. The time of the game was 58 minutes for the shortest nine-inning game in Cub history.

1971 — Ron Santo hits his 300th homer as the Cubs and Burt Hooton blank the Mets and Tom Seaver, 3-0, at Wrigley Field.

September 22

1925 — The Cubs complete a triple play in the eighth inning against the Dodgers at Wrigley Field, shortstop Sparky Adams to second baseman Gale Staley to first baseman Charlie Grimm to catcher Gabby Hartnett. Cubs win, 3-2, in 12 innings.

1938 — Bill Lee pitches his fourth consecutive shutout to tie Mordecai Brown and Ed Reulbach for the Cub record, beating the Phillies, 4-0, at Shibe Park.

September 23

1907 — The Cubs clinch the pennant, beating the Phillies, 4-1, in a rain-shortened, seven and one-half inning game. Ed Reulbach, in relief of Mordecai Brown, gains the victory at West Side Grounds. In the fifth inning the Cubs pull a triple play, first baseman George Howard to shortstop Joe Tinker.

1908 — The Merkle Boner! Fred Merkle of the Giants fails to touch second base as the apparent winning run crosses the plate in the ninth inning at the Polo Grounds. The game is declared a 1-1 tie and is rescheduled for October 8.

1930 — Second baseman Rogers Hornsby replaces Joe McCarthy as manager of the Cubs.

September 24

1899 — Sam Mertes hits two homers and Clark Griffith pitches the Cubs to a 21-5 victory at Cincinnati.

1943 — Andy Pafko drives in four runs with a double and single in three at bats during his major league debut to lead the Cubs to a 7-4 victory over the Phillies. Unfortunately, due to inclement weather, a Wrigley Field record low of only 314 paid fans witnesses the contest which is finally called after five innings.

September 25

1885 — The Cubs play a "home" game in Milwaukee, beating Providence, 21-3. Cubs get 26 hits while Providence commits 20 errors.

1934 — Phil Cavarretta goes four-for-five with two triples, two runs and four RBI's. Dewey Williams drives in four runs with two singles. Bill Nicholson drives in three with a double and a triple, and Lou Novikoff hits his final Cub homer.

1935 — A year later to the day, Phil Cavarretta homers as the Cubs blank the hosting Cardinals, 1-0, to move the Cubs to a tie for first place. It was the Cubs' 19th straight victory.

1966 — Cubs rookie pitcher Ken Holtzman loses his no-hitter in the ninth inning, but outduels the Dodgers' Sandy Koufax for a 2-1 victory at Wrigley Field. Holtzman settled for a two-hitter.

1968 — Ron Santo's grandslam homer in the ninth inning off Bill Singer gives the Cubs a 4-1 victory over the Dodgers at Wrigley Field.

September 26

1876 — The Cubs score six runs in the sixth inning and clinch the first National League pennant at 23rd Street Park, beating Hartford, 7-6. Hartford's four-run rally in the ninth inning fell short.

1908 — A double shutout! Ed Reulbach becomes the only pitcher in major league history to pitch a doubleheader shutout, beating the Dodgers, 5-0 and 3-0, in Brooklyn.

1944 — Hank Wyse hurls a four hitter as the Cubs bomb the Phillies, 15-0, at Shibe Park. Phil Cavarretta goes four-for-five with two triples, two runs and four RBI. Dewey Williams drives in four runs with two singles, Bill Nicholson drives in three with a double and a triple, and Lou Novikoff hits his final Cub homer.

1959 — Bobby Thomson goes four-for-four and Al Dark hits a three-run homer as the Cubs bounce the Dodgers, 12-2, at Wrigley Field to force a pennant playoff between the Dodgers and Braves.

1971 — Ernie Banks plays his final game (2,528th), getting his 2,583rd hit, a first-inning single off Ken Reynolds, but the Cubs lose, 5-1, to the Phillies at Wrigley Field.

September 27

1881 — The Cubs play their final game of the season in a driving rainstorm in Troy, N.Y. The paid attendance is 12, the smallest crowd in major league history. The Cubs win, 10-8.

1884 — The Cubs score 10 runs in the first inning and pummel Providence, 15-10. George Gore and Abner Dalrymple collect two hits each in the inning. Dalrymple goes ' five-for-six with a homer and scores three runs, while Tommy Burns goes four-for-five and scores three times at Lakefront Park.

1930 — Hack Wilson hits two homers, giving a him a National League record 56 for the season, Gabby Hartnett also homers and Pat Malone wins his 20th game as the Cubs beat the Reds, 13-8, at Wrigley Field.

1935 — The Cubs win their 21st game in a row and clinch the pennant, sweeping the

Cardinals, 6-2 and 5-3, at Sportsman's Park. Fred Lindstrom drives in four runs with three hits and Bill Lee wins his 20th game in the opener.

1936— Walt Alston strikes out in his only major league appearance as a Cardinal. The Cubs beat St. Louis, 6-3, behind Lon Warneke at Sportsman's Park. Alston later managed the Dodgers for 23 years, winning seven pennants and four World Series.

September 28

1897— Dave Wright allows 17 hits in his only major league victory as the Cubs score 11 runs in the fifth inning to pelt Pittsburgh, 15-14, in a game called after seven innings because of darkness at Pittsburgh. Jimmy Ryan and Barry McCormick had four hits each for the Cubs.

1912— Frank Chance is released as Cubs player-manager. In 7-1/2 seasons Chance led the Cubs to four pennants and two World Series victories. His teams won 753 games and lost only 379 for a .665 percentage, highest among Cub managers.

1930— Hack Wilson drives in his 189th and 190th runs on the final day of the season to set an all-time major league RBI record as the Cubs beat the Reds, 13-11, at Wrigley Field.

1938— Homer in the Gloamin! Gabby Hartnett hits his famed home run off Mace Brown as darkness sets in in the ninth inning at Wrigley Field to beat the Pirates, 6-5, and virtually clinch the pennant for Chicago.

1952— On the last day of the season, Stan Musial pitches to Frankie Baumholtz of the Cubs with two out and nobody on in the first inning, and Baumholtz reaches first on an error. Paul Minner and the Cubs beat Harvey Haddix and the Cardinals, 3-0, at Sportsman's Park, but Musial beats out Baumholtz for the batting title, .336 to .325. Since it was the end of the season, the teams decided to have Baumholtz and Musial face each other. It was Musial's only major league pitching appearance.

1959— Charlie Grimm begins his third term as Cub manager, replacing Bob Scheffing, who had given the Cubs their best record (74-80) since 1952 (77-77).

September 29

1882— The Cubs clinch the pennant with an 11-5 romp over Buffalo at Lakefront Park. Abner Dalrymple and King Kelly collect three hits each and Silver Flint hits a two-run homer.

1926— Charlie Root limits the White Sox to four hits as the Cubs win the City Series opener, 6-0, at Wrigley Field.

1935— Augie Galan played his 154th game of season for the Cubs without hitting into a doubleplay to set the current major league record as Cubs lose 2-1 at St. Louis.

September 30

1882— Sixteen-year-old Milton Scott, a substitute first baseman, is the youngest player in Cub history and goes two-for-five and scores once as the Cubs trip Buffalo, 6-5, at Lakefront Park. Larry Corcoran goes all the way, and Ed Williamson goes five-for-five with an RBI, a stolen base, and scores the winning run in the ninth inning on King Kelly's single. It was also Corcoran's 10th straight win.

1884 — John Clarkson strikes out seven batters in a row in the second, third and fourth innings as the Cubs beat the Giants, 17-2, at Chicago. Clarkson fans 13 for the game.

1885 — The Cubs clinch the pennant on Fred Pfeffer's seventh inning homer. John Clarkson edges Tim Keefe and the Giants, 2-1, at West Side Park.

1889 — Jimmy Ryan hits George Haddock's first pitch for a homer, his sixth leadoff homer of the season. This is the major league record until Bobby Bonds hit seven leadoff homers in 1973. Ryan adds a double and two sacrifice flies as the Cubs beat Washington, 9-5, at West Side Park.

1933 — Babe Herman hits for the cycle and Guy Bush wins his 20th game as the Cubs rip the Cardinals and Dizzy Dean, 12-2, at Sportsman's Park.

1962 — The Cubs complete a triple play in the eighth inning, second baseman Ken Hubbs to first baseman Ernie Banks to shortstop Andre Rodgers as the Cubs beat the Mets, 5-1, at Wrigley Field.

OCTOBER

October 1

1903 — In the first City Series game played between the Cubs and the White Sox, Jack Taylor whitewashes the Sox, 11-0, at West Side Grounds. Taylor loses his next three starts, as the series ends in a draw, each side winning seven games.

1906 — Ed Reulbach wins his 12th consecutive game as the Cubs edge the Phillies, 4-3, in a contest called after six innings because of darkness, at Philadelphia. Cubs won the first game, 4-0, on Carl Lundgren's two-hitter.

1908 — Ed Reulbach pitches his fourth straight shutout, tying a club record set by Mordecai Brown earlier in the year, as the Cubs beat the Reds, 6-0, at West Side Grounds.

1920 — Grover Alexander of the Cubs and Jesse Haines of the Cardinals, both future Hall of Famers, go the distance as the Cubs outlast the Redbirds, 3-2, in 17 innings at Wrigley Field.

1924 — In the first Chicago baseball game ever broadcast on radio, with Sen Kaney at the mike for WGN, the Cubs beat the White Sox, 10-7, in the City Series opener at Wrigley Field. Cub second baseman George Grantham drives in four runs with a two-run homer and a two-run single, Whitey Sheely belts two home runs for the Sox, and Grover Alexander goes the route for the Cubs, collecting two singles and scoring twice. But the Sox came back to win the series, four games to two.

1932 — Babe Ruth points toward the Wrigley Field bleachers and reputedly "calls his shot", hitting a home run in the fifth inning off Charlie Root of the Cubs in the third game of the World Series. Ruth and Lou Gehrig had two homers apiece as the Yankees beat the Cubs, 7-5.

1938 — Cubs clinch the pennant with a 10-3 win over the Cardinals in the second game of a doubleheader at St. Louis. Charlie Root goes the route and Billy Herman gets four hits.

1972 — Milt Pappas wins his 11th straight game as the Cubs beat the Cardinals, 3-0, at Wrigley Field.

October 2

1910 — Cubs clinch the pennant with an 8-4 win over the Reds at Cincinnati, highlighted by a third inning triple play, leftfielder Jimmy Sheckard to catcher Johnny Kling to first baseman Jimmy Archer.

1925 — Grover Alexander of the Cubs and Ted Blankenship of the Sox go the route in a 19 inning, 2-2, tie in the City Series, at Comiskey Park.

1932 — Yankees bomb the Cubs, 13-6, to complete four game sweep of the World Series, at Wrigley Field. Lou Gehrig hit .529 for the series with three homers and eight RBI's.

1935 — Lon Warneke pitches a four-hitter as the Cubs blank the Tigers, 2-0, in the World Series opener at Briggs Stadium.

1979 — Preston Gomez is hired as Cub manager, to replace interim boss Joe Amalfitano, who took Herman Franks' place September 24.

October 3

1890 — John Luby wins his 17th consecutive game, a Cub record, as the Cubs beat the Giants and Amos Rusie at West Side Park, 3-2, in a game that is called after seven innings because of darkness.

1897 — Cap Anson closes out his career, hitting two home runs as the Cardinals beat the Cubs, 10-9, in the first game of a doubleheader, at St. Louis. At 46, Anson was the oldest player to hit a home run in the majors. Cubs win second game, 7-1, but Anson goes zero for three.

1945 — Cubs rip the Tigers, 9-0, in the World Series opener at Detroit, behind Hank Borowy's six-hitter.

1965 — Cubs make their third triple play of the year, to tie the major league record, first baseman Ernie Banks to shortstop Don Kessinger in the fifth inning, but the Pirates win, 6-3, at Forbes Field. Bill Faul was the Cub pitcher on all three occasions.

1976 — Bill Madlock goes four-for-four on the final day of the season to win the batting title with a .339 mark a the Cubs beat the Expos, 8-2, at Wrigley Field.

October 4

1906 — Jack Pfiester shuts out the hosting Pittsburgh Pirates, 4-0, for the Cubs' record

116th win of the season and Pfiester's 20th. Cub pitcher Carl Lundgren plays the entire game at second base.

1908 — Cubs beat the Pirates, 5-2, before 30,247 at West Side Grounds, behind Mordecai Brown, to clinch a tie for the pennant, while a woman gives birth in the grandstand.

1928 — First baseman Art Shires' muff in the top of the ninth inning allows the Cubs to tie the score, and they go on to beat the White Sox, 5-3, in 14 innings in the City Series at Comiskey Park.

1939 — Before a crowd of 42,267 at Comiskey Park, Bill Nicholson hits a two-run homer in the top of the ninth to tie the White Sox, 9-9, in the City Series opener. Cubs win, 10-9, in the tenth when Augie Galan drives in Stan Hack with the winning run.

1948 — Cubs trade popular slugger Bill Nicholson to the Phillies for outfielder Harry Walker.

October 5

1930 — A crowd of 45,104 — the largest to attend a City Series game — sees the Cubs beat the White Sox, 6-4, at Wrigley Field.

1933 — Red Faber, 45 years old, pitches the final game of his career, going all the way to beat 24-year-old Lon Warneke and the Cubs, 2-0, in the second game of the City Series, at Wrigley Field.

1935 — Lon Warneke wins his second game of the World Series, beating the Tigers, 3-1, in the fifth game, at Wrigley Field.

1945 — Claude Passeau pitches a one-hitter (a third inning single by Rudy York) as the Cubs beat the Tigers, 3-0, in the third game of the World Series, at Briggs Stadium.

October 6

1930 — Hack Wilson hits a home run in the fifth inning to help the Cubs to a 6-4 victory over the White Sox at Comiskey Park, clinching the City Series, four games to two. Throughout the game, Cub fans shower White Sox centerfielder Carl Reynolds with lemons in retaliation to Sox fans throwing tomatoes and other objects at Hack Wilson during the previous five games.

1938 — Dizzy Dean holds the Yankees to two runs for seven innings with his "nothing ball" in the second game of the World Series, at Wrigley Field. But the Cubs lose their 3-2 lead in the eighth inning on Frank Crosetti's two-run homer. Joe DiMaggio also hits a two-run homer in the ninth inning as the Yanks win, 6-3.

October 7

1935 — Goose Goslin singles home Mickey Cochrane with the winning run in the ninth inning as the Detroit Tigers beat the Cubs, 4-3, to win the World Series in six games, at Detroit.

1939 — With two out and two on, and the Cubs behind, 3-2, Hank Leiber smashes a three-run homer in the bottom of the ninth to beat the White Sox, 5-3, at Wrigley Field. The Sox had taken the lead earlier on pitcher Edgar Smith's inside-the-park homer with Gee Walker on base in the seventh. This victory gives the Cubs a 3-1 edge in the City Series, but the Sox reel off three straight victories to win the series, four games to three.

October 8

1885 — Jimmy Ryan makes his major league debut, at shortstop, and gets one hit in four trips as the Phillies beat the Cubs, 5-3, at Philadelphia.

1899 — In an unusual doubleheader, the Cubs play Cleveland in the morning and Louisville in the afternoon contest, which is called because of darkness after five innings, at West Side Grounds. Cubs take both games, 13-0 over Cleveland, and 7-3 over Louisville. In the first game, Jack Taylor pitches his first major league shutout and his 39th complete game of the season, a post-1892 Cub record. In the first inning of game two, Bill Lange doubles, steals third on Rube Waddell's next pitch, and steals home on the next pitch. Sam Mertes then hits an inside-the-park home run for the Cubs' second run.

1907 — With the Tigers leading the Cubs, 3-2, with two out in the bottom of the ninth of the World Series opener, catcher Charlie Schmidt drops pitcher Bill Donovan's third strike, allowing the tying run to score from third base. The teams go on to a 12 inning, 3-3 tie, called because of darkness at West Side Grounds.

1929 — Surprise starter Howard Ehmke sets a World Series record (since broken) by fanning 13 Cubs as the Athletics win the series opener, 3-1, at Wrigley Field.

1936 — Cubs trade pitcher Lon Warneke to the St. Louis Cardinals for first baseman Rip Collins and pitcher Leroy Parmelee.

1945 — Cubs beat the Tigers, 8-7, in the sixth game of the World Series at Wrigley Field when Stan Hack's double bounces over Hank Greenberg's shoulder in the bottom of the 12th inning.

October 9

1886 — Cubs clinch the pennant by beating the Braves, 12-3, at Boston, in a game called after seven innings because of darkness. Pitcher John Clarkson gets two hits and goes the route.

1906 — Nick Altrock outduels Mordecai Brown as the White Sox edge the Cubs, 2-1, in the first game of the only all-Chicago World Series, at West Side Grounds.

1907 — Cubs beat the Tigers, 3-1, behind Jack Pfiester, in the second game of the World Series, at West Side Grounds.

1925 — Cubs draft Hack Wilson from the Giants Toledo farm club for $5,000.

1928 — Cubs crush the White Sox, 13-2, at Comiskey Park, to win the City Series, four games to three.

1938— Yanks again sweep the Cubs in four straight, winning the World Series, 8-3, at Yankee Stadium.

October 10

1906— Cubs even up the World Series as Ed Reulbach downs the White Sox, 7-1, on a one-hitter at South Side Grounds, the only hit being a single by Jiggs Donahue in the seventh inning. Sox score their only run in the sixth on an error and a wild pitch.

1907— Cubs tame the Tigers, 5-1, in the third game of the World Series, behind Ed Reulbach at West Side Grounds.

1908— Cubs score five runs in the ninth inning to beat the Tigers, 10-6, in the World Series opener at Navin Field. Mordecai Brown is the winning pitcher.

1945— Tigers beat the Cubs, 9-3, behind the pitching of Hal Newhouser in the seventh game of the World Series at Wrigley Field.

October 11

1906— Ed Walsh fans 12 batters as the White Sox beat the Cubs, 3-0, at West Side Grounds, in game three of the World Series.

1907— Cubs beat the Tigers, 6-1, behind Orval Overall in the fourth game of the World Series, at Detroit's Navin Field.

1908— Joe Tinker hits the first Cub home run in World Series play as the Cubs beat the Tigers, 6-1, in the second game behind Orval Overall at West Side Grounds.

1929— Cubs win their lone game of the World Series as Guy Bush outduels George Earnshaw of the A's in the third game, at Shibe Park, 3-1.

October 12

1906— Mordecai Brown pitches the first Cub shutout in a World Series as the Cubs edge the White Sox, 1-0, at South Side Grounds.

1907— Cubs celebrate Columbus Day by winning the World Series, behind Mordecai Brown's 2-0 victory over the Tigers at Navin Field. Cubs stole 18 bases in the series, including six by Jimmy Slagle, while their leading hitter is Harry Steinfeldt at .471.

1929— With the Cubs leading, 8-0, the Athletics score 10 runs in the seventh inning to beat the Cubs, 10-8, at Shibe Park, in the fourth game of the World Series. Cubs centerfielder Hack Wilson loses a fly ball in the sun, and the ball rolls to the fence for a three-run inside-the-park home run by Mule Haas to highlight the rally. Cynical sportswriters began calling Wilson "Sunny Boy" as a result.

October 13

1906— White Sox take the edge in the World Series as they beat the Cubs, 8-6, at West Side Grounds.

1908 — Mordecai Brown pitches his third World Series shutout as the Cubs beat the Tigers, 3-0, in the fourth game, at Navin Field.

1925 — Cubs sign Joe McCarthy as manager. After rebuilding the Cubs and leading them to the 1929 pennant, McCarthy leaves late September, 1930. The following year he signs as manager of the New York Yankees, bringing them eight pennants and seven world championships before he was replaced by Bill Dickey on May 24, 1946. As manager of the Red Sox from 1948 to June 23, 1950, he brings the team home in second place twice. In spite of the fact that he never played a major league game, McCarthy wins 2,126 games as a manager while losing only 1,335 for a percentage of .614, the best in major league history.

1929 — Athletics score three runs in the ninth inning to win the World Series, 3-2, in five games at Shibe Park. Despite being the "goat", according to some who witnessed the lost fly ball, Hack Wilson hit .471 for the Cubs.

October 14

1885 — Cubs score four runs in the eighth inning to tie the American Association St. Louis Browns, 5-5, (managed by Charles Comiskey) in the Championship Series opener at Chicago. Game is called after eight innings because of darkness, at West Side Park.

1906 — White Sox win the World Series in six games, beating the Cubs, 8-3, at South Side Grounds.

1908 — Cubs win their second straight World Series, beating the Tigers in five games as Orval Overall goes the route for a 2-0 victory. Frank Chance leads Cub hitters with a .421 average.

October 15

1885 — Cubs score three runs in the sixth inning to lead the Browns, 5-4, in the second game of the Championship Series at St. Louis. However, the game is called after the sixth and forfeited to the Cubs, 9-0, after the Browns stomp off the field, kicking about umpire Dan Sullivan.

1909 — Cubs win the City Series, four games to one, as Mordecai Brown holds the White Sox to one hit (a single by Freddie Parent in the fifth) en route to a 1-0 victory, at West Side Grounds.

1922 — Cubs win their first City title in 13 years as Grover Alexander shuts out the White Sox, 2-0, in the seventh game, before 32,000 at Comiskey Park. Hack Miller drives in Ray Grimes with the first and winning run in the sixth inning, and the Cubs bat last even though they are the visiting team.

October 16

1885 — Cap Anson agrees to let a certain William Medart umpire the third game in St. Louis, and the Browns win, 7-4, to square the Championship Series at one apiece. Medart allegedly gives every close decision to the home team and barely escapes violence at the hands of Chicago's Jim McCormick and Billy Sunday.

October 17

1885 — Browns beat the Cubs, 3-2, to take a 2-1 edge in the Championship Series. There are no incidents in St. Louis.

October 18

1886 — Cubs win the opener of the Championship Series, beating the Browns, 6-0, behind John Clarkson at West Side Park.

October 19

1886 — The Browns even the Series, clouting the Cubs, 12-0, behind Bob Caruthers at West Side Park. Tip O'Neill hits two homers for St. Louis.

October 20

1886 — Cubs take the Series lead, beating the Browns, 11-4, behind John Clarkson. King Kelly and George Gore homer for the Cubs. Game was played at West Side Park.

October 21

1886 — Browns even the Series, beating the Cubs, 8-5, behind Dave Foutz at Sportsman's Park in St. Louis.

October 22

1885 — There was a five day delay allowing the Browns to play the City Series with the Maroons, the St. Louis N.L. team at the time. The fifth game of the Browns vs. Cubs Championship Series is played in Pittsburgh before a neutral crowd with the Cubs winning, 9-2, behind Jim McCormick. Abner Dalrymple and Cap Anson get three hits each.

1886 — The Browns take a 3-2 lead in the Championship Series, pounding the Cubs, 10-3, behind Nat Hudson at Sportsman's Park.

1910 — Cubs get their lone victory of the World Series as Mordecai Brown earns a 10-inning, 4-3, win in the fourth game, at West Side Grounds. Cubs tie the game in the ninth, then win with two out in the 10th on Jimmy Archer's double and Jimmy Sheckard's single.

1981 — Lee Elia is named manager of the Cubs replacing Joey Amalfitano.

October 23

1885 — The teams move to Cincinnati and the Cubs again win, 9-2, behind Jim McCormick, taking a 3-2 lead in the series. Fred Pfeffer paces the Cubs with three hits.

1886 — Browns win the Championship Series in six games, beating the Cubs, 4-3, behind Bob Caruthers at Sportsman's Park. The Browns' Tip O'Neill is the leading hitter with a .400 average.

1910 — Athletics beat the Cubs in the fifth and final game of the World Series, 7-2, behind Jack Coombs at West Side Grounds.

1974 — Cubs trade outfielder Billy Williams to the Oakland A's for pitchers Darold Knowles and Bob Locker, and second baseman Manny Trillo.

October 24

1885 — Browns crush the Cubs, 13-4, to square the Championship Series at three games apiece. A special committee calls the series a standoff with no clear champion. Cap Anson leads all batters with 11 hits in 26 at bats for a .423 average. Fred Pfeffer is next with 11 safeties in 27 trips for a .407 mark. The final game was played at Cincinnati.

October 25

1965 — Leo Durocher is named manager of the Cubs, thereby flunking out the so-called College of Coaches, which reigned for five seasons.

1973 — Cubs trade pitcher Fergie Jenkins to the Texas Rangers for second baseman Vic Harris and third baseman Bill Madlock.

October 27

1924 — Cubs trade pitcher Vic Aldridge, first baseman Al Niehaus, and second baseman George Grantham to the Pirates for pitcher Wilbur Cooper, shortstop Rabbit Maranville, and first baseman Charlie Grimm.

NOVEMBER

November 4

1959 — Ernie Banks becomes the first National League player to win the Most Valuable Player Award two years in a row.

November 5

1955 — Bert Wilson, the radio voice of the Cubs on station WIND since 1943, dies at age 44 from high blood pressure.

November 7

1928 — Cubs trade infielder Fred Maguire, catcher Doc Leggett, pitchers Percy Jones, Harry Siebold and Bruce Cunningham, plus $200,000, to the Braves for second baseman Rogers Hornsby.

November 11

1917 — Cubs trade pitcher Mike Prendergast and catcher Pickles Dilhoefer, plus $60,000, to the Phillies for pitcher Grover Cleveland Alexander and catcher Bill Killefer.

November 13

1940 — After 19 years with the Cubs, the last two and a half as manager, Gabby Hartnett is fired.

November 18

1888 — Cub owner Albert Spalding takes the Cubs and assorted players from other teams on a world-wide tour, leaving San Francisco and sailing to Hawaii, New Zealand, Australia, Ceylon, India, Egypt, Italy, France, and England. Games are played in Sydney, Melbourne, Cairo, Naples, Rome, Paris, and London. In Egypt one of the pyramids is used as a backstop.

November 21

1933 — Cubs trade outfielder Harvey Hendrick, infielder Mark Koenig, pitcher Ted Kleinhans — plus $65,000 — to the Phillies for outfielder Chuck Klein.

November 22

1934 — Cubs trade outfielder Babe Herman, pitcher Guy Bush and pitcher Jim Weaver to the Pirates for outfielder Fred Lindstrom and pitcher Larry French.

November 24

1948 — Hack Wilson dies penniless at age 48 in Baltimore. His 56 runs and 190 RBI in 1930 are unmatched in National League history. The latter is a Major League monument which experts claim will never be surpassed.

November 28

1927 — Cubs trade infielder Sparky Adams and outfielder Floyd Scott to the Pirates for outfielder Kiki Cuyler.

DECEMBER

December 6

1938 — Cubs trade shortstop Billy Jurges, outfielder Frank Demaree, and catcher Ken O'Dea to the Giants for shortstop Dick Bartell, outfielder Hank Leiber, and catcher Gus Mancuso.

December 9

1980 — Cubs trade Bruce Sutter to Cardinals for first baseman-outfielder Leon Durham, third baseman Ken Reitz, and infielder Tye Waller.

December 10

1931 — Cubs trade outfielder Hack Wilson and pitcher Art Teachout to the Cardinals for pitcher Burleigh Grimes. The Cards trade Wilson to the Dodgers later in the winter.

December 12

1903 — Cubs trade pitcher Jack Taylor and catcher Al McLean to the Cardinals for pitcher Mordecai Brown and catcher Jack O'Neill.

1913 — Cubs release second baseman-manager Johnny Evers.

December 15

1912 — Cubs trade shortstop Joe Tinker, pitcher Grover Lowdermilk, and catcher Harry Chapman to the Reds for pitcher Bert Humphries, infielders Pete Knisely, Red Corriden, and Art Phelan, and outfielder Mike Mitchell.

December 20

1972 — All-time great Cub catcher Gabby Hartnett dies on his 72nd birthday, in Chicago.

December 21

1960 — Cub owner P.K. Wrigley announces that the Cubs will no longer have a manager but will instead be run by a "college" of eight coaches, including Rip Collins, Charlie Grimm, Elvin Tappe, Goldie Holt, Vedie Himsl, Harry Craft, Bobby Adams, and Rube Walker. Others who float in and out before the system is junked in October 1965 include Bob Kennedy, Buck O'Neill, Lou Klein, Charlie Metro, Al Dark, Freddie Martin, Mel Wright and Mel Harder.

First Cub Champions — Seven of the nine players in this 1876-77 photograph were regulars on the first title team: (Center) A.G. Spalding, manager-pitcher; (top and continuing clockwise) Ross Barnes; John Peters; Adrian "Cap" Anson; George Bradley (1877); Charles Waitt (1877); Paul Hines; Cal McVey; and John Glenn.

2
TEAM AND MANAGER
WON-LOSS RECORDS

Where the Cubs Finished, 1876 to Date

Year	W	L	Pct.	Pos.	Manager	Attendance
1876	52	14	.788	1	Al Spalding	
1877	26	33	.441	5	Al Spalding	
1878	30	30	.500	4	Bob Ferguson	
1879	46	33	.582	4	Cap Anson	
1880	67	17	.798	1	Cap Anson	
1881	56	28	.667	1	Cap Anson	
1882	55	29	.655	1	Cap Anson	
1883	59	39	.602	2	Cap Anson	
1884	62	50	.554	4t	Cap Anson	
1885	87	25	.777	1	Cap Anson	
1886	90	34	.726	1	Cap Anson	
1887	71	50	.587	3	Cap Anson	
1888	77	58	.578	2	Cap Anson	
1889	67	65	.508	3	Cap Anson	
1890	84	53	.613	2	Cap Anson	
1891	82	53	.607	2	Cap Anson	
1892	70	76	.479	7	Cap Anson	91,892
1893	56	71	.441	9	Cap Anson	223,514
1894	57	75	.432	8	Cap Anson	238,958
1895	72	58	.555	4	Cap Anson	382,299
1896	71	57	.556	5	Cap Anson	317,548
1897	59	73	.447	9	Cap Anson	327,675
1898	85	65	.567	4	Tom Burns	401,092
1899	75	73	.507	8	Tom Burns	393,609
1900	65	75	.464	5t	Tom Loftus	286,918
1901	53	86	.381	6	Tom Loftus	205,071
1902	68	69	.496	5	Frank Selee	263,700
1903	82	56	.594	3	Frank Selee	386,205
1904	93	60	.608	2	Frank Selee	439,100
1905	92	61	.601	3	Frank Selee	509,900

The 1908 World Champions.

Where the Cubs Finished, 1876 to Date (Continued)

Year	W	L	Pct.	Pos.	Manager	Attendance
1906	116	36	.763	1	Frank Chance	654,300
1907	107	45	.704	1	Frank Chance	422,550
1908	99	55	.643	1	Frank Chance	665,325
1909	104	49	.680	2	Frank Chance	633,480
1910	104	50	.675	1	Frank Chance	526,152
1911	92	62	.597	2	Frank Chance	576,000
1912	91	59	.607	3	Frank Chance	514,000
1913	88	65	.575	3	Johnny Evers	419,000
1914	78	76	.506	4	Hank O'Day	202,516
1915	73	80	.477	4	Roger Bresnahan	217,058
1916	67	86	.438	5	Joe Tinker	454,609
1917	74	80	.481	5	Fred Mitchell	363,748
1918	84	45	.651	1	Fred Mitchell	338,802
1919	75	65	.536	3	Fred Mitchell	421,680
1920	75	79	.487	5t	Fred Mitchell	481,183
1921	64	89	.418	7	Johnny Evers Bill Killefer	410,110
1922	80	74	.519	5	Bill Killefer	541,993
1923	83	71	.539	4	Bill Killefer	705,049
1924	81	72	.529	5	Bill Killefer	720,962
1925	68	86	.442	8	Bill Killefer Rabbit Maranville George Gibson	623,030
1926	82	72	.532	4	Joe McCarthy	886,925
1927	85	68	.556	4	Joe McCarthy	1,163,347
1928	91	63	.591	3	Joe McCarthy	1,148,053
1929	98	54	.645	1	Joe McCarthy	1,485,166
1930	90	64	.584	2	Joe McCarthy Rogers Hornsby	1,467,881
1931	84	70	.545	3	Rogers Hornsby	1,089,449
1932	90	64	.584	1	Rogers Hornsby Charlie Grimm	976,449
1933	86	68	.558	3	Charlie Grimm	594,879
1934	86	65	.570	3	Charlie Grimm	709,245
1935	100	54	.649	1	Charlie Grimm	690,576
1936	87	67	.565	2t	Charlie Grimm	701,111
1937	93	61	.604	2	Charlie Grimm	897,852
1938	89	63	.586	1	Charlie Grimm Gabby Hartnett	955,401
1939	84	70	.545	4	Gabby Hartnett	729,309
1940	75	79	.487	5	Gabby Hartnett	534,878
1941	70	84	.455	6	Jimmy Wilson	545,159
1942	68	86	.442	6	Jimmy Wilson	590,972
1943	74	79	.484	5	Jimmy Wilson	508,247
1944	75	79	.487	4	Jimmy Wilson Roy Johnson Charlie Grimm	640,110
1945	98	56	.636	1	Charlie Grimm	1,036,386

Where the Cubs Finished, 1876 to Date (Continued)

Year	W	L	Pct.	Pos.	Manager	Attendance
1946	82	71	.536	3	Charlie Grimm	1,342,970
1947	69	85	.448	6	Charlie Grimm	1,364,039
1948	64	90	.416	8	Charlie Grimm	1,237,792
1949	61	93	.396	8	Charlie Grimm	1,143,139
					Frankie Frisch	
1950	64	89	.418	7	Frankie Frisch	1,165,944
1951	62	92	.403	8	Frankie Frisch	894,415
					Phil Cavarretta	
1952	77	77	.500	5	Phil Cavarretta	1,024,826
1953	65	89	.422	7	Phil Cavarretta	763,653
1954	64	90	.416	7	Stan Hack	748,183
1955	72	81	.471	6	Stan Hack	875,800
1956	60	94	.390	8	Stan Hack	720,118
1957	62	92	.403	7t	Bob Scheffing	670,629
1958	72	82	.468	5t	Bob Scheffing	979,904
1959	74	80	.481	5t	Bob Scheffing	858,255
1960	60	94	.390	7	Charlie Grimm	809,770
					Lou Boudreau	
1961	64	90	.416	7	None	673,057
1962	59	103	.364	9	None	609,802
1963	82	80	.506	7	None	979,551
1964	76	86	.469	8	None	751,647
1965	72	90	.444	8	None	641,361
1966	59	103	.364	10	Leo Durocher	635,891
1967	87	74	.540	3	Leo Durocher	977,226
1968	84	78	.519	3	Leo Durocher	1,043,409
1969*	92	70	.568	2	Leo Durocher	1,674,993
1970	84	78	.519	2	Leo Durocher	1,642,705
1971	83	79	.512	3t	Leo Durocher	1,653,007
1972	85	70	.548	2	Leo Durocher	1,299,163
					Whitey Lockman	
1973	77	84	.478	5	Whitey Lockman	1,351,705
1974	66	96	.407	6	Whitey Lockman	1,015,378
					Jim Marshall	
1975	75	87	.463	5t	Jim Marshall	1,034,819
1976	75	87	.463	4	Jim Marshall	1,026,217
1977	81	81	.500	4	Herman Franks	1,439,834
1978	79	83	.488	3	Herman Franks	1,525,311
1979	80	82	.494	5	Herman Franks	1,648,587
					Joe Amalfitano	
1980	64	98	.395	6	Preston Gomez	1,206,776
					Joe Amalfitano	
1981	38	65	.369	6	Joe Amalfitano	565,637

Notes: The National League had only six clubs in 1877 and 1878. From 1892 through 1899 there were twelve. In all other years there were eight, until 1962, when it was expanded to a ten club circuit. Divisional play began in 1969, with six clubs in each of the two divisions, the Cubs being in the Eastern division. The 1981 season was shortened by a players' strike. Team home attendance figures prior to 1916 are unofficial estimates.
*Eastern Division Play began.

Leo Durocher was never known to be shy with umpires. Here he loses a bout with Mel Steiner and heads for the showers.

Charlie Grimm, the most popular of past Cub managers, led the Cubs to three pennants.

Cubs Managers Records

Manager	Years	Won	Lost	Pct.
Albert Spalding	(1876-1877)	78	47	.624
Bob Ferguson	(1878)	30	30	.500
Cap Anson	(1879-1897)	1288	944	.577
Tommy Burns	(1898-1899)	160	138	.537
Tom Loftus	(1900-1901)	118	161	.423
Frank Selee	(1902-1905)	295	223	.569
Frank Chance	(1905-1912)	778	396	.649
Johnny Evers	(1913) (1921)	130	121	.517
Hank O'Day	(1914)	78	76	.506
Roger Bresnahan	(1915)	73	80	.477
Joe Tinker	(1916)	67	86	.438
Fred Mitchell	(1917-1920)	308	269	.534
Bill Killefer	(1921-1925)	299	292	.506
Rabbit Maranville	(1925)	23	30	.434
George Gibson	(1925)	12	14	.462
Joe McCarthy	(1926-1930)	442	321	.579
Rogers Hornsby	(1930-1932)	141	114	.553
Charlie Grimm	(1932-1938) (1944-1949)			
	(1960)	846	784	.519
Gabby Hartnett	(1938-1940)	203	176	.536
Jimmy Wilson	(1941-1944)	213	258	.452
Roy Johnson	(1944)	0	1	.000
Frankie Frisch	(1949-1951)	141	196	.418
Phil Cavarretta	(1951-1953)	169	213	.442
Stan Hack	(1954-1956)	196	265	.425
Bob Scheffing	(1957-1959)	208	254	.450
Lou Boudreau	(1960)	54	83	.394
*Vedie Himsl	(1961)	10	21	.323
*Harry Craft	(1961)	7	9	.438
*Elvin Tappe	(1961-1962)	46	69	.400
*Lou Klein	(1961-1962) (1965)	65	83	.439
*Charlie Metro	(1962)	43	69	.384
*Bob Kennedy	(1963-1965)	182	198	.479
Leo Durocher	(1966-1972)	452	447	.503
Whitey Lockman	(1972-1974)	157	162	.492
Jim Marshall	(1974-1976)	175	218	.445
Herman Franks	(1977-1979)	238	241	·497
Joe Amalfitano	(1979-1980) (1981)	66	116	.363
Preston Gomez	(1980)	38	52	.422

*College of Coaches

Adrian "Cap" Anson was a 22-year player for the Cubs. He became the first member of the 3000-hit club while batting over .300 for twenty seasons. As a manager he won five pennants.

3
BATTING RECORDS

BATTING AVERAGES

Leading Cub Hitters, 1876 to Present

Year	Player	Batting Average	Year	Player	Batting Average
1876*	Ross Barnes	.429	1895	Bill Lange	.389
1877	Cal McVey	.368	1896	Bill Dahlen	.361
1878	Bob Ferguson	.351	1897	Bill Lange	.340
1879*	Cap Anson	.396	1898	Jimmy Ryan	.323
1880*	George Gore	.360	1899	Bill Lange	.325
1881*	Cap Anson	.399	1900	Danny Green	.298
1882	Cap Anson	.362	1901	Topsy Hartsel	.335
1883	George Gore	.334	1902	Jimmy Slagle	.315
1884	Mike Kelly	.354	1903	Frank Chance	.327
1885	George Gore	.312	1904	Frank Chance	.310
1886*	Mike Kelly	.388	1905	Frank Chance	.316
1887*	Cap Anson	.421	1906	Harry Steinfeldt	.327
		(.347 without	1907	Frank Chance	.292
		bases on balls)	1908	Johnny Evers	.300
1888*	Cap Anson	.344	1909	Artie Hofman	.285
1889	Cap Anson	.342	1910	Artie Hofman	.325
1890	Cap Anson	.312	1911	Heinie Zimmerman	.307
1891	Cap Anson	.291	1912*	Heinie Zimmerman	.372
1892	Bill Dahlen	.295	1913	Heinie Zimmerman	.313
1893	Cap Anson	.314	1914	Heinie Zimmerman	.296
1894	Cap Anson	.395	1915	Bob Fisher	.287

*League Leader

Leading Cub Hitters, 1876 to Present (Continued)

Year	Player	Batting Average	Year	Player	Batting Average
1916	Heinie Zimmerman	.286	1947	Phil Cavarretta	.314
1917	Les Mann	.273	1948	Andy Pafko	.312
1918	Charlie Hollocher	.316	1949	Phil Cavarretta	.294
1919	Max Flack	.294	1950	Andy Pafko	.304
1920	Charlie Hollocher	.319	1951	Frankie Baumholtz	.284
1921	Ray Grimes	.321	1952	Frankie Baumholtz	.325
1922	Ray Grimes	.354	1953	Dee Fondy	.309
1923	Jigger Statz	.319	1954	Hank Sauer	.288
	Bob O'Farrell	.319	1955	Ernie Banks	.295
1924	George Grantham	.316	1956	Ernie Banks	.297
1925	Charlie Grimm	.306	1957	Dale Long	.305
1926	Hack Wilson	.321	1958	Ernie Banks	.313
1927	Riggs Stephenson	.344	1959	Ernie Banks	.304
1928	Riggs Stephenson	.324	1960	Richie Ashburn	.291
1929	Rogers Hornsby	.380	1961	George Altman	.303
1930	Riggs Stephenson	.367	1962	George Altman	.318
1931	Charlie Grimm	.331	1963	Ron Santo	.297
	Rogers Hornsby	.331	1964	Ron Santo	.313
1932	Riggs Stephenson	.324	1965	Billy Williams	.315
1933	Riggs Stephenson	.329	1966	Ron Santo	.312
1934	Kiki Cuyler	.338	1967	Ron Santo	.300
1935	Gabby Hartnett	.344	1968	Glenn Beckert	.294
1936	Frank Demaree	.350	1969	Billy Williams	.293
1937	Gabby Hartnett	.354	1970	Billy Williams	.322
1938	Stan Hack	.320	1971	Glenn Beckert	.342
1939	Hank Leiber	.310	1972*	Billy Williams	.333
1940	Stan Hack	.317	1973	Jose Cardenal	.302
1941	Stan Hack	.317	1974	Bill Madlock	.313
1942	Stan Hack	.300	1975*	Bill Madlock	.354
	Lou Novikoff	.300	1976*	Bill Madlock	.339
1943	Bill Nicholson	.309	1977	Steve Ontiveros	.299
1944	Phil Cavarretta	.321	1978	Bill Buckner	.323
1945*	Phil Cavarretta	.355	1979	Dave Klingman	.288
1946	Eddie Waitkus	.304	1980*	Bill Buckner	.324
			1981	Bill Buckner	.311

*League leader

(Note: In 1887, bases on balls were counted as base hits. Without the walks, Anson's average was second in the league to Sam Thompson of Detroit, who batted .372.)

(Note: Long batted .298 for season. .305 in Cub uniform)

Cub .300 Hitters, 1876 to Date

From the year 1884 (first 100 game schedule) on, only those batters with at least 300 at bats are listed.

Year	Player	Average	Year	Player	Average
1876	Ross Barnes	.429	1890	Cap Anson	.312
	John Peters	.351	1893	Cap Anson	.314
	Cal McVey	.347		Bill Dahlen	.301
	Cap Anson	.343		Walt Wilmot	.301
	Jim White	.343	1894	Cap Anson	.395
	Paul Hines	.331		Bill Dahlen	.362
1877	Cal McVey	.368		Jimmy Ryan	.360
	Cap Anson	.337		Walt Wilmot	.330
	John Peters	.317		Bill Lange	.328
1878	Bob Ferguson	.351		George Decker	.313
	Joe Start	.351	1895	Bill Lange	.389
	Cap Anson	.341		Bill Everett	.358
1879	Cap Anson	.396		Cap Anson	.335
	George Shaffer	.304		Jimmy Ryan	.323
1880	George Gore	.360	1896	Bill Dahlen	.361
	Cap Anson	.337		Cap Anson	.331
	Abner Dalrymple	.330		Bill Lange	.326
	Tommy Burns	.309		Bill Everett	.320
1881	Cap Anson	.399		Jimmy Ryan	.312
	Abner Dalrymple	.323	1897	Bill Lange	.340
	King Kelly	.323		Bill Everett	.314
1882	Cap Anson	.362		Jimmy Ryan	.308
	George Gore	.319		Cap Anson	.302
	King Kelly	.305	1898	Jimmy Ryan	.323
1883	George Gore	.334		Bill Lange	.319
	Cap Anson	.308		Bill Everett	.319
1884	King Kelly	.354	1899	Bill Lange	.325
	Cap Anson	.335		Bill Everett	.310
	George Gore	.318		Jimmy Ryan	.301
	Abner Dalrymple	.309	1901	Topsy Hartsel	.335
1885	George Gore	.312		Danny Green	.313
	Cap Anson	.310	1902	Jimmy Slagle	.315
1886	King Kelly	.388	1903	Frank Chance	.327
	Cap Anson	.371	1904	Frank Chance	.310
	Jimmy Ryan	.306	1905	Frank Chance	.316
	George Gore	.304	1906	Harry Steinfeldt	.327
1887	Cap Anson	.347		Frank Chance	.319
		(.421)		Johnny Kling	.312
1888	Cap Anson	.344	1908	Johnny Evers	.300
	Jimmy Ryan	.332	1910	Artie Hofman	.325
1889	Cap Anson	.342		Frank Schulte	.301
	Jimmy Ryan	.325	1911	Heinie Zimmerman	.307
	George Van Haltren	.309		Frank Schulte	.300
	Hugh Duffy	.305			

Cub .300 Hitters, 1876 to Date (Continued)

Year	Player	Average	Year	Player	Average
1912	Heinie Zimmerman	.372		Charlie Grimm	.307
	Johnny Evers	.341		Johnny Moore	.305
1913	Heinie Zimmerman	.313	1933	Riggs Stephenson	.329
1918	Charlie Hollocher	.316	1934	Kiki Cuyler	.338
1920	Charlie Hollocher	.319		Tuck Stainback	.306
	Max Flack	.302		Babe Herman	.304
	Dave Robertson	.300		Billy Herman	.303
1921	Ray Grimes	.321		Chuck Klein	.301
	Turner Barber	.314	1935	Gabby Hartnett	.344
	George Maisel	.310		Billy Herman	.341
	Max Flack	.301		Frank Demaree	.325
1922	Ray Grimes	.354		Augie Galan	.314
	Hack Miller	.352		Stan Hack	.311
	Charlie Hollocher	.340	1936	Frank Demaree	.350
	Bob O'Farrell	.324		Billy Herman	.334
1923	Arnold Statz	.319		Gabby Hartnett	.307
	Bob O'Farrell	.319	1937	Gabby Hartnett	.354
	Barney Friberg	.318		Billy Herman	.335
	Hack Miller	.301		Frank Demaree	.324
1924	George Grantham	.316	1938	Stan Hack	.320
	Cliff Heathcote	.309		Carl Reynolds	.302
1925	Charlie Grimm	.306	1939	Hank Leiber	.310
1926	Hack Wilson	.321		Billy Herman	.307
	Sparky Adams	.309		Augie Galan	.304
1927	Riggs Stephenson	.344	1940	Stan Hack	.317
	Hack Wilson	.318		Jimmy Gleeson	.313
	Charlie Grimm	.311		Hank Leiber	.302
	Earl Webb	.301	1941	Stan Hack	.317
1928	Riggs Stephenson	.324	1942	Stan Hack	.300
	Hack Wilson	.313		Lou Novikoff	.300
	Gabby Hartnett	.302	1943	Bill Nicholson	.309
1929	Rogers Hornsby	.380	1944	Phil Cavarretta	.321
	Riggs Stephenson	.362		Dom Dallessandro	.304
	Kiki Cuyler	.360	1945	Phil Cavarretta	.355
	Hack Wilson	.345		Stan Hack	.323
1930	Riggs Stephenson	.367		Don Johnson	.302
	Hack Wilson	.356	1946	Eddie Waitkus	.304
	Kiki Cuyler	.355	1947	Phil Cavarretta	.314
	Gabby Hartnett	.339		Andy Pafko	.302
	Woody English	.335	1948	Andy Pafko	.312
1931	Charlie Grimm	.331	1950	Andy Pafko	.304
	Rogers Hornsby	.331	1952	Frankie Baumholtz	.325
	Kiki Cuyler	.330		Dee Fondy	.300
	Woody English	.319	1953	Dee Fondy	.309
1932	Riggs Stephenson	.324		Frankie Baumholtz	.306
	Billy Herman	.314			

Cub .300 Hitters, 1876 to Date (Continued)

Year	Player	Average	Year	Player	Average
1958	Ernie Banks	.313	1971	Glenn Beckert	.342
	Lee Walls	.304		Billy Williams	.301
1959	Ernie Banks	.304	1972	Billy Williams	.333
1961	George Altman	.303		Ron Santo	.302
1962	George Altman	.318	1973	Jose Cardenal	.302
1964	Ron Santo	.313	1974	Bill Madlock	.316
	Billy Williams	.312	1975	Bill Madlock	.354
1965	Billy Williams	.315		Jose Cardenal	.317
1966	Ron Santo	.312	1976	Bill Madlock	.339
1967	Ron Santo	.300	1978	Bill Buckner	.323
1970	Billy Williams	.322	1980	Bill Buckner	.324
	Jim Hickman	.315	1981	Bill Buckner	.311

Bill Buckner has been the most productive Cub at the plate in recent years.

.300 Lifetime Hitters (500-game minimum)

Player	Years	Average
Riggs Stephenson	(1926-1934)	.336
Cap Anson	(1876-1897)	.333
Bill Lange	(1893-1899)	.330
Kiki Cuyler	(1928-1935)	.325
Bill Everett	(1895-1900)	.323
Hack Wilson	(1926-1931)	.322
Mike Kelly	(1880-1886)	.316
George Gore	(1879-1886)	.315
Billy Herman	(1931-1941)	.309
Jimmy Ryan	(1885-1889;1891-1900)	.308
Frank Demaree	(1932-1938)	.308
Bill Buckner	(1977-1981)	.305
Heinie Zimmerman	(1907-1916)	.304
Charlie Hollocher	(1918-1924)	.304
Bill Dahlen	(1891-1898)	.303
Stan Hack	(1932-1947)	.301

Riggs Stephenson had a lifetime batting average of .336, higher than any other Cub.

.290 Lifetime Hitters (500-game minimum)

Player	Years	Average
Frank Chance	(1898-1912)	.298
Gabby Hartnett	(1922-1940)	.297
Charlie Grimm	(1925-1936)	.296
Billy Williams	(1959-1974)	.296
Jose Cardenal	(1972-1977)	.296
Frankie Baumholtz	(1949;1951-1955)	.295
Andy Pafko	(1943-1951)	.294
Sparky Adams	(1922-1927)	.292
Phil Cavarretta	(1934-1953)	.292
Woody English	(1927-1936)	.291

.280 Lifetime Hitters (500-game minimum)

Player	Years	Average
Dee Fondy	(1951-1957)	.286
Walt Wilmot	(1890-1895)	.284
Glenn Beckert	(1965-1973)	.283
Abner Dalrymple	(1879-1886)	.282
Cliff Heathcote	(1922-1930)	.280

Another hit for Phil Cavarretta.

Ron Santo belts another one out of the park.

.270 Lifetime Hitters (500-game minimum)

Player	Years	Average
Bob O'Farrell	(1915-1925;1934)	.279
Ron Santo	(1960-1973)	.279
George Decker	(1892-1897)	.278
Fred Merkle	(1917-1920)	.278
Peanuts Lowrey	(1942-1943;1945-1949)	.278
Augie Galan	(1934-1941)	.277
Jerry Morales	(1974-1977;1981)	.277
Johnny Evers	(1902-1913)	.276
George Altman	(1959-1962;1965-1967)	.276
Max Flack	(1915-1922)	.274
Ernie Banks	(1953-1971)	.274
Frank Schulte	(1904-1916)	.273
Don Johnson	(1943-1948)	.273
Artie Hofman	(1904-1912;1916)	.272
Bill Nicholson	(1939-1948)	.272
Walt Moryn	(1956-1960)	.272
Johnny Kling	(1900-1908;1910-1911)	.271
Dom Dallessandro	(1940-1944;1946-1947)	.270
Rick Monday	(1972-1976)	.270

.260 Lifetime Hitters (500-game minimum)

Player	Years	Average
Harry Steinfeldt	(1906-1910)	.269
Hank Sauer	(1949-1955)	.269
Jimmy Slagle	(1902-1908)	.268
Jim Hickman	(1968-1973)	.267
Ivan DeJesus	(1977-1981)	.266
Vic Saier	(1911-1917)	.265
Ransom Jackson	(1950-1955;1959)	.265
Tommy Burns	(1880-1891)	.264
Charlie Deal	(1916-1921)	.262
Jimmy Archer	(1909-1917)	.261

.250 Lifetime Hitters (500-game minimum)

Player	Years	Average
Joe Tinker	(1902-1912;1916)	.259
Jimmy Sheckard	(1906-1912)	.257
Manny Trillo	(1975-1978)	.256
Hal Jeffcoat	(1948-1955)	.255
Billy Jurges	(1931-1938;1946-1947)	.254
Cy Williams	(1912-1917)	.251
Bill Serena	(1949-1954)	.251
Fred Pfeffer	(1883-1889;1891; 1896-1897)	.250

.240 Lifetime Hitters (500-game minimum)

Player	Years	Average
Clyde McCullough	(1940-1943;1946-1948; 1953-1956)	.249
Barry McCormick	(1896-1901)	.244
Eddie Miksis	(1951-1956)	.243
Frank Flint	(1879-1889)	.241
Lennie Merullo	(1941-1947)	.240
Randy Hundley	(1966-1973;1976-1977)	.240

Below .240 Lifetime Hitters (500-game minimum)

Player	Years	Average
Roy Smalley	(1948-1953)	.232
Malachi Kittredge	(1890-1897)	.219

Batting Average By Position (Season)
Modern

1B	Phil Cavarretta	1945	.355
2B	Rogers Hornsby	1929	.380
SS	Charlie Hollocher	1922	.340
3B	Heinie Zimmerman	1912	.372
OF	Riggs Stephenson	1930	.367
OF	Kiki Cuyler	1929	.360
OF	Hack Wilson	1930	.356
C	Gabby Hartnett	1937	.354

19th Century

1B	Cap Anson	1881	.399
2B	Ross Barnes	1876	.429
SS	Bill Dahlen	1894	.362
3B	Bill Everett	1895	.358
OF	Bill Lange	1895	.389
OF	Jimmy Ryan	1894	.361
OF	George Gore	1880	.360
C	King Kelly	1886	.388

All-Time

1B	Cap Anson	1881	.399
2B	Ross Barnes	1876	.429
SS	Bill Dahlen	1894	.362
3B	Heinie Zimmerman	1912	.372
OF	Bill Lange	1895	.389
OF	Riggs Stephenson	1930	.367
OF	Jimmy Ryan	1894	.361
C	King Kelly	1886	.388

LEADERS IN HITS

Year-by-Year Leader in Base Hits

Year	Player	Total	Year	Player	Total
1876*	Ross Barnes	138	1921	Max Flack	172
1877	Cal McVey	98	1922	Charlie Hollocher	201
1878*	Joe Start	100	1923	Jigger Statz	209
1879	Abner Dalrymple	97	1924	Jigger Statz	152
1880*	Abner Dalrymple	126	1925	Sparky Adams	180
1881*	Cap Anson	137	1926	Sparky Adams	193
1882	Cap Anson	126	1927	Riggs Stephenson	199
1883	George Gore	131	1928	Riggs Stephenson	166
1884	Abner Dalrymple	161	1929	Rogers Hornsby	229
1885	Cap Anson	144	1930	Kiki Cuyler	228
1886	Cap Anson	187	1931	Kiki Cuyler	202
1887	Cap Anson	164		Woody English	202
1888*	Jimmy Ryan	182	1932	Billy Herman	206
1889	Jimmy Ryan	187	1933	Billy Herman	173
1890	Cliff Carroll	166	1934	Kiki Cuyler	189
1891	Cap Anson	157	1935*	Billy Herman	227
1892	Bill Dahlen	173	1936	Frank Demaree	212
1893	Bill Dahlen	146	1937	Frank Demaree	199
1894	Walt Wilmot	197	1938	Stan Hack	195
1895	Bill Everett	197	1939	Stan Hack	191
1896	Bill Everett	184		Billy Herman	191
1897	Bill Lange	163	1940*	Stan Hack	191
1898	Bill Everett	190	1941*	Stan Hack	186
1899	Bill Everett	166	1942	Bill Nicholson	173
1900	Jack McCarthy	148	1943	Bill Nicholson	188
1901	Topsy Hartsel	187	1944*	Phil Cavarretta	197
1902	Jimmy Slagle	143	1945	Stan Hack	193
1903	Jimmy Slagle	162	1946	Phil Cavarretta	150
1904	Doc Casey	147	1947	Andy Pafko	155
1905	Jimmy Slagle	153	1948	Andy Pafko	171
1906*	Harry Steinfeldt	176	1949	Andy Pafko	146
1907	Harry Steinfeldt	144	1950	Andy Pafko	156
1908	Joe Tinker	146	1951	Frank Baumholtz	159
1909	Solly Hofman	150	1952	Dee Fondy	166
1910	Frank Schulte	168	1953	Dee Fondy	184
1911	Frank Schulte	173	1954	Ernie Banks	163
1912*	Heinie Zimmerman	207	1955	Ernie Banks	176
1913	Heinie Zimmerman	140	1956	Ernie Banks	160
1914	Heinie Zimmerman	167	1957	Ernie Banks	169
1915	Bob Fisher	163	1958	Ernie Banks	193
1916	Vic Saier	126	1959	Ernie Banks	179
1917	Fred Merkle	146	1960	Ernie Banks	162
1918*	Charlie Hollocher	161	1961	Ron Santo	164
1919	Max Flack	138	1962	Billy Williams	184
1920	Max Flack	157	1963	Ron Santo	187
			1964	Billy Williams	201

*League Leader

Year-by-Year Leader in Base Hits (Continued)

Year	Player	Total	Year	Player	Total
1965	Billy Williams	203	1974	Jose Cardenal	159
1966	Glenn Beckert	188	1975	Jose Cardenal	182
1967	Ron Santo	176		Bill Madlock	182
	Billy Williams	176	1976	Bill Madlock	174
1968	Glenn Beckert	189	1977	Ivan DeJesus	166
1969	Billy Williams	188	1978	Ivan DeJesus	172
1970*	Billy Williams	205	1979	Ivan DeJesus	180
1971	Glenn Beckert	181	1980	Bill Buckner	187
1972	Billy Williams	191	1981	Bill Buckner	131
1973	Billy Williams	166			

*League Leader

All-Star Bill Madlock led the Cubs in base hits in 1976 and tied for the lead with Jose Cardenal in 1975.

200 Base Hits in One Season

Year	Player	Total
1912	Heinie Zimmerman	207
1922	Charlie Hollocher	201
1923	Jigger Statz	209
1929	Rogers Hornsby	229
1930	Kiki Cuyler	228
	Woody English	214
	Hack Wilson	208
1931	Kiki Cuyler	202
	Woody English	202
1932	Billy Herman	206
1935	Billy Herman	227
	Augie Galan	203
1936	Frank Demaree	212
	Billy Herman	211
1964	Billy Williams	201
1965	Billy Williams	203
1970	Billy Williams	205

The great Rogers Hornsby had 229 hits during the 1929 season, a record that has not been matched to this day by any Cub.

100-or-More Hits, Season

Year	Player	Total	Year	Player	Total
1876	Ross Barnes	138	1888	Jimmy Ryan	182
	John Peters	111		Cap Anson	177
	Cap Anson	110		Fred Pfeffer	129
	Cal McVey	107		Tommy Burns	115
	Jim White	104		Ed Williamson	113
	Paul Hines	101	1889	Jimmy Ryan	187
1878	Joe Start	100		Hugh Duffy	178
1880	Abner Dalrymple	126		Cap Anson	177
	Cap Anson	120		George Van Haltren	168
	George Gore	116		Tommy Burns	127
	Tommy Burns	103		Fred Pfeffer	121
	King Kelly	100		Duke Farrell	101
1881	Cap Anson	137	1890	Cliff Carroll	166
	Abner Dalrymple	117		Walt Wilmot	159
	King Kelly	114		Cap Anson	157
1882	Cap Anson	126		Jimmy Cooney	156
	Abner Dalrymple	117		Tommy Burns	149
	George Gore	117	1891	Cap Anson	157
	King Kelly	115		Bill Dahlen	145
1883	George Gore	131		Jimmy Ryan	145
	Cap Anson	127		Walt Wilmot	139
	Tommy Burns	119		Cliff Carroll	132
	Ed Williamson	111		Fred Pfeffer	123
	King Kelly	109		Jimmy Cooney	114
	Abner Dalrymple	108	1892	Bill Dahlen	173
1884	Abner Dalrymple	161		Cap Anson	152
	King Kelly	160		Jimmy Ryan	148
	Cap Anson	159		Sam Dungan	123
	Fred Pfeffer	135	1893	Bill Dahlen	146
	George Gore	134		Sam Dungan	138
	Ed Williamson	116		Bill Lange	132
1885	Cap Anson	144		Cap Anson	125
	George Gore	138		Walt Wilmot	118
	Abner Dalrymple	135		Jiggs Parrott	111
	King Kelly	126		Jimmy Ryan	102
	Tommy Burns	121	1894	Walt Wilmot	197
	Fred Pfeffer	113		Bill Dahlen	184
1886	Cap Anson	187		Jimmy Ryan	173
	Mike Kelly	75		Bill Lange	145
	George Gore	135		Charlie Irwin	144
	Fred Pfeffer	125		Jiggs Parrott	139
	Tommy Burns	123		Cap Anson	137
	Jimmy Ryan	100		George Decker	120
1887	Cap Anson	164	1895	Bill Everett	197
	Jimmy Ryan	145		Bill Lange	186
	Marty Sullivan	134		Cap Anson	159
	Fred Pfeffer	133		Jimmy Ryan	143
	Ed Williamson	117		Bill Dahlen	139
	Tommy Burns	112		Walt Wilmot	132

100-or-More Hits, Season (Continued)

Year	Player	Total	Year	Player	Total
1896	Bill Everett	184		Johnny Evers	141
	Bill Dahlen	172		Jimmy Slagle	125
	Bill Lange	153		Jack McCarthy	114
	Jimmy Ryan	153		Johnny Kling	110
	Cap Anson	133		Joe Tinker	108
	George Decker	118	1905	Jimmy Slagle	153
1897	Bill Lange	163		Bill Maloney	145
	Jimmy Ryan	160		Frank Schulte	135
	Cap Anson	128		Joe Tinker	135
	George Decker	124		Frank Chance	124
	Bill Everett	119		Doc Casey	122
	Barry McCormick	112	1906	Harry Steinfeldt	176
	Jimmy Callahan	105		Frank Schulte	158
1898	Bill Everett	190		Frank Chance	151
	Jimmy Ryan	185		Jimmy Sheckard	144
	Bill Dahlen	152		Johnny Evers	136
	Bill Lange	141		Joe Tinker	122
	Barry McCormick	131		Jimmy Slagle	119
	Jim Connor	114		Johnny Kling	107
1899	Bill Everett	166	1907	Harry Steinfeldt	144
	Jimmy Ryan	158		Johnny Evers	127
	Danny Green	140		Jimmy Sheckard	127
	Bill Lange	135		Artie Hofman	125
	Sam Mertes	127		Jimmy Slagle	125
	Harry Wolverton	111		Frank Chance	111
1900	Jack McCarthy	148	1908	Joe Tinker	146
	Sam Mertes	142		Harry Steinfeldt	130
	Bill Bradley	128		Johnny Evers	125
	Clarence Childs	128		Frank Chance	123
	Danny Green	116		Johnny Kling	117
	Jimmy Ryan	115		Artie Hofman	100
1901	Topsy Hartsel	187	1909	Artie Hofman	150
	Danny Green	168		Frank Schulte	142
	Charlie Dexter	123		Jimmy Sheckard	134
	Fred Raymer	108		Harry Steinfeldt	133
	Barry McCormick	100		Joe Tinker	132
1902	Jimmy Slagle	143		Johnny Evers	122
	Joe Tinker	129	1910	Frank Schulte	168
	Johnny Kling	123		Artie Hofman	155
	Bobby Lowe	116		Joe Tinker	136
1903	Jimmy Slagle	162		Jimmy Sheckard	130
	Johnny Kling	146		Johnny Evers	114
	Frank Chance	144		Harry Steinfeldt	113
	Davy Jones	140	1911	Frank Schulte	173
	Johnny Evers	136		Heinie Zimmerman	164
	Joe Tinker	134		Jimmy Sheckard	149
	Doc Casey	126		Joe Tinker	149
1904	Doc Casey	147		Jim Doyle	133
	Frank Chance	140		Artie Hofman	129

100-or-More Hits, Season (Continued)

Year	Player	Total	Year	Player	Total
1912	Heinie Zimmerman	207		Zeb Terry	139
	Johnny Evers	163		George Paskert	136
	Joe Tinker	155		Charlie Deal	108
	Frank Schulte	146	1921	Max Flack	172
	Jimmy Archer	109		Ray Grimes	170
	Vic Saier	130		Charlie Hollocher	161
	Jimmy Sheckard	128		Turner Barber	142
1913	Vic Saier	150		Zeb Terry	134
	Heinie Zimmerman	140		George Maisel	133
	Frank Schulte	138		John Kelleher	130
	Tommy Leach	131		Charlie Deal	122
	Johnny Evers	126	1922	Charlie Hollocher	201
1914	Heinie Zimmerman	167		Ray Grimes	180
	Wilbur Good	158		Hack Miller	164
	Tommy Leach	152		Zeb Terry	142
	Vic Saier	129		Arnold Statz	137
	Frank Schulte	112		Bob O'Farrell	127
	Bill Sweeney	101		Marty Krug	124
1915	Bob Fisher	163	1923	Arnold Statz	209
	Heinie Zimmerman	138		Barney Friberg	174
	Frank Schulte	137		George Grantham	160
	Cy Williams	133		Hack Miller	146
	Vic Saier	131		Bob O'Farrell	124
	Wilbur Good	126	1924	Arnold Statz	152
1916	Vic Saier	126		George Grantham	148
	Max Flack	120		Barney Friberg	138
	Heinie Zimmerman	116		Denver Grigsby	123
	Les Mann	113		Cliff Heathcote	121
	Cy Williams	113		Sparky Adams	117
1917	Fred Merkle	146		Gabby Hartnett	106
	Larry Doyle	121	1925	Sparky Adams	180
	Les Mann	121		Charlie Grimm	159
	Charlie Deal	114		Howie Freigau	146
	Cy Williams	113		Gabby Hartnett	115
	Max Flack	111	1926	Sparky Adams	193
1918	Charlie Hollocher	161		Hack Wilson	170
	Fred Merkle	143		Charlie Grimm	145
	Les Mann	141		Cliff Heathcote	141
	George Paskert	132		Howie Freigau	137
	Max Flack	123		Jimmy Cooney	129
1919	Max Flack	138	1927	Riggs Stephenson	199
	Fred Merkle	133		Sparky Adams	189
	Charlie Deal	117		Hack Wilson	175
	Charlie Hollocher	116		Charlie Grimm	169
1920	Max Flack	157		Gabby Hartnett	132
	Dave Robertson	150		Earl Webb	100

100-or-More Hits, Season (Continued)

Year	Player	Total	Year	Player	Total
1928	Riggs Stephenson	166		Stan Hack	116
	Hack Wilson	163	1935	Billy Herman	221
	Charlie Grimm	161		Augie Galan	203
	Fred Maguire	160		Phil Cavarretta	162
	Kiki Cuyler	142		Gabby Hartnett	142
	Woody English	142		Stan Hack	133
	Gabby Hartnett	117		Chuck Klein	127
1929	Rogers Hornsby	229		Frank Demaree	125
	Hack Wilson	198		Billy Jurges	125
	Kiki Cuyler	183	1936	Frank Demaree	212
	Riggs Stephenson	179		Billy Herman	211
	Woody English	168		Stan Hack	167
	Charlie Grimm	138		Augie Galan	152
	Norm McMillan	134		Gabby Hartnett	130
1930	Kiki Cuyler	228		Phil Cavarretta	125
	Woody English	214		Billy Jurges	120
	Hack Wilson	208		Ethan Allen	110
	Gabby Hartnett	172	1937	Frank Demaree	199
	Footsie Blair	158		Billy Herman	189
	Riggs Stephenson	125		Stan Hack	173
	Charlie Grimm	124		Augie Galan	154
1931	Kiki Cuyler	202		Billy Jurges	134
	Woody English	202		Gabby Hartnett	126
	Charlie Grimm	176		Rip Collins	125
	Rogers Hornsby	118	1938	Stan Hack	195
	Gabby Hartnett	107		Billy Herman	173
	Hack Wilson	103		Carl Reynolds	150
1932	Billy Herman	206		Rip Collins	131
	Riggs Stephenson	189		Frank Demaree	130
	Charlie Grimm	175		Billy Jurges	114
	Woody English	142		Augie Galan	113
	Johnny Moore	135	1939	Stan Hack	191
	Kiki Cuyler	130		Billy Herman	191
	Gabby Hartnett	110		Augie Galan	167
	Billy Jurges	100		Glen Russell	148
1933	Billy Herman	173		Hank Leiber	113
	Babe Herman	147	1940	Stan Hack	191
	Frank Demaree	140		Billy Herman	163
	Gabby Hartnett	135		Jimmy Gleeson	152
	Billy Jurges	131		Bill Nicholson	146
	Riggs Stephenson	114		Hank Leiber	133
	Woody English	104	1941	Stan Hack	186
1934	Kiki Cuyler	189		Bill Nicholson	135
	Babe Herman	142		Dom Dallessandro	132
	Billy Herman	138		Lou Stringer	126
	Chuck Klein	134		Bobby Sturgeon	106
	Gabby Hartnett	131		Babe Dahlgren	101
	Woody English	117			

Stan Hack held down the third base job for 16 years. He was an outstanding gloveman and a great hitter. He filed a career batting average of .301.

100-or-More Hits, Season (Continued)

Year	Player	Total	Year	Player	Total
1942	Bill Nicholson	173		Wayne Terwilliger	116
	Stan Hack	166		Bill Serena	104
	Lou Novikoff	145	1951	Frankie Baumholtz	159
	Lennie Merullo	132		Randy Jackson	153
	Phil Cavarretta	130		Hank Sauer	138
1943	Bill Nicholson	188		Eddie Miksis	112
	Phil Cavarretta	154	1952	Dee Fondy	166
	Stan Hack	154		Hank Sauer	153
	P-Nuts Lowrey	140		Frankie Baumholtz	135
	Ed Stanky	125		Bill Serena	107
	Lennie Merullo	115		Toby Atwell	105
1944	Phil Cavarretta	197	1953	Dee Fondy	184
	Don Johnson	169		Frankie Baumholtz	159
	Bill Nicholson	167		Eddie Miksis	145
	Roy Hughes	137		Randy Jackson	142
	Andy Pafko	126		Ralph Kiner	117
	Dom Dallessandro	116		Hank Sauer	104
	Stan Hack	108	1954	Ernie Banks	163
1945	Stan Hack	193		Dee Fondy	162
	Phil Cavarretta	177		Ralph Kiner	159
	Don Johnson	168		Gene Baker	149
	Andy Pafko	159		Hank Sauer	150
	P-Nuts Lowrey	148		Randy Jackson	132
	Bill Nicholson	136	1955	Ernie Banks	176
1946	Phil Cavarretta	150		Gene Baker	163
	P-Nuts Lowrey	139		Dee Fondy	152
	Eddie Waitkus	134		Randy Jackson	132
	Marv Rickert	103		Eddie Miksis	113
1947	Andy Pafko	155	1956	Ernie Banks	160
	Eddie Waitkus	150		Walt Moryn	151
	Phil Cavarretta	144		Dee Fondy	146
	P-nuts Lowrey	126		Gene Baker	141
	Bill Nicholson	119	1957	Ernie Banks	169
	Don Johnson	104		Walt Moryn	164
1948	Andy Pafko	171		Dale Long	121
	Eddie Waitkus	166		Cal Neeman	107
	Hal Jeffcoat	132	1958	Ernie Banks	193
	Bill Nicholson	129		Lee Walls	156
	P-Nuts Lowrey	128		Bobby Thomson	155
1949	Andy Pafko	146		Al Dark	137
	Roy Smalley	117		Walt Moryn	135
	Herman Reich	108		Dale Long	130
	Phil Cavarretta	106		Tony Taylor	117
	Hank Sauer	104	1959	Ernie Banks	179
1950	Andy Pafko	156		Tony Taylor	175
	Hank Sauer	148		Al Dark	126
	Roy Smalley	128		George Altman	103

Action at third — Ron Santo records another out.

Cincinnati's Johnny Bench puts tag on the Cubs' Joe Pepitone.

100-or-More Hits, Season (Continued)

Year	Player	Total	Year	Player	Total
1960	Ernie Banks	162		Don Kessinger	157
	Richie Ashburn	159		Ron Santo	142
	Bob Will	121		Ernie Banks	136
	Frank Thomas	114		Randy Hundley	125
1961	Ron Santo	164		Adolfo Phillips	106
	George Altman	157	1969	Billy Williams	188
	Billy Williams	147		Don Kessinger	181
	Ernie Banks	142		Ron Santo	166
	Don Zimmer	120		Glenn Beckert	158
1962	Billy Williams	184		Ernie Banks	143
	Ken Hubbs	172		Randy Hundley	133
	George Altman	170	1970	Billy Williams	205
	Ernie Banks	164		Glenn Beckert	170
	Ron Santo	137		Don Kessinger	168
	Andre Rodgers	128		Jim Hickman	162
	Lou Brock	114		Ron Santo	148
1963	Ron Santo	187		Johnny Callison	126
	Billy Williams	175	1971	Glenn Beckert	181
	Lou Brock	141		Billy Williams	179
	Ken Hubbs	133		Don Kessinger	159
	Andre Rodgers	118		Ron Santo	148
1964	Billy Williams	201		Joe Pepitone	131
	Ron Santo	185	1972	Billy Williams	191
	Ernie Banks	156		Don Kessinger	158
	Billy Cowan	120		Jose Cardenal	155
	Andre Rodgers	107		Ron Santo	140
	Jimmy Stewart	105		Glenn Beckert	128
1965	Billy Williams	203		Rick Monday	108
	Ron Santo	173		Jim Hickman	100
	Ernie Banks	162	1973	Billy Williams	166
	Glenn Beckert	147		Jose Cardenal	158
1966	Glenn Beckert	188		Don Kessinger	151
	Billy Williams	179		Rick Monday	148
	Ron Santo	175		Ron Santo	143
	Don Kessinger	146	1974	Jose Cardenal	159
	Ernie Banks	139		Rick Monday	158
	Randy Hundley	124		Don Kessinger	155
	Adolfo Phillips	109		Jerry Morales	146
	Byron Browne	102		Bill Madlock	142
1967	Ron Santo	176		Billy Williams	113
	Billy Williams	176	1975	Jose Cardenal	182
	Glenn Beckert	167		Bill Madlock	182
	Ernie Banks	158		Jerry Morales	156
	Randy Hundley	144		Don Kessinger	146
	Don Kessinger	134		Manny Trillo	135
	Adolfo Phillips	120		Rick Monday	131
1968	Glenn Beckert	189		Andy Thornton	109
	Billy Williams	185			

100-or-More Hits, Season (Continued)

Year	Player	Total	Year	Player	Total
1976	Bill Madlock	174		Bobby Murcer	140
	Jose Cardenal	156		Dave Kingman	105
	Jerry Morales	147	1979	Ivan DeJesus	180
	Rick Monday	145		Bill Buckner	168
	Manny Trillo	139		Dave Kingman	153
1977	Ivan DeJesus	166		Steve Ontiveros	147
	Steve Ontiveros	163		Jerry Martin	145
	Larry Biittner	147		Barry Foote	109
	Bobby Murcer	147		Scot Thompson	101
	Jerry Morales	142	1980	Bill Buckner	187
	Manny Trillo	141		Ivan DeJesus	159
	Bill Buckner	121		Lenny Randle	135
1978	Ivan DeJesus	172		Jerry Martin	112
	Bill Buckner	144	1981	Bill Buckner	131
	Manny Trillo	144			

Manny Trillo cracks another single.

Kiki Cuyler was a member of the famous "Murderer's Row" of the 1929 Cubs. Other members were Hack Wilson, Rogers Hornsby, and Riggs Stephenson.

Base Hits by Position (Season)

Modern

1B	Phil Cavarretta	1944	197
2B	Rogers Hornsby	1929	229
SS	Woody English	1930	214
3B	Heinie Zimmerman	1912	207
OF	Kiki Cuyler	1930	228
OF	Frank Demaree	1936	212
OF	Jigger Statz	1923	209
C	Gabby Hartnett	1930	172

19th Century

1B	Bill Everett	1898	190
2B	Ross Barnes	1876	138
SS	Bill Dahlen	1894	184
3B	Bill Everett	1895	197
OF	Walt Wilmot	1894	197
OF	Bill Lange	1895	186
OF	Jimmy Ryan	1889	187
C	King Kelly	1886	175

All-Time

1B	Phil Cavarretta	1944	197
2B	Rogers Hornsby	1929	229
SS	Woody English	1930	214
3B	Heinie Zimmerman	1912	207
OF	Kiki Cuyler	1930	228
OF	Frank Demaree	1936	212
OF	Jigger Statz	1923	209
C	King Kelly	1886	175

Ernie Banks proudly displays the ball he hit allowing him to reach 2500 career base hits.

Career Leaders in Base Hits

Player	Total	Player	Total
Cap Anson	3041	Charlie Hollocher	894
Ernie Banks	2583	Bill Everett	880
Billy Williams	2510	Dee Fondy	872
Stan Hack	2193	Jose Cardenal	864
Ron Santo	2171	Hank Sauer	852
Jimmy Ryan	2102	Solly Hofman	841
Phil Cavarretta	1927	Max Flack	833
Gabby Hartnett	1867	Walt Wilmot	827
Billy Herman	1710	Frank Demaree	820
Don Kessinger	1619	Sparky Adams	777
Frank Schulte	1590	Randy Hundley	758
Charlie Grimm	1454	Ivan DeJesus	756
Joe Tinker	1435	Bill Buckner	751
Glenn Beckert	1423	Cliff Heathcote	743
Johnny Evers	1339	Vic Saier	738
Bill Nicholson	1323	P-Nuts Lowrey	722
Tom Burns	1291	Harry Steinfeldt	696
Frank Chance	1267	Randy Jackson	690
Woody English	1248	Rick Monday	690
Kiki Cuyler	1199	Jimmy Archer	673
Bill Dahlen	1193	Jerry Morales	661
Riggs Stephenson	1167	Frank Baumholtz	659
Heinie Zimmerman	1112	Silver Flint	625
Fred Pfeffer	1078	George Altman	608
Bill Lange	1055	George Decker	599
Ed Williamson	1050	Walt Moryn	571
Andy Pafko	1048	Eddie Miksis	564
Hack Wilson	1017	Charlie Deal	562
Johnny Kling	960	Barry McCormick	560
Abner Dalrymple	938	Manny Trillo	559
George Gore	933	Clyde McCullough	540
Billy Jurges	928	Jigger Statz	536
Augie Galan	912	Jim Hickman	531
Jimmy Sheckard	905	Bob O'Farrell	529
Jimmy Slagle	905	Don Johnson	528
King Kelly	899	Fred Merkle	526

DOUBLES

Year-by-Year Leaders In Doubles

Year	Player	Total	Year	Player	Total
1876*	Ross Barnes	21	1913	Heinie Zimmerman	28
	Paul Hines		1914	Heinie Zimmerman	36
1877*	Cap Anson	19	1915	Vic Saier	35
1878	Cap Anson	12	1916	Vic Saier	25
	Bill Harbridge	12		Heinie Zimmerman	25
	Joe Start	12	1917	Fred Merkle	31
1879	Abner Dalrymple	25	1918	Les Mann	27
1880	Abner Dalrymple	27	1919	Charlie Deal	23
1881*	King Kelly	27	1920	Max Flack	30
1882*	King Kelly	37	1921	Ray Grimes	38
1883*	Ed Williamson	49	1922	Ray Grimes	45
1884	Cap Anson	30	1923	George Grantham	36
1885*	Cap Anson	35	1924	Jigger Statz	21
1886	Cap Anson	35	1925	Sparky Adams	29
1887	Cap Anson	33		Charlie Grimm	29
1888*	Jimmy Ryan	33	1926	Hack Wilson	36
1889	Cap Anson	32	1927*	Riggs Stephenson	46
1890	Jimmy Cooney	19	1928	Riggs Stephenson	36
1891	Cap Anson	24	1929	Rogers Hornsby	47
1892	Cap Anson	25	1930	Kiki Cuyler	50
1893	Bill Dahlen	28	1931	Woody English	38
1894	Walt Wilmot	45	1932	Riggs Stephenson	49
1895	Bill Lange	27	1933	Babe Herman	36
1896	Bill Dahlen	30	1934	Kiki Cuyler	42
1897	Jimmy Ryan	33	1935*	Billy Herman	57
1898	Bill Dahlen	35	1936	Billy Herman	57
1899	Bill Lange	21	1937	Frank Demaree	36
1900	Sam Mertes	25	1938	Billy Herman	34
	Jimmy Ryan	25		Stan Hack	34
1901	Topsy Hartsel	25	1939	Augie Galan	36
1902	Johnny Kling	19	1940	Jim Gleeson	39
	Joe Tinker	19	1941	Dom Dallessandro	36
1903	Johnny Kling	29	1942	Stan Hack	36
1904	Doc Casey	20	1943	Bill Nicholson	30
1905	Doc Casey	21	1944	Don Johnson	37
1906	Jimmy Sheckard	27	1945	Phil Cavarretta	34
	Harry Steinfeldt	27	1946	Phil Cavarretta	28
1907	Harry Steinfeldt	25	1947	Bill Nicholson	28
1908	Frank Chance	27		Eddie Waitkus	28
1909	Jimmy Sheckard	29	1948	Andy Pafko	30
1910	Frank Schulte	29	1949	Andy Pafko	29
1911	Frank Schulte	30	1950	Hank Sauer	32
1912*	Heinie Zimmerman	41	1951	Frank Baumholtz	28

*League Leader

Year-by-Year Leaders In Doubles (Continued)

Year	Player	Total	Year	Player	Total
1952	Hank Sauer	31	1967	Glenn Beckert	32
1953	Frank Baumholtz	36	1968	Billy Williams	30
1954	Ralph Kiner	36	1969	Don Kessinger	38
1955	Ernie Banks	29	1970	Billy Williams	34
	Gene Baker	29	1971	Billy Williams	27
1956	Walt Moryn	27	1972	Billy Williams	34
1957	Ernie Banks	34	1973	Jose Cardenal	33
1958	Bobby Thomson	27	1974	Jose Cardenal	35
1959	Tony Taylor	30	1975	Jose Cardenal	30
1960	Ernie Banks	32	1976	Bill Madlock	36
1961	Ron Santo	32	1977	Jerry Morales	34
1962	George Altman	27	1978	Bill Buckner	26
1963	Billy Williams	36	1979	Bill Buckner	34
1964	Billy Williams	39		Jerry Martin	34
1965	Billy Williams	39	1980	Bill Buckner	41
1966	Adolfo Phillips	29	1981	Bill Buckner	35

Glenn Beckert slides home as the ball (arrow) flies to San Diego catcher Pat Corrules. The run scored on a Billy Williams' double; manager Leo Durocher watches the action from his third base coaching position.

30-or-More Doubles in One Season

1882		
King Kelly	37	
1883		
Ed Williamson	49	
Tommy Burns	37	
Cap Anson	36	
George Gore	30	
1884		
Cap Anson	30	
1885		
Cap Anson	35	
1886		
Cap Anson	35	
King Kelly	32	
1887		
Cap Anson	33	
1888		
Jimmy Ryan	33	
1889		
Cap Anson	32	
Jimmy Ryan	31	
1894		
Walt Wilmot	45	
Jimmy Ryan	37	
Bill Dahlen	32	
1896		
Bill Dahlen	30	
1897		
Jimmy Ryan	33	
1898		
Bill Dahlen	35	
Jimmy Ryan	32	
1911		
Frank Schulte	30	
1912		
Heinie Zimmerman	41	
1914		
Heinie Zimmerman	36	

1915	
Vic Saier	35
1917	
Fred Merkle	31
1920	
Max Flack	30
1921	
Ray Grimes	38
Max Flack	31
1922	
Ray Grimes	45
Charlie Hollocher	37
1923	
George Grantham	36
Jigger Statz	33
1926	
Hack Wilson	36
Sparky Adams	35
Cliff Heathcote	33
Charlie Grimm	30
1927	
Riggs Stephenson	46
Gabby Hartnett	32
Hack Wilson	30
1928	
Riggs Stephenson	36
Hack Wilson	32
1929	
Rogers Hornsby	47
Riggs Stephenson	36
Norm McMillan	35
Hack Wilson	30
1930	
Kiki Cuyler	50
Woody English	36
Hack Wilson	36
Gabby Hartnett	31

30-or-More Doubles in One Season (Continued)

1931		1941	
Woody English	38	Dom Dallessandro	36
Kiki Cuyler	37	Stan Hack	33
Rogers Hornsby	37	Lou Stringer	31
Charlie Grimm	33	**1942**	
Gabby Hartnett	32	Stan Hack	36
1932		**1943**	
Riggs Stephenson	49	Bill Nicholson	30
Charlie Grimm	42	**1944**	
Billy Herman	42	Don Johnson	37
1933		Phil Cavarretta	35
Babe Herman	36	Bill Nicholson	35
Billy Herman	35	**1945**	
1934		Phil Cavarretta	34
Kiki Cuyler	42	**1948**	
Babe Herman	34	Andy Pafko	30
1935		**1950**	
Billy Herman	57	Hank Sauer	32
Augie Galan	41	**1952**	
Billy Jurges	33	Hank Sauer	31
Gabby Hartnett	32	**1953**	
1936		Frank Baumholtz	36
Billy Herman	57	**1954**	
Frank Demaree	34	Ralph Kiner	36
1937		Gene Baker	32
Frank Demaree	36	Dee Fondy	30
Billy Herman	35	**1957**	
1938		Ernie Banks	34
Stan Hack	34	Walt Moryn	33
Billy Herman	34	**1959**	
1939		Tony Taylor	30
Augie Galan	36	**1960**	
Billy Herman	34	Ernie Banks	32
1940		**1961**	
Jim Gleeson	39	Ron Santo	32
Stan Hack	38		

30-or-More Doubles in One Season (Continued)

1963	
Billy Williams	36

1964	
Billy Williams	39
Ron Santo	33

1965	
Billy Williams	39
Ron Santo	30

1967	
Glenn Beckert	32

1968	
Billy Williams	30

1969	
Don Kessinger	38
Billy Williams	33

1970	
Billy Williams	34
Jim Hickman	33
Ron Santo	30

1972	
Billy Williams	34

1973	
Jose Cardenal	33

1974	
Jose Cardenal	35

1975	
Jose Cardenal	30

1976	
Bill Madlock	36

1977	
Jerry Morales	34
Steve Ontiveros	32
Ivan DeJesus	31

1979	
Bill Buckner	34
Jerry Martin	34

1980	
Bill Buckner	41

1981	
Bill Buckner	35

Don Kessinger in pursuit of the ball.

Lifetime Leaders in Doubles

Player	Total	Player	Total
Cap Anson	532	Augie Galan	166
Ernie Banks	407	Bill Buckner	163
Billy Williams	402	George Gore	162
Gabby Hartnett	391	Andy Pafko	162
Stan Hack	363	Jose Cardenal	159
Jimmy Ryan	362	Johnny Kling	157
Ron Santo	353	Charlie Hollocher	145
Billy Herman	346	Hank Sauer	141
Phil Cavarretta	341	Dee Fondy	140
Charlie Grimm	270	Vic Saier	140
Frank Schulte	254	Cliff Heathcote	135
Bill Nicholson	245	Bill Lange	133
Riggs Stephenson	237	Max Flack	132
Tommy Burns	235	Frank Demaree	131
Kiki Cuyler	220	Silver Flint	122
Joe Tinker	220	Fred Pfeffer	121
Woody English	218	Harry Steinfeldt	120
Heinie Zimmerman	210	Ivan DeJesus	115
Ed Williamson	209	Rick Monday	114
Bill Dahlen	203	Randy Hundley	111
Don Kessinger	201	Walt Wilmot	111
Frank Chance	199	Frankie Baumholtz	109
Glenn Beckert	194	Sparky Adams	106
Mike Kelly	193	P-Nuts Lowrey	105
Hack Wilson	185	Jimmy Archer	104
Johnny Evers	181	Art Hofman	104
Billy Jurges	176	Walt Moryn	104
Abner Dalrymple	173	Dom Dallessandro	103
Jimmy Sheckard	171	George Altman	100

The 1932 infield — ONE OF THE GREATEST — Woody English, 3b; Bill Jurges, ss; Billy Herman, 2b, and Charlie Grimm, 1b.

Gabby Hartnett, known as a hard-hitting catcher, poses with pitcher Lou Warneke.

Doubles by Position (Season)

Modern

1B	Ray Grimes	1922	45
2B	Billy Herman	1935-1936	57
SS	Woody English	1931	38
	Don Kessinger	1969	38
3B	Heinie Zimmerman	1912	41
OF	Kiki Cuyler	1930	50
OF	Riggs Stephenson	1932	49
OF	Augie Galan	1935	41
C	Gabby Hartnett	1927-1931-1935	32

19th Century

1B	Cap Anson	1883	36
2B	Fred Pfeffer	1888	22
SS	Tommy Burns	1883	37
3B	Ed Williamson	1883	49
OF	Walt Wilmot	1894	45

Batting Records

OF	Jimmy Ryan	1894	37
OF	George Gore	1883	30
C	King Kelly	1882	37

All-Time

1B	Ray Grimes	1922	45
2B	Billy Herman	1935-1936	57
SS	Woody English	1931	38
	Don Kessinger	1969	38
3B	Ed Williamson	1883	49
OF	Kiki Cuyler	1930	50
OF	Riggs Stephenson	1932	49
OF	Walt Wilmot	1894	45
C	King Kelly	1882	37

Second baseman, Bill Herman, shows his hitting style.

Billy Williams safe at third — another triple.

TRIPLES

Most Triples, Season

Year	Player	Total	Year	Player	Total
1876*	Ross Barnes	14	1895	Bill Lange	16
1877	Paul Hines	7	1896	Bill Dahlen	19
	Cal McVey	7	1897	Jimmy Ryan	17
1878	Joe Start	5	1898	Jimmy Ryan	13
1879	Ed Williamson	13	1899	Sam Mertes	16
1880	Abner Dalrymple	12	1900	Bill Bradley	7
1881	George Gore	9		Jack McCarthy	7
1882	Abner Dalrymple	11	1901	Topsy Hartsel	16
1883	Mike Kelly	10	1902	Joe Tinker	5
1884	Fred Pfeffer	10	1903	Johnny Kling	13
1885	George Gore	13	1904	Joe Tinker	13
1886	George Gore	12	1905	Bill Maloney	14
	Abner Dalrymple	12		Frank Schulte	14
1887	Marty Sullivan	16	1906*	Frank Schulte	13
1888	George Van Haltren	14	1907	Johnny Kling	8
	Ed Williamson	14	1908	Joe Tinker	14
1889	Jimmy Ryan	14	1909	Joe Tinker	11
1890	Walt Wilmot	12		Frank Schulte	11
1891	Jimmy Ryan	15	1910	Art Hofman	16
1892	Bill Dahlen	19	1911	Frank Schulte	21
1893	Bill Dahlen	15	1912	Vic Saier	14
1894	Bill Dahlen	14		Heinie Zimmerman	14

Most Triples, Season (Continued)

Year	Player	Total	Year	Player	Total
1913*	Vic Saier	21	1946	Phil Cavarretta	10
1914	Heinie Zimmerman	12	1947	Andy Pafko	7
1915	Vic Saier	11	1948	Eddie Waitkus	10
	Heinie Zimmerman	11	1949	Roy Smalley	10
1916	Les Mann	9	1950	Roy Smalley	9
	Cy Williams	9	1951	Frankie Baumholtz	10
1917	Les Mann	10	1952	Dee Fondy	9
1918	Max Flack	10	1953	Dee Fondy	11
1919	Les Mann	9	1954	Ernie Banks	7
1920	Dave Robertson	11	1955	Ernie Banks	9
1921	Charlie Deal	8	1956	Dee Fondy	9
	Charlie Hollocher	8	1957	Ernie Banks	6
1922	Ray Grimes	12	1958	Ernie Banks	11
1923	Barney Friberg	11	1959	Al Dark	9
1924	Gabby Hartnett	7	1960	Bob Will	9
	Cliff Heathcote	7	1961*	George Altman	12
1925	Howie Freigau	10	1962	Ken Hubbs	9
1926	Hack Wilson	8	1963	Lou Brock	11
1927	Hack Wilson	12	1964*	Ron Santo	13
1928	Kiki Cuyler	9	1965	Billy Williams	6
	Hack Wilson	9	1966	Ron Santo	8
	Gabby Hartnett	9	1967	Billy Williams	12
	Riggs Stephenson	9	1968	Billy Williams	8
1929	Kiki Cuyler	7	1969	Billy Williams	10
	Rogers Hornsby	7	1970	Don Kessinger	14
1930	Kiki Cuyler	17	1971	Don Kessinger	6
	Woody English	17	1972	Don Kessinger	6
1931	Kiki Cuyler	12		Jose Cardenal	6
1932	Kiki Cuyler	9		Billy Williams	6
1933	Babe Herman	12	1973	Rick Monday	5
1934	Kiki Cuyler	8	1974	Don Kessinger	7
1935	Phil Cavarretta	12		Rick Monday	7
1936	Billy Herman	7		Jerry Morales	7
1937	Billy Herman	11	1975	Don Kessinger	10
1938	Stan Hack	11	1976	Rick Monday	5
1939*	Billy Herman	18		Joe Wallis	5
1940	Jimmy Gleeson	11	1977	Ivan DeJesus	7
1941	Stan Hack	5	1978	Ivan DeJesus	7
1942	Bill Nicholson	11		Greg Gross	7
1943	P-Nuts Lowrey	12	1979	Ivan DeJesus	10
1944	Phil Cavarretta	15	1980	Lenny Randle	6
1945	Andy Pafko	12	1981	Bull Durham	6

*Led League

15-or-More Triples in One Season

Year	Player	Total	Year	Player	Total
1911	Frank Schulte	21	1887	Marty Sullivan	16
1913	Vic Saier	21	1895	Bill Lange	16
1892	Bill Dahlen	19	1899	Sam Mertes	16
1896	Bill Dahlen	19	1901	Topsy Hartsel	16
1939	Billy Herman	18	1910	Solly Hofman	16
1897	Jimmy Ryan	17	1891	Jimmy Ryan	15
1911	Heinie Zimmerman	17	1893	Bill Dahlen	15
1930	Kiki Cuyler	17	1910	Frank Schulte	15
1930	Woody English	17	1944	Phil Cavarretta	15

Lifetime Leaders in Triples

Player	Total	Player	Total
Jimmy Ryan	142	King Kelly	49
Cap Anson	124	Augie Galan	46
Frank Schulte	117	George Decker	46
Bill Dahlen	106	Jimmy Sheckard	46
Phil Cavarretta	99	Dee Fondy	44
Joe Tinker	93	Hack Wilson	44
Ernie Banks	90	Charlie Grimm	43
Billy Williams	87	Andy Pafko	40
Stan Hack	81	Riggs Stephenson	40
Ed Williamson	80	Solly Hofman	37
Heinie Zimmerman	80	Jimmy Slagle	37
Frank Chance	79	Randy Jackson	36
Bill Lange	79	Charlie Hollocher	35
Don Kessinger	71	Les Mann	35
Tommy Burns	69	Frank Baumholtz	34
Billy Herman	69	Max Flack	34
Kiki Cuyler	66	Silver Flint	34
Ron Santo	66	Billy Jurges	34
Abner Dalrymple	65	Barry McCormick	33
Johnny Evers	64	P-Nuts Lowrey	32
Gabby Hartnett	64	Jimmy Archer	31
Fred Pfeffer	64	Glenn Beckert	31
George Gore	60	Bill Everett	31
Vic Saier	58	Danny Green	31
Bill Nicholson	53	Bob O'Farrell	31
Johnny Kling	51	Ivan DeJesus	31
Walt Wilmot	51	Cliff Heathcote	30
Woody English	50		

Triples by Position, Season

Modern

1B	Vic Saier	1913	21
2B	Billy Herman	1939	18
SS	Woody English	1930	21
3B	Heinie Zimmerman	1911	17
OF	Frank Schulte	1911	17
OF	Kiki Cuyler	1930	17
OF	Topsy Hartsel	1901	16
	Solly Hofman	1910	16
C	Johnny Kling	1903	13

19th Century

1B	Cap Anson	1887	13
2B	Ross Barnes	1876	14
SS	Bill Dahlen	1892-1896	19
3B	Ed Williamson	1879	13
OF	Jimmy Ryan	1897	17
OF	Bill Lange	1895	16
OF	Sam Mertes	1899	16
C	King Kelly	1886	11

All-Time

1B	Vic Saier	1913	21
2B	Billy Herman	1939	18
SS	Bill Dahlen	1892-1896	19
3B	Heinie Zimmerman	1911	17
OF	Frank Schulte	1911	21
OF	Kiki Cuyler	1930	17
OF	Jimmy Ryan	1897	17
C	Johnny Kling	1903	13

The speedy Joe Tinker is ranked sixth in lifetime triples with 93.

Ernie Banks is the all-time Cubs leader in career home runs with 512.

HOME RUNS

Year-by-Year Home Run Leaders

Year	Player	Total	Year	Player	Total
1876	Paul Hines	2	1910*	Frank Schulte	10
1877	None	0	1911*	Frank Schulte	21
1878	Frank Hankinson	1	1912*	Heinie Zimmerman	14
	John Remsen	1	1913	Vic Saier	14
	Joe Start	1	1914	Vic Saier	18
1879	Silver Flint	1	1915	Cy Williams	13
	John Peters	1	1916	Cy Williams	12
	Ed Williamson	1	1917	Larry Doyle	6
1880	George Gore	2	1918	Max Flack	4
1881	Tom Burns	4	1919	Max Flack	6
1882	Silver Flint	4	1920	Dave Robertson	10
1883	King Kelly	3	1921	Max Flack	6
1884*	Ed Williamson	27		Ray Grimes	6
1885*	Abner Dalrymple	11	1922	Ray Grimes	14
1886	Cap Anson	10	1923	Hack Miller	20
1887	Fred Pfeffer	16	1924	Gabby Hartnett	16
1888*	Jimmy Ryan	16	1925	Gabby Hartnett	24
1889	Jimmy Ryan	17	1926*	Hack Wilson	21
1890*	Walt Wilmot	14	1927*	Hack Wilson	30
1891	Walt Wilmot	11	1928*	Hack Wilson	31
1892	Jimmy Ryan	10	1929	Rogers Hornsby	39
1893	Bill Lange	8		Hack Wilson	39
1894	Bill Dahlen	15	1930*	Hack Wilson	56
1895	Bill Lange	10	1931	Rogers Hornsby	16
1896	Bill Dahlen	9	1932	Johnny Moore	13
1897	Bill Dahlen	6	1933	Gabby Hartnett	16
1898	Bill Lange	6		Babe Herman	16
1899	Sam Mertes	9	1934	Gabby Hartnett	22
1900	Sam Mertes	7	1935	Chuck Klein	21
1901	Topsy Hartsel	7	1936	Frank Demaree	16
1902	Charles Dexter	2	1937	Augie Galan	18
	Joe Tinker	2	1938	Ripper Collins	13
1903	Johnny Kling	3	1939	Hank Leiber	24
1904	Frank Chance	6	1940	Bill Nicholson	25
1905	Frank Chance	2	1941	Bill Nicholson	26
	Bill Maloney	2	1942	Bill Nicholson	21
	Joe Tinker	2	1943*	Bill Nicholson	29
1906	Frank Schulte	7	1944*	Bill Nicholson	33
1907	Johnny Evers	2	1945	Bill Nicholson	13
	Frank Schulte	2	1946	Bill Nicholson	8
1908	Joe Tinker	7		Phil Cavarretta	8
1909	Frank Schulte	4	1947	Bill Nicholson	26
	Joe Tinker	4	1948	Andy Pafko	26

*Led League

Hack Wilson, the home run king of the major leagues, signs his contract for the 1931 season as Bill Veeck Sr. looks on.

Year-by-Year Home Run Leaders (Continued)

Year	Player	Total	Year	Player	Total
1949	Hank Sauer	27	1965	Billy Williams	34
1950	Andy Pafko	36	1966	Ron Santo	30
1951	Hank Sauer	30	1967	Ron Santo	31
1952*	Hank Sauer	37	1968	Ernie Banks	32
1953	Ralph Kiner	28	1969	Ron Santo	29
1954	Hank Sauer	41	1970	Billy Williams	42
1955	Ernie Banks	44	1971	Billy Williams	28
1956	Ernie Banks	28	1972	Billy Williams	37
1957	Ernie Banks	43	1973	Rick Monday	26
1958*	Ernie Banks	47	1974	Rick Monday	20
1959	Ernie Banks	45	1975	Andy Thornton	18
1960*	Ernie Banks	41	1976	Rick Monday	32
1961	Ernie Banks	29	1977	Bobby Murcer	27
1962	Ernie Banks	37	1978	Dave Kingman	28
1963	Ron Santo	25	1979*	Dave Kingman	48
	Billy Williams	25	1980	Jerry Martin	23
1964	Billy Williams	33	1981	Bill Buckner	10
				Leon Durham	10

*Led League

20-or-More Home Runs, Season

Year	Player	HR	Year	Player	HR
1884	Ed Williamson	27	1949	Hank Sauer	27
	Fred Pfeffer	25	1950	Andy Pafko	36
	Abner Dalrymple	22		Hank Sauer	32
	Cap Anson	21		Roy Smalley	21
1911	Frank Schulte	21	1951	Hank Sauer	30
1923	Hack Miller	20	1952	Hank Sauer	37
1925	Gabby Hartnett	24	1953	Ralph Kiner	28
1926	Hack Wilson	21	1954	Hank Sauer	41
1927	Hack Wilson	30	1955	Ernie Banks	44
1928	Hack Wilson	31		Randy Jackson	21
1929	Rogers Hornsby	40	1956	Ernie Banks	28
	Hack Wilson	39		Walt Moryn	23
1930	Hack Wilson	56	1957	Ernie Banks	43
	Gabby Hartnett	37	1958	Ernie Banks	47
1934	Gabby Hartnett	22		Walt Moryn	26
	Chuck Klein	20		Lee Walls	24
1935	Chuck Klein	21		Bobby Thomson	21
1939	Hank Leiber	24		Dale Long	20
1940	Bill Nicholson	25	1959	Ernie Banks	45
1941	Bill Nicholson	26	1960	Ernie Banks	41
1942	Bill Nicholson	21		Frank Thomas	21
1943	Bill Nicholson	29	1961	Ernie Banks	29
1944	Bill Nicholson	33		George Altman	27
1947	Bill Nicholson	26		Billy Williams	25
1948	Andy Pafko	26		Ron Santo	23

20-or-More Home Runs, Season (Continued)

Year	Player	HR	Year	Player	HR
1962	Ernie Banks	37	1969	Ron Santo	29
	George Altman	22		Ernie Banks	23
	Billy Williams	22		Billy Williams	21
1963	Ron Santo	25		Jim Hickman	21
	Billy Williams	25	1970	Billy Williams	42
1964	Billy Williams	33		Jim Hickman	32
	Ron Santo	30		Ron Santo	26
	Ernie Banks	23	1971	Billy Williams	28
1965	Billy Wiflliams	34		Ron Santo	21
	Ron Santo	33	1972	Billy Williams	37
	Ernie Banks	28	1973	Rick Monday	26
1966	Ron Santo	30		Ron Santo	20
	Billy Williams	29		Billy Williams	20
1967	Ron Santo	31	1974	Rick Monday	20
	Billy Williams	28	1976	Rick Monday	32
	Ernie Banks	23	1977	Bobby Murcer	27
1968	Ernie Banks	32	1978	Dave Kingman	28
	Billy Williams	30	1979	Dave Kingman	48
	Ron Santo	26	1980	Jerry Martin	23

Home run hitter, Rick Monday, does it all as he makes another spectacular catch.

Slugger Bill "Swish" Nicholson hit over 20 home runs in 5 consecutive seasons for the Cubs (1940-1944).

20-Homer Club, Lifetime

Player	Total	Player	Total
Ernie Banks	512	Bill Lange	40
Billy Williams	392	Joe Pepitone	39
Ron Santo	337	Hack Miller	38
Gabby Hartnett	231	Lee Walls	38
Bill Nicholson	205	Gene Baker	37
Hank Sauer	198	Billy Herman	37
Hack Wilson	190	Eddie Miksis	34
Andy Pafko	126	Cy Williams	34
Rick Monday	106	Cliff Heathcote	33
Jimmy Ryan	99	King Kelly	33
Jim Hickman	97	Clyde McCullough	33
Cap Anson	96	Bobby Thomson	32
Dave Kingman	94	Woody English	31
Phil Cavarretta	92	Bill Madlock	31
Frank Schulte	91	Babe Herman	30
Randy Jackson	88	Sammy Taylor	30
Walt Moryn	84	Andre Thornton	30
George Altman	83	Ripper Collins	29
Randy Hundley	80	Joe Tinker	29
Kiki Cuyler	79	Andre Rodgers	28
Fred Pfeffer	79	Bob Speake	28
Dee Fondy	66	Johnny Callison	27
Jose Cardenal	61	Ray Grimes	27
Charlie Grimm	61	Bob O'Farrell	27
Ed Williamson	61	Jim King	26
Augie Galan	59	George Mitterwald	26
Rogers Hornsby	58	Bob Neeman	25
Bill Dahlen	57	George Gore	24
Stan Hack	57	Frank Thomas	23
Dale Long	55	George Decker	23
Jerry Morales	55	Barry Foote	22
Vic Saier	53	Glenn Beckert	22
Roy Smalley	52	Dom Dallessandro	22
Bill Buckner	50	Hal Jeffcoat	22
Ralph Kiner	50	P-Nuts Lowrey	22
Frank Demaree	49	Rip Russell	22
Riggs Stephenson	49	Manny Trillo	22
Hank Leiber	48	Silver Flint	21
Bill Serena	48	Lou Brock	20
Heinie Zimmerman	47	Frank Chance	20
Chuck Klein	46	Harry Chiti	20
Adolfo Phillips	46	Billy Cowan	20
Bobby Murcer	43	Carmen Fanzone	20
Walt Wilmot	43	George Grantham	20
Jerry Martin	42	Danny Green	20
Tommy Burns	40	Billy Jurges	20
Abner Dalrymple	40	Larry Biittner	20

Grand-Slam Home Runs

Date		Player	Team-Pitcher	In.	Site
1882	June 20	Larry Corcoran	Worcester-Richmond	9	H
1884	June 21	Fred Pfeffer	Braves-Whitney	1	H
	Aug. 14	King Kelly	Buffalo-Seard	2	H
1886	Sept. 8	Jimmy Ryan	Giants-Welch	6	H
1889	May 9	Addison Gumbert	Pirates-Conway	4	H
	Aug. 17	Jimmy Ryan	Washington-Sullivan	6	H
1890	May 8	Howard Earl	Reds-Viau	6	H
	June 26	Howard Earl	Dodgers-Lovett	1	H
	Aug. 16	Tommy Burns	Pirates-Phillips	5	H
	Aug. 16	Malachi Kittredge	Pirates-Phillips	5	H
	Sept. 8	Elmer Foster	Pirates-Anderson	1	H
1893	July 11	Bill Lange	Washington-Duryea	1	H
	Sept. 3	Malachi Kittredge	Baltimore-Mullane	5	H
	Sept. 10	Jiggs Parrott	Washington-Maul	4	H
1894	July 29	Walt Wilmot	Reds-Flynn	8	A
	Aug. 1	Cap Anson	Cardinals-Mason	5	H
	Aug. 11	Charlie Irwin	Cleveland-Cuppy	5	H
1895	May 20	Asa Stewart	Phillies-Carsey	8	H
	Aug. 24	Jimmy Ryan	Washington-Anderson	1	A
1896	May 18	Bill Lange	Giants-Campfield	6	H
1897	June 29	Jimmy Ryan	Louisville-Frazer	2	H
1899	Aug. 28	Bill Everett	Giants-Gettig	5	H
1902	Aug. 4	Frank Chance	Phillies-White	12	A
1904	Aug. 17	Jack O'Neil	Braves-Fisher	4	A
1905	June 25	Bill Maloney	Reds-Harper	5	H
1908	June 6	Johnny Kling	Braves-Young	3	A
	Sept. 12	Johnny Kling	Cardinals-Lush	12	A
1911	June 3	Frank Schulte	Giants-Marquard	8	H
	July 4	Frank Schulte	Reds-Keefe	3	H
	July 15	Joe Tinker	Braves-Mattern	7	A
	July 18	Frank Schulte	Braves-Tyler	6	A
	Aug. 16	Frank Schulte	Braves-R. Brown	4	A
	Sept. 21	Vic Saier	Phillies-Chalmers	3-2dG	H
1913	May 25	Vic Saier	Cardinals-Steel	1	H
	Aug. 25	Cy Williams	Dodgers-Rucker	2	H
	Sept. 6	Vic Saier	Reds-Johnson	1	H
1914	Aug. 18	Heinie Zimmerman	Dodgers-Ragan	5	H
1918	June 25	Max Flack	Cardinals-Sherdel	4	H
1921	Aug. 6	Bob O'Farrell	Giants-Ryan	4	H
1922	June 27	Elwood Wirts	Pirates-Glazner	5	H
	Sept. 16	Hack Miller	Dodgers-Ruether	1	A
1923	June 12	Hack Miller	Braves-F. Miller	5	H
	June 14	Bob O'Farrell	Dodgers-Vance	1	H
	July 15	Barney Friberg	Giants-Jonnard	10	A
1924	May 16	George Grantham	Giants-Oeschger	5	H
	Aug. 9	Jigger Statz	Braves-Benton	10	A
1925	Aug. 25	Mandy Brooks	Phillies-Mitchell	9	A
1926	June 1	Gabby Hartnett	Cardinals-Sherdel	3	H
	Sept. 11	Floyd Scott	Phillies-Knight	7	A

Grand-Slam Home Runs (Continued)

Date		Player	Team-Pitcher	In.	Site
1927*	May 1	Clyde Tolson	Pirates-Kremer	7	H
1928	Apr. 19	Hack Wilson	Reds-Luque	2	H
	July 3	Riggs Stephenson	Cardinals-Haid	9	A
1929	Apr. 17	Rogers Hornsby	Pirates-Fussell	8	H
	Apr. 18	Charlie Grimm	Pirates-Petty	3	H
	May 17	Hack Wilson	Reds-Donohue	6	H
	June 15	Rogers Hornsby	Phillies-Collins	7	H
	June 18	Hack Wilson	Cardinals-Haid	5	H
	June 29	Charlie Grimm	Cardinals-Sherdel	1	A
	July 1	Riggs Stephenson	Cardinals-Haines	1	A
	Aug. 26	Norm McMillan	Reds-Ehrhardt	8	H
	Sept. 17	Kiki Cuyler	Dodgers-Vance	5	H
1930	Apr. 29	Les Bell	Pirates-Kremer	3	H
	June 16	Charlie Grimm	Giants-Hubbell	9	A
	Aug. 22	Gabby Hartnett	Giants-Parmelee	8	H
1931	June 30	Rogers Hornsby	Phillies-Dudley	5	A
	Sept. 13*	Rogers Hornsby	Braves-Cunningham	11	A
	Sept. 27	Vince Barton	Pirates-Brame	7	H
1933	July 20	Babe Herman	Phillies-Liska	8	H
	July 23	Harvey Hendrick	Phillies-Collins	10	H
	Sept. 23	Gabby Hartnett	Reds-Kolp	6	H
1934	May 18	Tuck Stainback	Phillies-Holley	3	A
	June 22	Chuck Klein	Giants-Castleman	4	H
1935	July 27	Gabby Hartnett	Reds-Freitas	4	H
	Sept. 4	Augie Galan	Phillies-Bivin	8	H
1936	May 16	Phil Cavarretta	Phillies-Johnson	8	A
1937	May 5	Frank Demaree	Phillies-Sivess	6	A
	June 29	Billy Herman	Cardinals-Harrell	7	A
	Aug. 28	Clay Bryant	Braves-Gable	10	A
1938	May 24	Augie Galan	Dodgers-Mungo	4	A
	Sept. 14	Gabby Hartnett	Braves-Fette	3	A
1939	June 22	Augie Galan	Braves-Errickson	2	H
	Sept. 12	Hank Leiber	Braves-Posedel	1	H
1940	Apr. 26	Bill Nicholson	Reds-Thompson	1	H
	June 30	Jim Gleeson	Reds-Walters	5	A
	July 5	Rip Russell	Cardinals-Doyle	5	A
	July 19	Hank Leiber	Dodgers-Wyatt	1	H
	Sept. 7	Bill Nicholson	Reds-Derringer	4	H
1941	May 19	Claude Passeau	Dodgers-Casey	2	H
	May 21	Bill Nicholson	Phillies-Hoerst	5	H
	June 10	Hank Leiber	Giants-McGee	1	A
	July 5	Dom Dallessandro	Pirates-Sullivan	7	A
	July 29	Bill Nicholson	Phillies-Melton	8	H
	Aug. 26	Dom Dallessandro	Phillies-Beck	4	A
1941*	Sept. 20	Bob Scheffing	Cardinals-Krist	9	A
1942	June 3	Rip Russell	Giants-Sunkel	1	H
	June 21*	Dom Dallessandro	Giants-McGee	9	A
1944	June 28	Bill Nicholson	Dodgers-Webber	6	H

*Pinch-Hit Home Run

Billy Williams hit 392 career home runs and ranks second behind Banks on the Cubs all-time list.

Grand-Slam Home Runs (Continued)

Date		Player	Team-Pitcher	In.	Site
	Aug. 16	Bill Nicholson	Braves-Rich	3	H
	Aug. 20	Lennie Merullo	Giants-Feldman	4	H
1945	Aug. 15	Paul Gillespie	Dodgers-Herring	1	A
	Sept. 3	Andy Pafko	Reds-Heusser	1	H
	Sept. 23	Andy Pafko	Pirates-Roe	3	H
1946*	June 6	Frank Secory	Giants-Koslo	12	H
	Sept. 16	Bill Nicholson	Dodgers-Minner	7	A
1947	Apr. 20	Bill Nicholson	Cardinals-Pollet	5	A
	Aug. 24	Eddie Waitkus	Giants-Iott	5	A
	Sept. 8	John Miller	Pirates-Higbe	2	A
	Sept. 9*	Cliff Aberson	Dodgers-Lombardi	8	H
1949	Sept. 4	Andy Pafko	Pirates-Sewell	4	H
	Sept. 9	Andy Pafko	Pirates-Poat	5	A
1950	May 18	Rube Walker	Giants-Hartung	6	A
	May 26	Roy Smalley	Pirates-Queen	4	A
	Sept. 18*	Ron Northey	Dodgers-Bankhead	7	A
1951	May 3	Andy Pafko	Braves-Sufkont	6	A
	May 18	Jack Cusick	Phillies-Johnson	4	H
	July 29*	Phil Cavarretta	Phillies-Roberts	7-2dG	H
	Aug. 18	Randy Jackson	Pirates-Pollet	1	A
1952	Apr. 15	Hank Sauer	Reds-Wehmeier	3	A
	July 22	Dee Fondy	Braves-Bickford	4	A
1953	June 14	Ralph Kiner	Dodgers-Erskine	9	A
	June 19	Randy Jackson	Dodgers-Loes	5	H
	Aug. 14*	Bill Serena	Braves-Jolly	6	H
1954	May 17	Hank Sauer	Pirates-Purkey	5	A
	May 29	Walker Cooper	Reds-Baczewski	4	H
	July 18	Walker Cooper	Dodgers-Meyer	4	H
	Aug. 17	Clyde McCullough	Reds-Podbelian	4	H
1955	May 11	Ernie Banks	Dodgers-Meyer	1	H
	May 29	Ernie Banks	Braves-Burdette	3	H
	July 1	Gene Baker	Cardinals-Lawrence	2	H
	July 17	Ernie Banks	Phillies-Negray	6	A
	Aug. 2	Ernie Banks	Pirates-Littlefield	5	H
	Sept. 19	Ernie Banks	Cardinals-McDaniel	7	A
1956	July 8	Monte Irvin	Braves-Conley	9	A
	July 15	Gene Baker	Dodgers-Newcombe	3	H
	Aug. 23	Gene Baker	Giants-Surkont	7	H
1957	Apr. 30	Moose Moryn	Dodgers-Labine	7	A
1959*	May 12	Earl Averill	Braves-Burdette	9	H
	May 13	Ernie Banks	Reds-Purkey	3	H
	July 22	Earl Averill	Dodgers-McDevitt	2	A
	Aug. 13	Alvin Dark	Giants-McCormick	7	H
	Aug. 29	Ernie Banks	Braves-Spahn	3	H
1960	Apr. 14	Ernie Banks	Giants-Sanford	3	A
	Aug. 14	Ron Santo	Phillies-Green	6	A
1961	Apr. 15	Al Heist	Braves-Nottebart	9	H
	May 2	Billy Williams	Giants-Fisher	2	H

*Pinch-Hit Home Run

Grand-Slam Home Runs (Continued)

Date		Player	Team-Pitcher	In.	Site
	May 28	Ernie Banks	Giants-Miller	8	H
	June 16	Billy Williams	Giants-Jones	3	A
1962	May 20	Lou Brock	Phillies-Owens	2	A
	Sept. 16	Nellie Mathews	Dodgers-Williams	1	H
1963	Aug. 31	Ellis Burton	Colts-Woodeshick	9	H
	Sept. 2	Ron Santo	Giants-Fisher	5	H
1964	June 12	Joe Amalfitano	Pirates-Face	6	H
	May 1	Billy Williams	Colts-Hoerner	1	A
	Sept. 27	Ernie Banks	Giants-Bolin	5	H
1965	July 22	Ed Bailey	Phillies-Warner	5	H
	Aug. 27	Billy Williams	Braves-Johnson	5	A
1966	June 8	Randy Hundley	Dodgers-Drysdale	4	H
1967	May 20	Randy Hundley	Dodgers-Lee	7	H
	July 13	Adolfo Phillips	Giants-Perry	6	A
1968	July 7	Ernie Banks	Pirates-Blass	1	H
	July 14	Billy Williams	Pirates-McBean	7	A
	Sept. 25	Ron Santo	Dodgers-Singer	9	H
1969	May 24	Ernie Banks	Padres-Baldschun	5	A
	Aug. 23	Jim Hickman	Astros-Gladding	7	H
	May 28	Randy Hundley	Giants-Sadecki	3	A
1970	Apr. 26	Ron Santo	Astros-Dierker	6	H
	July 3	Billy Williams	Pirates-Gibbon	2	H
	July 6	Ron Santo	Expos-Wegener	1	H
	Aug. 14	Joe Pepitone	Dodgers-Sutton	1	H
1971	Aug. 18	Johnny Callison	Braves-P. Niekro	8	A
	Sept. 11	Paul Popovich	Cardinals-Reuss	3	H
1972	June 20	Randy Hundley	Giants-Carrithers	1	H
	Sept. 15	Jim Hickman	Mets-Gentry	3	H
	Sept. 16	Burt Hooton	Mets-Seaver	3	H
	Sept. 27	Billy Williams	Expos-Renko	5	A
1973	July 6	Rick Monday	Padres-Kirby	5	A
1974	Apr. 17	George Mitterwald	Pirates-Reuss	1	H
	July 26	Billy Williams	Pirates-Hernaiz	6	H
	Aug. 20	Carmen Fanzone	Dodgers-Hough	8	H
	Aug. 28*	Bill Madlock	Dodgers-Sutton	8	A
	Sept. 8	Jerry Morales	Phillies-Christenson	9	H
	Sept. 21	Steve Swisher	Cardinals-Lersch	6	A
1975*	Aug. 23*	Champ Summers	Astros-York	7	H
	Sept. 8*	Pete LaCock	Cardinals-Gibson	7	A
	Sept. 14*	Tim Hosley	Phillies-Lerch	9	H
1976	June 18	Bill Madlock	Braves-Leon	7	A
1978	April 26	Bobby Murcer	Phillies-Carlton	3	A
	June 6	Dave Kingman	Astros-Zamora	6	H
	June 26	Dave Rader	Mets-Murray	5	H
1979	Apr. 20	Dave Kingman	Expos-Rogers	3	H
	May 15	Barry Foote	Phillies-Espinosa	5	H
	May 17	Bill Buckner	Phillies-McGraw	5	H
	June 30	Mike Vail	Mets-Murray	11	H
	Sept. 9	Barry Foote	Phillies-Kucek	4	H

*Pinch-Hit Home Run

Grand-Slam Home Runs (Continued)

Date		Player	Team-Pitcher	In.	Site
1980	Apr. 19	Dave Kingman	Mets-Allen	8	H
	Apr. 22	Barry Foote	Cardinals-Littell	9	H
	June 18	Jerry Martin	Reds-Bair	7	H
	July 12	Cliff Johnson	Expos-Bahnsen	7-2dG	A
	Aug. 8	Cliff Johnson	Expos-Murray	14	H

Pinch-Hit Home Runs

Date		Player	Team-Pitcher	In.	On Base	Site
1913	June 19	Wilbur Good	Phillies-Alexander	8	0	H
	Sept. 5	Art Phelan	Reds-Packard	3	2	H
	Sept. 11	Cy Williams	Dodgers-Reulbach	7	1	H
1914	June 10	Red Corriden	Giants-Marquard	8	0	A
1915	Sept. 28	Wilbur Good	Reds-Lear	9	0	H
1916	June 30	Cy Williams	Cardinals-Doak	5	2	A
1923	May 4	Hack Miller	Cardinals-Toney	8	0	A
1924	Sept. 12	Hack Miller	Phillies-Ring	8	0	A
1925	Aug. 24	Tommy Griffith	Dodgers-Grimes	9-1stG	1	A
1926	June 23	Chick Tolson	Reds-Rixey	10	1	A
1927	Apr. 26	Earl Webb	Reds-Lucas	9	0	A
	May 1	Chick Tolson	Pirates-Kremer	7	3	H
1928	Apr. 18	Earl Webb	Reds-Lucas	8	2	H
1929	May 12	Gabby Hartnett	Giants-Hubbell	7	2	A
1930	Apr. 27	Cliff Heathcote	Pirates-Swetonic	9	1	H
	July 6	Gabby Hartnett	Reds-Benton	8-2dG	1	A
1931	Aug. 13	Hack Wilson	Phillies-Collins	7	2	A
	Aug. 26	Rogers Hornsby	Giants-Fitzsimmons	9-2dG	0	A
	Sept. 13	Rogers Hornsby	Braves-Cunningham	11	3	H
1932	June 20	Marv Gudat	Phillies-Holley	9	2	A
1933	July 7	Mark Koenig	Giants-Luque	8	2	H
	July 23	Harvey Hendrick	Phillies-Collins	10-1stG	3	H
1934	May 21	Babe Phelps	Dodgers-Beck	9	1	A
	Aug. 21	Augie Galan	Phillies-Collins	8	0	H
1936	June 21	Charlie Grimm	Dodgers-Mungo	8-2dG	0	A
	Aug. 16	John Gill	Reds-Derringer	7-2dG	0	A
	Aug. 29	John Gill	Braves-Lanning	7	1	H
1939	May 26	Carl Reynolds	Pirates-Tobin	5	0	H
	July 4	Gabby Hartnett	Cardinals-P. Dean	8-2dG	0	H
1940	June 3	Bill Nicholson	Dodgers-Casey	8	0	H
	June 27	Billy Rogell	Dodgers-Carleton	8	1	A
	Aug. 25	Bill Nicholson	Giants-P. Dean	6-2dG	2	H
1941	Sept. 20	Bob Scheffing	Cardinals-Krist	9	3	A
1942	June 21	Dom Dallessandro	Giants-McGee	9-2dG	3	A
1944	May 30	Lou Novikoff	Giants-Feldman	8-1stG	0	A

Pinch-Hit Home Runs (Continued)

Date	Player	Team-Pitcher	In.	On Base	Site
	Sept. 26 Lou Novikoff	Phillies-McKee	9-1stG	0	A
1946	June 6 Frank Secory	Giants-Koslo	12	3	H
	June 2 Bill Nicholson	Braves-Cooper	7-1stG	0	H
	July 6 Frank Secory	Reds-Beggs	12	1	H
1947	July 18 Marv Rickert	Phillies-Rowe	3	0	A
	Sept. 9 Cliff Aberson	Dodgers-Lombardi	8	3	H
1948	June 24 Clarence Maddern	Giants-Jensen	9-1stG	1	A
	July 28 Rube Walker	Phillies-Donnelly	7	0	A
	Sept. 12 Hal Jeffcoat	Pirates-Sewell	8	0	H
1949	May 17 Smoky Burgess	Dodgers-Branca	8	1	H
	Aug. 24 Frank Baumholtz	Giants-Jones	8	1	A
1950	Sept. 9 Phil Cavarretta	Reds-Smith	9-2dG	2	A
	Sept. 18 Ron Northey	Dodgers-Bankhead	7	3	A
1951	May 6 Hal Jeffcoat	Phillies-Roberts	3-2dG	1	A
	July 29 Phil Cavarretta	Phillies-Roberts	7-2dG	3	H
	Sept. 17 Gene Hermanski	Dodgers-King	7	1	H
1952	June 18 Bob Addis	Dodgers-Black	9	2	H
	Aug. 18 Phil Cavarretta	Pirates-Dickson	9	1	H
1953	July 29 Carl Sawatski	Dodgers-Meyer	7	2	H
	Aug. 14 Bill Serena	Braves-Jolly	6	3	H
	Sept. 17 Tommy Brown	Phillies-Simmons	5	2	H
1954	Apr. 18 Frankie Baumholtz	Cardinals-Raschi	7	0	H
	June 9 Joe Garagiola	Phillies-Miller	7-2dG	0	H
	June 9 Bill Serena	Phillies-Miller	9-2dG	0	H
1955	May 5 Ted Tappe	Giants-Grissom	7	0	A
	June 5 Frankie Baumholtz	Giants-Grissom	9-2dG	2	A
1956	July 17 Hobie Landrith	Phillies-Negray	9	0	H
1957	June 18 Jim Bolger	Phillies-Sanford	5	0	H
	July 4 Bob Will	Cardinals-McDaniel	7-stG	1	H
	July 14 Bob Speake	Giants-Crone	4	2	A
1958	Apr. 23 Chuck Tanner	Dodgers-Erskine	9	0	A
	May 2 Jim Bolger	Braves-Conley	7	2	H
	Aug. 2 Walt Moryn	Phillies-Miller	3	2	A
	Aug. 24 Dale Long	Phillies-Farrell	9-1stG	1	H
	Aug. 30 Dale Long	Cardinals-S. Jones	10	1	H
	Aug. 31 Chuck Tanner	Cardinals-Maglie	3	2	A
	Sept. 14 Chuck Tanner	Pirates-Raydon	5-1stG	2	A
1959	Apr. 29 Johnny Goryl	Reds-Lawrence	5	1	A
	May 12 Earl Averill	Braves-Burdette	9	3	H
	June 18 Jim Marshall	Pirates-Kline	8	0	H
	Aug. 13 Dale Long	Giants-Fischer	7	1	H
	Aug. 14 Dale Long	Giants-S. Jones	7	1	H
1960	Apr. 16 Walt Moryn	Giants-S. Jones	8	0	A
	Apr. 24 Earl Averill	Giants-O'Dell	7	0	H
	June 4 Sammy Taylor	Dodgers-Roebuck	8	0	A
1961	July 26 Ernie Banks	Cardinals-Bauta	8	2	H
	Aug. 6 Don Zimmer	Dodgers-Padres	7	0	A

Pinch-Hit Home Runs (Continued)

Date	Player		Team-Pitcher	In.	On Base	Site
1962	May 18	Bob Will	Phillies-Baldschun	8	0	A
	May 29	Bob Will	Braves-Burdette	8	0	H
	June 10	Ernie Banks	Mets-C. Anderson	9-2dG	2	H
	July 14	Dick Bertell	Reds-O'Toole	5	0	H
1963	June 8	Merritt Ranew	Dodgers-Sherry	6	1	H
	Aug. 2	Leo Burke	Giants-Bolin	8	2	H
1964	June 13	Leo Burke	Pirates-Law	6	2	H
	July 9	Len Gabrielson	Giants-Perry	5	0	H
1965	May 18	Len Gabrielson	Giants-Sanford	2	1	H
	May 26	George Altman	Mets-Ribant	10	1	A
1966	May 21	George Altman	Braves-Cloninger	7	0	A
	Sept. 17	Adolfo Phillips	Cardinals-Hoerner	9	0	H
1967	June 5	Ted Savage	Phillies-Loughlin	6	2	A
	Aug. 9	Clarence Jones	Pirates-McBean	8-2dG	0	H
1968	May 19	Ernie Banks	Giants-Gibbon	6-2dG	2	A
	July 4	Dick Nen	Phillies-Farrell	8-1stG	1	H
1969	Apr. 8	Willie Smith	Phillies-Lersch	11	1	H
	June 1	Jim Hickman	Graves-Raymond	6	1	H
	June 10	Willie Smith	Braves-Reed	8	0	H
	Sept. 11	Willie Smith	Phillies-James	9	0	A
1970	June 24	Ernie Banks	Mets-Seaver	9-1stG	2	H
	July 28	Al Spangler	Astros-Billingham	6	0	H
	Sept. 7	Willie Smith	Pirates-Moose	7-1stG	1	A
1971	July 21	Ernie Banks	Mets-McGraw	6	0	H
	Sept. 8	Carmen Fanzone	Pirates-Blass	8	0	A
	Sept. 15	Billy Williams	Mets-Frisella	9-1stG	0	A
1973	May 6	Adrian Garrett	Giants-Willoughby	7-2dG	1	A
	July 20	Pat Bourque	Giants-Marichal	9	0	H
1974	May 11	Andre Thornton	Mets-Sadecki	8	1	H
	July 31	Carmen Fanzone	Expos-Taylor	9-1stG	1	H
	Aug. 28	Bill Madlock	Dodgers-Sutton	8	3	A
	Sept. 10	Carmen Fanzone	Pirates-Brett	3	1	H
	Sept. 10	Jim Tyrone	Pirates-Pizarro	8	0	H
1975	June 26	Tim Hosley	Pirates-Candelaria	8	0	A
	Aug. 23	Champ Summers	Astros-York	7	3	H
	Aug. 23	Rick Monday	Astros-J. Sosa	8	0	H
	Sept. 3	Pete LaCock	Cardinals-Gibson	7	3	A
	Sept. 5	George Mitterwald	Phillies-McGraw	9-2dG	0	A
	Sept. 14	Tim Hosley	Phillies-Lersch	9	3	H
1976	Apr. 25	Pete LaCock	Dodgers-Rhoden	5	0	A
	May 16	Rick Monday	Padres-Greif	6	2	H
	July 23	Jerry Morales	Cardinals-Rasmussen	7	0	A
	Sept. 11	Champ Summers	Phillies-Reed	12	2	A
1977	July 4	Bobby Murcer	Expos-Atkinson	9-2dG	0	H
	Sept. 9	Gene Clines	Mets-Apodaca	9	0	H
1978	June 26	Dave Rader	Mets-Murray	5	3	H
	July 2	Mike Vail	Phillies-Ruthven	7	2	H

Pinch-Hit Home Runs (Continued)

Date		Player	Team-Pitcher	In.	On Base	Site
	Aug. 15	Bobby Murcer	Braves-Garber	6	0	H
	Sept. 6	Dave Johnson	Phillies-Carlton	8	0	H
1979	June 30	Mike Vail	Mets-Murray	11	3	H
	July 24	Ken Henderson	Astros-Forsch	8	0	A
	Aug. 1	Larry Biittner	Expos-Bahnsen	9	1	A
	Sept. 4	Mike Vail	Cardinals-Vuckovich	9	1	H
1980	June 1	Larry Biittner	Phillies-Walk	6	1	H
	June 2	Ken Henderson	Expos-Elias Sosa	8	0	A
	July 6	Cliff Johnson	Pirates-Bert Blyleven	9	0	A
1981	May 10	Hector Cruz	Braves-Rick Camp	9	0	H
	June 6	Mike Tyson	Dodgers-Valenzuela	4	2	H
	Aug. 12	Mike Lum	Mets-Leach	7	1	H
	Aug. 13	Jerry Morales	Mets-Searage	5	1	H
	Sept. 12	Mel Hall	Expos-Sanderson	5	1	H

Four Home Runs in One Inning

Date		Players	In.	Opponent	Site
1930	May 12	(Heathcote, Wilson, Grimm, Beck)	7	Giants	H

Three Homers in One Inning

Date		Players	In.	Opponent	Site
1929	June 4	(Hornsby, Wilson, Grimm)	5	Giants	H
	June 28	(Wilson, Malone, Hornsby)	2	Cardinals	A
1937	May 4	(Collins, Marty, Bottarini)	8	Phillies	A
1939	Sept. 6	(Nicholson, Russell, French)	3	Cardinals	H
1941	Aug. 11	(Cavarretta, Hack, Nicholson)*	5	Cardinals	A
1947	June 27	(Dallessandro, Nicholson, Johnson)	6	Pirates	H
1950	June 13	(Ramazzotti, Cavarretta, Borkowski)	6	Dodgers	A
1954	May 31	(Minner, Jackson, Serena)	4	Cardinals	H
	Apr. 16	(Jackson, Banks, Fondy)*	2	Cardinals	A
	July 1	(Sauer, Jackson, Baker)	2	Cardinals	H
	Aug. 29	(Chiti, Fondy, Baker)	4	Giants	A
	Sept. 9	(Fondy, Banks, Miksis)	1-1stG	Dodgers	H
	Sept. 9	(Fondy, Baker, Banks)	8-2dG	Dodgers	H
1960	Sept. 18	(Zimmer, Santo, Altman)	6	Dodgers	H
1964	June 2	(Williams, Santo, Cowan)	4	Cardinals	H
1967	July 3	(Williams, Santo, Hundley)	1	Braves	A
1968	July 31	(Williams, Banks, Hickman)	4	Astros	H
1970	Aug. 19	(Pepitone, Callison, Beckert)	8	Padres	H
1973	May 1	(Williams, Santo, Cardenal)	4	Dodgers	A
	June 10	(Monday, Bourque, Santo)	1	Reds	H
1977	May 17	(Biittner, Ontiveros, Clines)	3	Padres	H
	May 17	(Biittner, Murcer, Morales)*	5	Padres	H

*Consecutive Homers

Three Home Runs in a Game

Date		Player	Opponent	Site
1884	May 30	Ed Williamson	Buffalo	Lakefront Park
	Aug. 6	Cap Anson*	Cleveland	Lakefront Park
1930	July 26	Hack Wilson	Phillies	Baker Bowl
1931	Apr. 24	Rogers Hornsby*	Pirates	Forbes Field
1933	July 20	Babe Herman	Phillies	Wrigley Field
1939	July 4	Hank Leiber*	Cardinals	Wrigley Field
1942	July 26	Clyde McCullough*	Braves	Braves Field
1944	July 23	Bill Nicholson*	Giants	Polo Grounds
1950	Aug. 2	Andy Pafko*	Giants	Polo Grounds
	Aug. 28	Hank Sauer*	Phillies	Wrigley Field
1952	June 11	Hank Sauer	Phillies	Wrigley Field
1955	Aug. 4	Ernie Banks	Pirates	Wrigley Field
1957	Sept. 14	Ernie Banks*	Pirates	Wrigley Field
1958	Apr. 24	Lee Walls	Dodgers	LA Coliseum
	May 30	Moose Moryn	Dodgers	Wrigley Field
1962	May 29	Ernie Banks	Braves	Wrigley Field
1963	June 9	Ernie Banks	Dodgers	Wrigley Field
1967	June 11	Adolfo Phillips	Mets	Wrigley Field
1968	Sept. 10	Billy Williams	Mets	Wrigley Field
1972	May 16	Rick Monday*	Phillies	Veterans Stadium
1974	Apr. 17	George Mitterwald	Pirates	Wrigley Field
1978	May 14	Dave Kingman	Dodgers	Dodger Stadium (15 innings)
1979	May 17	Dave Kingman	Phillies	Wrigley Field
	July 28	Dave Kingman	Mets	Shea Stadium

*Consecutive homers

Rick Monday was the Cubs most recent player to hit three consecutive homers in one game (May 16, 1972).

10-or-More Home Runs in One Month

HR	Player	Date
13	Hack Wilson	August 1930
13	Ernie Banks	July 1955
13	Ernie Banks	September 1957
13	Ernie Banks	August 1958
12	Hack Wilson	June 1929
12	Hack Wilson	June 1930
12	Hank Sauer	May 1954
12	Ernie Banks	June 1960
12	Dave Kingman	June 1979
11	Hack Wilson	July 1929
11	Hack Wilson	July 1930
11	Hank Sauer	July 1949
11	Andy Pafko	July 1950
11	Ernie Banks	July 1958
10	Ed Williamson	July 1884
10	Hack Wilson	May 1930
10	Hack Wilson	September 1930
10	Hank Leiber	September 1939
10	Andy Pafko	August 1950
10	Hank Sauer	June 1952
10	Bob Speake	May 1955
10	George Altman	June 1961
10	Jim Hickman	August 1969
10	Billy Williams	July 1970

World Series Home Runs

Date		Player	Game	In.	Pitcher	Team	Site
1908	Oct. 11	Joe Tinker	2	8	Donovan	Tigers	Navin Field
1929	Oct. 12	Charlie Grimm	4	4	Quinn	Athletics	Shibe Park
1932	Oct. 1	Kiki Cuyler	3	3	Pipgras	Yankees	Wrigley Field
	Oct. 1	Gabby Hartnett	3	9	Pipgras	Yankees	Wrigley Field
	Oct. 2	Frank Demaree	4	1	Allen	Yankees	Wrigley Field
1935	Oct. 2	Frank Demaree	1	9	Rowe	Tigers	Navin Field
	Oct. 4	Frank Demaree	3	2	Auker	Tigers	Wrigley Field
	Oct. 5	Gabby Hartnett	4	2	Crowder	Tigers	Wrigley Field
	Oct. 6	Chuck Klein	5	3	Rowe	Tigers	Wrigley Field
	Oct. 7	Billy Herman	6	5	Bridges	Tigers	Navin Field
1938	Oct. 8	Joe Marty	3	8	Pearson	Yankees	Yankee Stadium
	Oct. 9	Ken O'Dea	4	8	Ruffing	Yankees	Yankee Stadium
1945	Oct. 3	Phil Cavarretta	1	7	Tobin	Tigers	Briggs Stadium

Cubs All-Star Game Home Runs

Date		Player	In.	Pitcher	Site
1936	July 7	Augie Galan	5	Rowe	Braves Field (Bos.)
1952	July 8	Hank Sauer	4	Lemon	Shibe Park (Phil.)
1960	July 11	Ernie Banks	1-1stG	Monbouquette	Municipal Stadium (K.C.)
1961	July 11	George Altman	8-1stG	Bunning	Candlestick Park (SF)
1964	July 7	Billy Williams	4	Wyatt	Shea Stadium (NY)

Most Home Runs by Position, One Season

Modern

1B	Ernie Banks	37	1962
2B	Rogers Hornsby	39	1929
SS	Ernie Banks	47	1958
3B	Ron Santo	33	1965
OF	Hack Wilson	56	1930
OF	Dave Kingman	48	1979
OF	Billy Williams	42	1970
C	Gabby Hartnett	37	1930
P	Fergie Jenkins	6	1971

19th Century

1B	Cap Anson	21	1884
2B	Fred Pfeffer	25	1884
SS	Bill Dahlen	15	1894
3B	Ed Williamson	27	1884
OF	Abner Dalrymple	22	1884
OF	Jimmy Ryan	17	1889
OF	Walt Wilmot	14	1890
C	Mike Kelly	13	1884
P	John Clarkson	6	1887

Dave Kingman averaged one homer every 12.6 times at bat.

Home Run Frequency

Player	At Bats	Homers	Frequency
Dave Kingman	1182	94	12.6
Hank Sauer	3165	198	15.9
Hack Wilson	3154	190	16.6
Ernie Banks	9421	512	18.4
Rogers Hornsby	1121	58	19.3
Ralph Kiner	971	50	19.4
Jim Hickman	1992	97	20.5
Dale Long	1173	55	21.3
Billy Williams	8479	392	21.6
Ron Santo	7768	337	23.0
Bill Nicholson	4857	205	23.7
Rick Monday	2551	106	24.1
Walt Moryn	2099	84	24.9
George Altman	2205	83	26.6
Gabby Hartnett	6282	231	27.2
Andy Pafko	3567	126	28.3
Randy Jackson	2602	88	29.6

(The home run frequency is attained by dividing the number of at bats by the amount of home runs. Dave Kingman thus averages one homer every 12.6 at bats.)

Home Runs by Decades (Top Ten)

1870's

1.	Paul Hines	2
2.	John Peters	2
3.	Cap Anson	1
4.	Ross Barnes	1
5.	Silver Flint	1
6.	Frank Hankinson	1
7.	Cal McVey	1
8.	John Remsen	1
9.	Joe Start	1
10.	Jim White	1
	Ed Williamson	1

1880's

1.	Fred Pfeffer	70
2.	Ed Williamson	60
3.	Cap Anson	57
4.	Jimmy Ryan	48
5.	Abner Dalrymple	40
6.	Tommy Burns	33
7.	King Kelly	33
8.	George Gore	24
9.	Silver Flint	20
10.	Hugh Duffy	19

1890's

1.	Bill Dahlen	57
2.	Jimmy Ryan	46
3.	Walt Wilmot	43
4.	Bill Lange	40
5.	Cap Anson	28
6.	George Decker	23
7.	Sam Carroll	14
8.	Bill Everett	13
9.	Malachi Kittredge	12
10.	Bill Hutchison	11

1900's

1.	Joe Tinker	22
2.	Frank Chance	17
3.	Frank Schulte	17
4,	Johnny Kling	13
5.	Danny Green	10
6.	Artie Hofman	9
7.	Topsy Hartsel	7
8.	Sam Mertes	7
9.	Harry Steinfeldt	7
10.	Jimmy Ryan	5
	Johnny Evers	5
	Jimmy Sheckard	5

1910's

1.	Frank Schulte	74
2.	Vic Saier	53
3.	Heinie Zimmerman	47
4.	Cy Williams	34
5.	Jimmy Archer	15
6.	Tommy Leach	15
7.	Max Flack	13
8.	Jimmy Sheckard	12
9.	Fred Merkle	9
10.	Larry Doyle	7

1920's

1.	Hack Wilson	121
2.	Gabby Hartnett	81
3.	Hack Miller	38
4.	Rogers Hornsby	39
5.	Charlie Grimm	35
6.	Riggs Stephenson	35
7.	Cliff Heathcote	33
8.	Kiki Cuyler	32
9.	Oscar Grimes	27
10.	Bob O'Farrell	26

1930's

1.	Gabby Hartnett	169
2.	Hack Wilson	69
3.	Augie Galan	55
4.	Frank Demaree	49
5.	Kiki Cuyler	47
6.	Chuck Klein	46
7.	Billy Herman	32
8.	Babe Herman	30
9.	Rip Collins	29
10.	Stan Hack	28

1940's

1.	Bill Nicholson	200
2.	Andy Pafko	78
3.	Phil Cavarretta	51
4.	Stan Hack	29
5.	Hank Sauer	27
6.	Clyde McCullough	24
7.	Dom Dallessandro	22
	P-Nuts Lowrey	22
9.	Lou Stringer	17
10.	Babe Dahlgren	16
	Bob Scheffing	16

Home Runs by Decades (Top Ten) (Continued)

1950's

1.	Ernie Banks	238
2.	Hank Sauer	171
3.	Randy Jackson	88
4.	Moose Moryn	82
5.	Dee Fondy	66
6.	Dale Long	55
7.	Ralph Kiner	50
8.	Andy Pafko	48
9.	Bill Serena	47
10.	Roy Smalley	40

1960's

1.	Ernie Banks	269
2.	Ron Santo	253
3.	Billy Williams	239
4.	George Altman	71
5.	Randy Hundley	58
6.	Adolfo Phillips	46
7.	Andre Rodgers	28
8.	Jim Hickman	26
9.	Frank Thomas	23
10.	Lou Brock	20
	Billy Cowan	20

1970's

1.	Billy Williams	143
2.	Rick Monday	106
3.	Ron Santo	84
4.	Dave Kingman	76
5.	Jim Hickman	71
6.	Jose Cardenal	61
7.	Jerry Morales	54
8.	Bobby Murcer	43
9.	Joe Pepitone	39
10.	Bill Madlock	31

1980's

1.	Jerry Martin	23
2.	Bill Buckner	20
3.	Dave Kingman	18
4.	Bull Durham	10
4.	Cliff Johnson	10
6.	Heity Cruz	7
7.	Bobby Bonds	6
	Steve Dillard	6
	Barry Foote	6
	Mike Vail	6

Ernie Banks greets Ron Santo as he heads for the plate after a game-winning homer.

EXTRA BASE HITS

Year-by-Year Leaders in Extra Base Hits

Year	Player	2B	3B	HR	Total
1876	Ross Barnes	21	14	1	36
1877	Cap Anson	19	1	0	20
1878	Joe Start	12	5	1	18
1879	Ed Williamson	20	13	1	34
1880	Abner Dalrymple	25	12	0	37
1881	King Kelly	27	3	2	32
1882	King Kelly	37	4	1	42
1883	Ed Williamson	49	5	2	56
1884	Cap Anson	30	3	21	54
1885	Abner Dalrymple	27	12	11	50
1886	Cap Anson	35	11	10	56
1887	Cap Anson	33	13	7	53
1888	Jimmy Ryan	33	10	16	59
1889	Jimmy Ryan	31	14	17	62
1890	Walt Wilmot	15	12	14	41
1891	Jimmy Ryan	22	15	9	46
1892	Bill Dahlen	23	19	5	47
1893	Bill Dahlen	28	15	5	48
1894	Walt Wilmot	45	12	5	62
1895	Bill Lange	27	16	10	53
1896	Bill Lange	30	19	9	58
1897	Jimmy Ryan	33	17	5	55
1898	Jimmy Ryan	32	13	4	49
1899	Sam Mertes	13	16	9	38
1900	Sam Mertes	25	4	7	36
1901	Topsy Hartsel	25	16	7	48
1902	Joe Tinker	19	5	2	26
1903	Johnny Kling	29	13	3	45
1904	Frank Chance	16	10	6	32
1905	Bill Maloney	17	14	2	33
1906	Harry Steinfeldt	27	10	3	40
1907	Harry Steinfeldt	25	5	1	31
1908	Joe Tinker	22	14	7	43
1909	Joe Tinker	26	11	4	41
1910	Frank Schulte	29	15	10	54
1911	Frank Schulte	30	21	21	72
1912	Heinie Zimmerman	41	14	14	69
1913	Vic Saier	15	21	14	50
1914	Heinie Zimmerman	36	12	3	51
1915	Vic Saier	35	11	11	57
1916	Cy Williams	19	9	12	40
1917	Fred Merkle	31	9	3	43
1918	Les Mann	27	7	2	36

Year-by-Year Leaders in Extra Base Hits (Continued)

Year	Player	2B	3B	HR	Total
1919	Charlie Deal (tie)	23	5	2	30
	Max Flack (tie)	20	4	6	30
1920	Dave Robertson	29	11	10	50
1921	Ray Grimes	38	6	6	50
1922	Ray Grimes	45	12	14	71
1923	George Grantham	36	8	8	52
1924	Gabby Hartnett	17	7	16	40
1925	Gabby Hartnett	28	3	24	55
1926	Hack Wilson	36	8	21	65
1927	Hack Wilson	30	12	30	72
1928	Hack Wilson	32	9	31	72
1929	Rogers Hornsby	47	7	39	93
1930	Hack Wilson	35	6	56	97
1931	Kiki Cuyler	37	12	9	58
1932	Riggs Stephenson	49	4	4	57
1933	Babe Herman	36	12	16	64
1934	Kiki Cuyler	42	8	6	56
1935	Billy Herman	57	6	7	70
1936	Billy Herman	57	7	5	69
1937	Frank Demaree	36	6	17	59
1938	Stan Hack	34	11	4	49
1939	Billy Herman	34	18	7	59
1940	Bill Nicholson	27	7	25	59
1941	Bill Nicholson	26	1	26	53
1942	Bill Nicholson	22	11	21	54
1943	Bill Nicholson	30	9	29	68
1944	Bill Nicholson	35	8	33	76
1945	Phil Cavarretta	34	10	6	50
1946	Phil Cavarretta	28	10	8	46
1947	Bill Nicholson	28	1	26	55
1948	Andy Pafko	30	2	26	58
1949	Andy Pafko	29	2	18	49
1950	Andy Pafko	24	8	36	68
1951	Hank Sauer	19	4	30	53
1952	Hank Sauer	31	3	37	71
1953	Dee Fondy	24	11	18	53
1954	Ralph Kiner	36	5	22	63
1955	Ernie Banks	29	9	44	82
1956	Ernie Banks	25	8	28	61
1957	Ernie Banks	34	6	43	83
1958	Ernie Banks	23	11	47	81
1959	Ernie Banks	26	5	45	76
1960	Ernie Banks	32	7	41	80
1961	George Altman	28	12	27	67
1962	Ernie Banks	20	6	37	63
1963	Billy Williams	36	9	25	70
1964	Ron Santo	33	13	30	76
1965	Billy Williams	39	6	34	79
1966	Ron Santo	21	8	30	59

Year-by-Year Leaders in Extra Base Hits (Continued)

Year	Player	2B	3B	HR	Total
1967	Billy Williams	21	12	28	61
1968	Billy Williams	30	8	30	68
1969	Billy Williams	33	10	21	64
1970	Billy Williams	34	4	42	80
1971	Billy Williams	27	5	28	60
1972	Billy Williams	34	6	37	77
1973	Rick Monday	24	5	26	55
1974	Jose Cardenal	35	3	13	51
1975	Rick Monday	29	4	17	50
1976	Rick Monday	20	5	32	57
1977	Jerry Morales	34	5	11	50
1978	Dave Kingman	17	4	28	49
1979	Dave Kingman	19	5	48	72
1980	Bill Buckner	41	3	10	54
1981	Bill Buckner	35	3	10	48

Phil Cavarretta led the 1945 World Champion Cubs in extra base hits and ranks fifth over-all in the Cubs all time list.

50 Extra Base Hits in One Season

Player	2B	Date	3B	HR	Total
Ed Williamson	49	1883	5	2	56
Cap Anson	30	1884	3	21	54
Ed Williamson	18		8	27	53
Abner Dalrymple	27	1885	12	11	50
Cap Anson	35	1886	11	10	56
Cap Anson	33	1887	13	7	53
Jimmy Ryan	33	1888	10	16	59
Jimmy Ryan	31	1889	14	17	62
Walt Wilmot	45	1894	12	5	62
Bill Dahlen	32		14	15	61
Bill Lange	27	1895	16	10	53
Bill Dahlen	30	1896	19	9	58
Jimmy Ryan	33	1897	17	5	55
Frank Schulte	29	1910	15	10	54
Frank Schulte	30	1911	21	21	72
Heinie Zimmerman	41	1912	14	14	69
Frank Schulte	27		11	12	50
Vic Saier	15	1913	21	14	50
Heinie Zimmerman	36	1914	12	3	51
Vic Saier	24		8	18	50
Vic Saier	35	1915	11	11	57
Dave Robertson	29	1920	11	10	50
Ray Grimes	38	1921	6	6	50

50 Extra Base Hits in One Season (Continued)

Player	2B	Date 3B	HR	Total
		1922		
Ray Grimes	45	12	14	71
		1923		
George Grantham	36	8	8	52
Jigger Statz	33	8	10	51
Barney Friberg	27	11	12	50
		1925		
Gabby Hartnett	28	3	24	55
		1926		
Hack Wilson	36	8	21	65
		1927		
Hack Wilson	30	12	30	72
Riggs Stephenson	46	9	7	62
		1928		
Hack Wilson	32	9	31	72
Riggs Stephenson	36	9	8	53
Kiki Cuyler	25	9	17	51
		1929		
Rogers Hornsby	47	7	39	93
Hack Wilson	30	5	39	74
Riggs Stephenson	36	6	17	59
Kiki Cuyler	29	7	15	51
		1930		
Hack Wilson	35	6	56	97
Kiki Cuyler	50	17	13	80
Gabby Hartnett	31	3	37	71
Woody English	36	17	14	67
		1931		
Kiki Cuyler	37	12	9	58
Rogers Hornsby	37	1	16	54
		1932		
Riggs Stephenson	49	4	4	57
Charlie Grimm	42	2	7	51
Billy Herman	42	7	1	50
		1933		
Babe Herman	36	12	16	64
		1934		
Kiki Cuyler	42	8	6	56
Babe Herman	34	5	14	53
		1935		
Billy Herman	57	6	7	70
Augie Galan	41	11	12	64
Gabby Hartnett	32	6	13	51

50 Extra Base Hits in One Season (Continued)

Player	2B	Date	3B	HR	Total
		1936			
Billy Herman	57		7	5	69
Frank Demaree	34		3	16	53
		1937			
Frank Demaree	36		6	17	59
Billy Herman	35		11	8	54
Augie Galan	24		10	18	52
		1939			
Billy Herman	34		18	7	59
Augie Galan	36		8	6	50
		1940			
Bill Nicholson	27		7	25	59
Jimmy Gleeson	39		11	5	55
Stan Hack	38		6	8	52
		1941			
Bill Nicholson	26		1	26	53
		1942			
Bill Nicholson	22		11	21	54
		1943			
Bill Nicholson	30		9	29	68
		1944			
Bill Nicholson	35		8	33	76
Phil Cavarretta	35		15	5	55
		1945			
Phil Cavarretta	34		10	6	50
		1947			
Bill Nicholson	28		1	26	55
		1948			
Andy Pafko	30		2	26	58
		1950			
Andy Pafko	24		8	36	68
Hank Sauer	32		2	32	66
Roy Smalley	21		9	21	51
		1951			
Hank Sauer	19		4	30	53
		1952			
Hank Sauer	31		3	37	71
		1953			
Dee Fondy	24		11	18	53
		1954			
Ralph Kiner	36		5	22	63
Hank Sauer	18		1	41	60
Gene Baker	32		5	13	50

50 Extra Base Hits in One Season (Continued)

Player	2B	Date	3B	HR	Total
		1955			
Ernie Banks	29		9	44	82
		1956			
Ernie Banks	25		8	28	61
Walt Moryn	27		3	23	53
		1957			
Ernie Banks	34		6	43	83
Walt Moryn	33		0	19	52
		1958			
Ernie Banks	23		11	47	81
Walt Moryn	26		7	26	59
Bobby Thomson	27		5	21	53
Dale Long	26		4	20	50
		1959			
Ernie Banks	26		5	45	76
		1960			
Ernie Banks	32		7	41	80
		1961			
George Altman	28		12	27	67
Ron Santo	32		6	23	61
Ernie Banks	22		4	29	55
Billy Williams	20		7	25	52
		1962			
Ernie Banks	20		6	37	63
George Altman	27		5	22	54
Billy Williams	22		8	22	52
		1963			
Billy Williams	36		9	25	70
Ron Santo	29		6	25	60
		1964			
Ron Santo	33		13	30	76
Billy Williams	39		2	33	74
Ernie Banks	29		6	23	58
		1965			
Billy Williams	39		6	34	79
Ron Santo	30		4	33	67
Ernie Banks	25		3	28	56
		1966			
Ron Santo	21		8	30	59
Billy Williams	23		5	29	57
		1967			
Billy Williams	21		12	28	61
Ron Santo	23		4	31	58
Ernie Banks	26		4	23	53

50 Extra Base Hits in One Season (Continued)

Play	2B	Date	3B	HR	Total
		1968			
Billy Williams	30		8	30	68
Ernie Banks	27		0	32	59
		1969			
Billy Williams	33		10	21	64
Ron Santo	18		4	29	51
		1970			
Billy Williams	34		4	42	80
Jim Hickman	33		4	32	69
Ron Santo	30		4	26	60
		1971			
Billy Williams	27		5	28	60
		1972			
Billy Williams	34		6	37	77
		1973			
Rick Monday	24		5	26	55
Ron Santo	29		2	20	51
		1974			
Jose Cardenal	35		3	13	51
		1975			
Rick Monday	29		4	17	50
		1976			
Rick Monday	20		5	32	57
Bill Madlock	36		1	15	52
		1977			
Jerry Morales	34		5	11	50
		1979			
Dave Kingman	19		5	48	72
Jerry Martin	34		3	19	56
Bill Buckner	34		7	14	55
		1980			
Bill Buckner	41		3	10	54

Players With 200-or-More Extra Base Hits

Player	2B	3B	HR	Total
Ernie Banks	407	90	512	1009
Billy Williams	402	87	392	881
Ron Santo	353	66	337	756
Cap Anson	532	124	96	752
Gabby Hartnett	391	64	231	686
Jimmy Ryan	362	140	99	601
Phil Cavarretta	341	99	92	532
Bill Nicholson	245	53	205	503
Stan Hack	363	81	57	501
Frank Schulte	254	117	91	462
Billy Herman	346	69	37	452
Hack Wilson	185	44	190	419
Charlie Grimm	270	43	61	374
Bill Dahlen	203	106	57	366
Kiki Cuyler	220	66	79	365
Hank Sauer	141	17	198	356
Ed Williamson	209	80	61	350
Joe Tinker	220	93	29	342
Tommy Burns	235	69	40	344
Heinie Zimmerman	210	80	47	337
Andy Pafko	162	40	126	328
Riggs Stephenson	237	40	49	326
Woody English	218	50	31	299
Frank Chance	199	79	20	298
Don Kessinger	201	71	11	283
Abner Dalrymple	173	65	40	278
King Kelly	193	49	33	275
Fred Pfeffer	132	64	79	275
Augie Galan	165	46	59	270
Johnny Evers	181	64	9	254
Bill Lange	133	79	40	252
Vic Saier	140	58	53	251
Dee Fondy	140	44	66	250
Glenn Beckert	194	31	22	247
George Gore	162	60	24	246
Rick Monday	114	26	106	246
Jose Cardenal	159	16	61	236
Jimmy Sheckard	171	46	17	234
Billy Jurges	176	34	20	230
Bill Buckner	163	14	50	227
Johnny Kling	157	51	16	224
Randy Jackson	93	36	88	217
George Altman	100	26	83	209
Frank Demaree	131	26	49	206
Walt Wilmot	111	51	43	205
Randy Hundley	111	12	80	203
Jim Hickman	89	15	97	201

Extra Base Hits by Position (Season)

		Modern	2B 3B HR Total
1B	Ray Grimes	1922	45-12-14—71
2B	Rogers Hornsby	1929	47- 7-39—93
SS	Ernie Banks	1957	34- 6-43—83
3B	Ron Santo	1964	33-13-30—76
OF	Hack Wilson	1930	35- 6-56—97
OF	Kiki Cuyler	1930	50-17-13—80
OF	Billy Williams	1970	34- 4-42—80
C	Gabby Hartnett	1930	31- 3-37—71

19th Century

1B	Cap Anson	1886	35-11-10—56
2B	Fred Pfeffer	1884	10-10-25—45
SS	Bill Dahlen	1894	32-14-15—61
3B	Ed Williamson	1883	49- 5- 2—56
OF	Jimmy Ryan	1889	31-14-17—62
OF	Walt Wilmot	1894	45-12- 5—62
OF	Bill Lange	1895	27-16-11—54
C	King Kelly	1886	32-11- 4—47

All-Time

(Same as Modern)

Roger Hornsby's personality might have left something to be desired, but his bat didn't. He had a record of 450 total bases in 1922, batted over .400 three times, and his .380 season for the Cubs in 1929 is still a club record.

LEADERS IN RUNS SCORED

Year-by-Year Leaders in Runs Scored

Year	Player	Total	Year	Player	Total
1876*	Ross Barnes	126	1918	Max Flack	74
1877	Cal McVey	58	1919	Max Flack	71
1878	Joe Start	58	1920	Max Flack	85
1879	Ed Williamson	66	1921	Ray Grimes	91
1880*	Abner Dalrymple	91	1922	Ray Grimes	99
1881*	George Gore	86	1923	Jigger Statz	110
1882*	George Gore	99	1924	George Grantham	85
1883	George Gore	105	1925	Sparky Adams	95
1884*	King Kelly	120	1926	Cliff Heathcote	98
1885*	King Kelly	124	1927	Hack Wilson	119
1886*	King Kelly	155	1928	Kiki Cuyler	92
1887	Jimmy Ryan	117	1929*	Rogers Hornsby	156
1888	Jimmy Ryan	115	1930	Kiki Cuyler	155
1889	Hugh Duffy	144	1931	Woody English	117
1890	Cliff Carroll	134	1932	Billy Herman	102
1891	Bill Dahlen	114	1933	Billy Herman	82
1892	Bill Dahlen	114	1934	Kiki Cuyler	80
1893	Bill Dahlen	113	1935*	Augie Galan	133
1894	Bill Dahlen	150	1936	Stan Hack	102
1895	Bill Everett	129	1937	Stan Hack	106
1896	Bill Dahlen	137		Billy Herman	106
1897	Bill Lange	119	1938	Stan Hack	109
1898	Jimmy Ryan	122	1939	Stan Hack	112
1899	Jimmy Ryan	91	1940	Stan Hack	101
1900	Sam Mertes	72	1941	Stan Hack	111
1901	Topsy Hartsel	111	1942	Stan Hack	91
1902	Jimmy Slagle	64	1943	Bill Nicholson	95
1903	Jimmy Slagle	104	1944*	Bill Nicholson	116
1904	Frank Chance	89	1945	Stan Hack	110
1905	Jimmy Slagle	96	1946	Phil Cavarretta	89
1906*	Frank Chance	103	1947	Bill Nicholson	69
1907	Jimmy Sheckard	75	1948	Eddie Waitkus	87
1908	Johnny Evers	83	1949	Andy Pafko	79
1909	Johnny Evers	88	1950	Andy Pafko	95
1910	Frank Schulte	93	1951	Randy Jackson	78
1911*	Jimmy Sheckard	121	1952	Hank Sauer	89
1912	Heinie Zimmerman	95	1953	Dee Fondy	79
1913*	Tommy Leach	99	1954	Hank Sauer	98
1914	Vic Saier	87	1955	Ernie Banks	98
1915	Vic Saier	74	1956	Ernie Banks	82
1916	Max Flack	65	1957	Ernie Banks	113
1917	Max Flack	65	1958	Ernie Banks	119
	Fred Merkle	65	1959	Ernie Banks	97

*Led League

THE CUBS ARE ...

Building a new tradition

LEE ELIA
Field Manager

DALLAS GREEN
General Manager

A
GREAT
PAST

EXCITEMENT

CHICAGO

SUPER FANS

SPECIAL

Year-by-Year Leaders in Runs Scored (Continued)

Year	Player	Total	Year	Player	Total
1960	Richie Ashburn	99	1971	Billy Williams	86
1961	Ron Santo	84	1972	Jose Cardenal	96
1962	Billy Williams	94	1973	Rick Monday	93
1963	Billy Williams	87	1974	Rick Monday	84
1964	Billy Williams	100	1975	Rick Monday	89
1965	Billy Williams	115	1976	Rick Monday	107
1966	Billy Williams	100	1977	Ivan DeJesus	91
1967	Ron Santo	107	1978*	Ivan DeJesus	104
1968*	Glenn Beckert	98	1979	Dave Kingman	97
1969	Don Kessinger	109	1980	Ivan DeJesus	78
1970*	Billy Williams	137	1981	Ivan DeJesus	49

*Led League

100-or-More Runs Scored in a Season

1876			1889	
Ross Barnes	126		Hugh Duffy	144
1883			Jimmy Ryan	140
George Gore	105		George Van Haltren	126
1884			Cap Anson	100
King Kelly	120		**1890**	
Abner Dalrymple	111		Cliff Carroll	134
Cap Anson	108		Walt Wilmot	114
Fred Pfeffer	105		**1891**	
George Gore	104		Bill Dahlen	114
1885			Jimmy Ryan	110
King Kelly	124		Walt Wilmot	102
George Gore	115		**1892**	
Abner Dalrymple	109		Bill Dahlen	114
Cap Anson	100		Jimmy Ryan	105
1886			**1893**	
King Kelly	155		Bill Dahlen	113
George Gore	150		**1894**	
Cap Anson	117		Bill Dahlen	150
1887			Walt Wilmot	134
Jimmy Ryan	117		Jimmy Ryan	132
Cap Anson	107		**1895**	
1888			Bill Everett	129
Jimmy Ryan	115		Bill Lange	121
Cap Anson	101		Bill Dahlen	106

100-or-More Runs Scored in a Season (Continued)

1896		1937	
Bill Dahlen	137	Stan Hack	106
Bill Everett	130	Billy Herman	106
Bill Lange	114	Frank Demaree	104
1897		Augie Galan	104
Bill Lange	119	**1938**	
Jimmy Ryan	103	Stan Hack	109
1898		**1939**	
Jimmy Ryan	122	Stan Hack	112
Bill Everett	102	Billy Herman	111
1901		Augie Galan	104
Topsy Hartsel	111	**1940**	
1903		Stan Hack	101
Jimmy Slagle	104	**1941**	
1906		Stan Hack	111
Frank Chance	103	. **1944**	
1911		Bill Nicholson	116
Jimmy Sheckard	121	Phil Cavarretta	106
Frank Schulte	105	**1945**	
1923		Stan Hack	110
Jigger Statz	110	**1957**	
1927		Ernie Banks	113
Hack Wilson	119	**1958**	
Riggs Stephenson	101	Ernie Banks	119
1929		**1964**	
Rogers Hornsby	156	Billy Williams	100
Hack Wilson	135	**1965**	
Woody English	131	Billy Williams	115
Kiki Cuyler	111	**1966**	
1930		Billy Williams	100
Kiki Cuyler	155	**1967**	
Woody English	152	Ron Santo	107
Hack Wilson	146	**1969**	
1931		Don Kessinger	109
Woody English	117	Billy Williams	103
Kiki Cuyler	110	**1970**	
1932		Billy Williams	137
Billy Herman	102	Jim Hickman	102
1935		Don Kessinger	100
Augie Galan	133	**1976**	
Billy Herman	113	Rick Monday	107
1936		**1978**	
Stan Hack	102	Ivan DeJesus	104
Billy Herman	101		

Career Leaders in Runs Scored

Player	Total	Player	Total
Cap Anson	1,719	Heinie Zimmerman	515
Jimmy Ryan	1,409	Hank Sauer	498
Billy Williams	1,306	Andy Pafko	486
Ernie Banks	1,305	Max Flack	447
Stan Hack	1,239	Rick Monday	441
Ron Santo	1,109	Vic Saier	436
Phil Cavarretta	968	Cliff Heathcote	435
Bill Dahlen	897	Jose Cardenal	433
Billy Herman	875	Billy Jurges	423
Gabby Hartnett	847	Ivan DeJesus	414
Frank Schulte	827	Charlie Hollocher	411
Frank Chance	794	Johnny Kling	398
George Gore	772	Sparky Adams	398
Don Kessinger	769	Frank Demaree	392
Woody English	747	Dee Fondy	372
Ed Williamson	744	George Decker	354
Johnny Evers	742	Randy Jackson	353
Bill Nicholson	738	Silver Flint	353
King Kelly	728	Harry Steinfeldt	339
Tommy Burns	715	P-Nuts Lowrey	331
Fred Pfeffer	707	Barry McCormick	313
Bill Lange	689	Jim Hickman	304
Glenn Beckert	672	George Altman	299
Joe Tinker	671	Randy Hundley	296
Abner Dalrymple	666	Jigger Statz	277
Kiki Cuyler	665	Walt Moryn	275
Hack Wilson	652	Frank Baumholtz	272
Charlie Grimm	596	Jerry Morales	271
Jimmy Sheckard	588	Eddie Miksis	268
Walt Wilmot	552	Bob O'Farrell	263
Augie Galan	549	Bill Buckner	263
Riggs Stephenson	533	Danny Green	261
Bill Everett	521	Ray Grimes	255
Jimmy Slagle	517		

Runs Scored by Position (Season)

Modern

	Player	Year	Total
1B	Phil Cavarretta	1944	106
2B	Rogers Hornsby	1929	156
SS	Woody English	1930	152
3B	Stan Hack	1939	112
OF	Kiki Cuyler	1930	155
OF	Hack Wilson	1930	146
OF	Billy Williams	1970	137
C	Gabby Hartnett	1930	84

Runs Scored by Position (Season) (Continued)
19th Century

1B	Cap Anson	1886	117
2B	Ross Barnes	1876	126
SS	Bill Dahlen	1894	150
3B	Bill Everett	1896	130
OF	George Gore	1886	150
OF	Hugh Duffy	1889	144
OF	Jimmy Ryan	1889	140
C	King Kelly	1886	155

All-Time

1B	Cap Anson	1886	117
2B	Rogers Hornsby	1929	156
SS	Woody English	1930	152
3B	Bill Everett	1896	130
OF	Kiki Cuyler	1930	155
OF	George Gore	1886	150
OF	Hack Wilson	1930	146
C	King Kelly	1886	155

The 1881 Chicago White Stockings' Cap Anson (center top) is the all-time club leader in runs scored in RBI's.

RBI RECORDS

All-Time RBI Leaders

Cap Anson	1879	Bill Buckner	344
Ernie Banks	1636	Jose Cardenal	343
Billy Williams	1354	Jim Hickman	336
Ron Santo	1290	Jerry Morales	334
Gabby Hartnett	1153	George Decker	333
Jimmy Ryan	914	Bill Everett	333
Phil Cavarretta	896	Harry Steinfeldt	332
Bill Nicholson	833	Randy Jackson	329
Hack Wilson	768	Dee Fondy	327
Frank Schulte	712	Abner Dalrymple	325
Charlie Grimm	697	P-Nuts Lowrey	311
Fred Pfeffer	689	George Altman	309
Joe Tinker	671	Solly Hofman	304
Stan Hack	642	Jimmy Sheckard	294
Ed Williamson	622	Rick Monday	293
Kiki Cuyler	602	Dom Dallessandro	292
Frank Chance	590	Walt Moryn	291
Riggs Stephenson	589	Barry McCormick	288
Hank Sauer	587	Jimmy Archer	282
Bill Lange	578	Cliff Heathcote	275
Billy Herman	577	Rogers Hornsby	264
Andy Pafko	575	Bob O'Farrell	257
Tommy Burns	567	Dave Kingman	249
Heinie Zimmerman	565	Ray Grimes	248
Bill Dahlen	560	Roy Smalley	242
King Kelly	480	Charlie Deal	241
Walt Wilmot	468	Charlie Hollocher	241
Johnny Evers	448	Jimmy Slagle	231
Johnny Kling	436	Clyde McCullough	230
Augie Galan	435	Fred Merkle	223
Don Kessinger	431	Barney Friberg	217
Frank Demaree	396	Cy Williams	215
Billy Jurges	390	Max Flack	209
George Gore	379	Malachi Kittredge	203
Woody English	374	Bill Madlock	202
Randy Hundley	372	Silver Flint	201
Vic Saier	363	Hack Miller	201
Glenn Beckert	353	Sparky Adams	200

100-or-More RBI's, Season

1884			1944	
Cap Anson	102		Bill Nicholson	122
Fred Pfeffer	101		1945	
1885			Andy Pafko	110
Cap Anson	114		1948	
1886			Andy Pafko	101
Cap Anson	147		1950	
1887			Hank Sauer	103
Cap Anson	102		1952	
1889			Hank Sauer	121
Cap Anson	117		1954	
1890			Hank Sauer	103
Cap Anson	107		1955	
1891			Ernie Banks	117
Cap Anson	120		1957	
1894			Ernie Banks	102
Walt Wilmot	130		1958	
Bill Dahlen	107		Ernie Banks	129
1911			1959	
Frank Schulte	107		Ernie Banks	143
1926			1960	
Hack Wilson	109		Ernie Banks	117
1927			1964	
Hack Wilson	129		Ron Santo	114
1928			1965	
Hack Wilson	120		Billy Williams	108
1929			Ernie Banks	106
Hack Wilson	159		Ron Santo	101
Rogers Hornsby	149		1969	
Riggs Stephenson	110		Ron Santo	123
Kiki Cuyler	102		Ernie Banks	106
1930			1970	
Hack Wilson	190		Billy Williams	129
Kiki Cuyler	134		Jim Hickman	115
Gabby Hartnett	122		Ron Santo	114
1937			1972	
Frank Demaree	115		Billy Williams	122
1943			1979	
Bill Nicholson	128		Dave Kingman	115

9 RBI's in One Game

HEINIE ZIMMERMAN
June 11, 1911
Cubs 20, Braves 2
At West Side, Chicago

First Inning — Homer	2 on
Fourth Inning — Triple	2 on
Sixth Inning — Homer	2 on
Seventh Inning — Single	1 on
	9 RBI's

8 RBI's in One Game

Rogers Hornsby
April 24, 1931
Cubs 10, Pirates 6
At Forbes Field, Pittsburgh

Third Inning — Homer	2 on
Fifth Inning — Homer	2 on
Sixth Inning — Homer	1 on
	8 RBI's

Babe Herman
July 20, 1933
Cubs 10, Phillies 1
At Wrigley Field, Chicago

Third Inning — Homer	1 on
Fifth Inning	1 on
Seventh Inning	3 on
	8 RBI's

Lee Walls
April 24, 1958
Cubs 15, Dodgers 2
At Coliseum, Los Angeles

First Inning — Homer	1 on
Fifth Inning — Homer	2 on
Seventh Inning — Homer	2 on
	8 RBI's

Ed Bailey
July 22, 1965
Cubs 10, Phillies 6
At Wrigley Field, Chicago

Second Inning — Homer	2 on
Fifth Inning — Homer	3 on
Seventh Inning — Single	1 on
	8 RBI's

Ron Santo
July 6, 1970
Cubs 14, Expos 2 (2nd Game)
At Wrigley Field, Chicago

First Inning — Homer	3 on
Fourth Inning — Walk	3 on
Sixth Inning — Homer	2 on
	8 RBI's

NOTE: Santo hit a two-run homer as the Cubs won the first game 3-2, giving him 10 RBI for the day.

George Mitterwald
April 17, 1974
Cubs 18, Pirates 9
At Wrigley Field, Chicago

First Inning — Homer	3 on
Third Inning — Homer	1 on
Sixth Inning — Homer	0 on
Eighth Inning — Dougle	1 on
	8 RBI's

Barry Foote
April 22, 1980
Cubs 16, Cardinals 12
At Wrigley Field, Chicago

Second Inning — Single	1 on
Third Inning — Double	2 on
Eighth Inning — Homer	1 RBI
Ninth Inning — Homer	3 on
	8 RBI's

Dave Kingman
May 14, 1978
Cubs 10, Dodgers 7 (15 innings)
At Dodger Stadium, Los Angeles

Sixth Inning — Homer	1 on
Seventh Inning — Force out	1 RBI
Ninth Inning — Homer	1 on
15th Inning — Homer	2 on
	8 RBI's

RBI Leaders
And All Cubs with 100-or-More RBI's

Year	Player	Total	Year	Player	Total
1876*	Jim White	60	1919	Fred Merkle	62
1877	John Peters	41	1920	Dave Robertson	75
1878	Cap Anson	40	1921	Ray Grimes	79
1879	Frank Flint	41	1922	Ray Grimes	99
1880	Cap Anson	74	1923	Barney Friberg	88
1881*	Cap Anson	82		Hack Miller	88
1882	Cap Anson	83	1924	Barney Friberg	82
1883	Cap Anson	62	1925	Charlie Grimm	76
	King Kelly	62	1926	Hack Wilson	109
1884*	Cap Anson	102	1927	Hack Wilson	129
1885	Cap Anson	114	1928	Hack Wilson	120
1886*	Cap Anson	147	1929*	Hack Wilson	159
1887	Cap Anson	102		Rogers Hornsby	149
1888*	Cap Anson	84		Riggs Stephenson	110
1889	Cap Anson	117		Kiki Cuyler	102
1890	Cap Anson	107	1930**	Hack Wilson	190
1891*	Cap Anson	120		Kiki Cuyler	134
1892	Cap Anson	74		Gabby Hartnett	122
1893	Cap Anson	91	1931	Rogers Hornsby	90
1894	Walt Wilmot	130	1932	Riggs Stephenson	85
	Bill Dahlen	107	1933	Babe Herman	93
1895	Bill Lange	98	1934	Gabby Hartnett	90
1896	Bill Lange	92	1935	Gabby Hartnett	91
1897	Jimmy Ryan	85	1936	Frank Demaree	96
1898	Jimmy Ryan	79	1937	Frank Demaree	115
	Bill Dahlen	79	1938	Augie Galan	69
1899	Sam Mertes	81	1939	Hank Leiber	88
1900	Sam Mertes	60	1940	Bill Nicholson	98
1901	Charlie Dexter	66	1941	Bill Nicholson	98
1902	Johnny Kling	57	1942	Bill Nicholson	78
1903	Frank Chance	81	1943*	Bill Nicholson	128
1904	Jack McCarthy	51	1944*	Bill Nicholson	122
1905	Frank Chance	70	1945	Andy Pafko	110
1906*	Harry Steinfeldt	83	1946	Phil Cavarretta	78
1907	Harry Steinfeldt	70	1947	Bill Nicholson	75
1908	Joe Tinker	69	1948	Andy Pafko	101
1909	Frank Schulte	60	1949	Hank Sauer	83
1910	Artie Hofman	86	1950	Hank Sauer	103
1911*	Frank Schulte	107	1951	Hank Sauer	89
1912	Heinie Zimmerman	98	1952*	Hank Sauer	121
1913	Heinie Zimmerman	95	1953	Ralph Kiner	87
1914	Heinie Zimmerman	87	1954	Hank Sauer	103
1915	Cy Williams	64	1955	Ernie Banks	117
	Vic Saier	64	1956	Ernie Banks	85
1916	Cy Williams	66	1957	Ernie Banks	102
1917	Larry Doyle	61			
1918	Fred Merkle	65			

*Led League

**Major League Record

RBI Leaders
And All Cubs with 100-or-More RBI's (Continued)

Year	Player	Total	Year	Player	Total
1958*	Ernie Banks	129	1970	Billy Williams	129
1959*	Ernie Banks	143		Jim Hickman	151
1960	Ernie Banks	117		Ron Santo	114
1961	George Altman	96	1971	Billy Williams	93
1962	Ernie Banks	104	1972	Billy Williams	122
1963	Ron Santo	99	1973	Billy Williams	86
1964	Ron Santo	114	1974	Jerry Morales	82
1965	Billy Williams	108	1975	Jerry Morales	91
	Ernie Banks	106	1976	Bill Madlock	84
	Ron Santo	101	1977	Bobby Murcer	89
1966	Ron Santo	94	1978	Dave Kingman	79
1967	Ron Santo	98	1979	Dave Kingman	115
1968	Ron Santo	98	1980	Jerry Martin	73
	Billy Williams	98	1981	Bill Buckner	75
1969	Ron Santo	123			
	Ernie Banks	106			

*Led League
**Major League Record

Miscellaneous RBI Records

Most RBI's, Lifetime	1879	Cap Anson (19th Century)
	1636	Ernie Banks (Modern)
Most RBI's, Season	190	Hack Wilson, 1930
Most RBI's, Two Consecutive Seasons	349	Hack Wilson, 1929 (159), 1930 (190)
Most RBI's, Game	9	Heinie Zimmerman, June 11, 1911
Most Years, 100 RBI's	8	Ernie Banks, 1955-57-58-59-60-62-65-69
Most RBI's, Right-Handed Batter	190	Hack Wilson, 1930
Most RBI's, Left-Handed Batter	129	Billy Williams, 1970

At the turn of the century, the slugging king of the Cubs was Hall-of-Famer Frank Chance. Slugging average is determined by dividing total bases of all safe hits by the total times at bat.

RBI's by Position (Season)

Modern

1B	Ernie Banks	1965-1969	106
2B	Rogers Hornsby	1929	149
SS	Ernie Banks	1959	143
3B	Ron Santo	1969	123
OF	Hack Wilson	1930	190
OF	Kiki Cuyler	1930	134
OF	Billy Williams	1970	129
C	Gabby Hartnett	1930	122

19th Century

1B	Cap Anson	1886	147
2B	Fred Pfeffer	1886	95
SS	Bill Dahlen	1894	107
3B	Bill Everett	1895	88
OF	Walt Wilmot	1894	130
OF	Bill Lange	1895	99
OF	Jimmy Ryan	1896	86
C	King Kelly	1886	79

All-Time

1B	Cap Anson	1886	147
2B	Rogers Hornsby	1929	149
SS	Ernie Banks	1959	143
3B	Ron Santo	1969	123
OF	Hack Wilson	1930	190
OF	Kiki Cuyler	1930	134
OF	Walt Wilmot	1894	130
C	Gabby Hartnett	1930	122

SLUGGING

Year-by-Year Leaders in Slugging Average

Year	Player	Total	Year	Player	Total
1876*	Ross Barnes	.590	1917	Fred Merkle	.373
1877	Cal McVey	.455	1918	Charlie Hollocher	.397
1878	Joe Start	.493	1919	Max Flack	.392
1879	Cap Anson	.447	1920	Dave Robertson	.462
1880*	George Gore	.463	1921	Ray Grimes	.449
1881	Cap Anson	.510	1922	Ray Grimes	.572
1882	Cap Anson	.500	1923	Hack Miller	.482
1883	George Gore	.472	1924	Gabby Hartnett	.523
1884	Ed Wiliamson	.554	1925	Gabby Hartnett	.555
1885	Cap Anson	.461	1926	Hack Wilson	.539
1886	Cap Anson	.544	1927	Hack Wilson	.579
1887	Cap Anson	.517	1928	Hack Wilson	.588
1888*	Jimmy Ryan	.515	1929*	Rogers Hornsby	.681
1889	Jimmy Ryan	.516	1930*	Hack Wilson	.723
1890	Walt Wilmot	.420	1931	Rogers Hornsby	.574
1891	Jimmy Ryan	.434	1932	Johnny Moore	.470
1892	Jimmy Ryan	.438	1933	Babe Herman	.502
1893	Bill Dahlen	.452	1934	Chuck Klein	.510
1894	Bill Dahlen	.569	1935	Gabby Hartnett	.545
1895	Bill Lange	.575	1936	Frank Demaree	.496
1896	Bill Dahlen	.561	1937	Gabby Hartnett	.548
1897	Bill Lange	.480	1938	Stan Hack	.432
1898	Jimmy Ryan	.446	1939	Hank Leiber	.556
1899	Sam Mertes	.467	1940	Bill Nicholson	.534
1900	Danny Green	.416	1941	Babe Dahlgren	.475
1901	Topsy Hartsel	.475	1942	Bill Nicholson	.476
1902	Jimmy Slagle	.357	1943	Bill Nicholson	.531
1903	Frank Chance	.440	1944	Bill Nicholson	.545
1904	Frank Chance	.430	1945	Phil Cavarretta	.500
1905	Frank Chance	.434	1946	Phil Cavarretta	.435
1906	Frank Chance	.430	1947	Bill Nicholson	.466
	Harry Steinfeldt	.430	1948	Andy Pafko	.516
1907	Frank Chance	.358	1949	Hank Sauer	.571
1908	Joe Tinker	.396	1950	Andy Pafko	.591
1909	Joe Tinker	.372	1951	Hank Sauer	.486
1910	Solly Hofman	.461	1952	Hank Sauer	.531
1911*	Frank Schulte	.534	1953	Ralph Kiner	.529
1912*	Heinie Zimmerman	.571	1954	Hank Sauer	.563
1913	Heinie Zimmerman	.490	1955	Ernie Banks	.596
1914	Heinie Zimmerman	.418	1956	Ernie Banks	.530
1915	Vic Saier	.445	1957	Ernie Banks	.579
1916	Cy Williams	.459	1958*	Ernie Banks	.614

*Led League

Year-by-Year Leaders in Slugging Average (Continued)

Year	Player	Total	Year	Player	Total
1959	Ernie Banks	.596	1971	Billy Williams	.505
1960	Ernie Banks	.554	1972*	Billy Williams	.606
1961	George Altman	.560	1973	Rick Monday	.469
1962	George Altman	.511	1974	Rick Monday	.467
1963	Billy Williams	.497	1975	Andy Thornton	.516
1964	Ron Santo	.564	1976	Rick Monday	.507
1965	Billy Williams	.552	1977	Bobby Murcer	.455
1966	Ron Santo	.538	1978	Dave Kingman	.542
1967	Ron Santo	.512	1979	Dave Kingman	.613
1968	Billy Williams	.500	1980	Bill Buckner	.457
1969	Ron Santo	.485	1981	Bill Buckner	.480
1970	Billy Williams	.586			

*Led League

.500 Sluggers in One Season

1876		1911	
Ross Barnes	.590	Frank Schulte	.534

1881		1912	
Cap Anson	.510	Heinie Zimmerman	.571

1882		1922	
Cap Anson	.500	Ray Grimes	.572
		Hack Miller	.511

1884

		1924	
Ed Williamson	.554	Gabby Hartnett	.523
Cap Anson	.543		
King Kelly	.524	1925	
Fred Pfeffer	.514	Gabby Hartnett	.555
Abner Dalrymple	.505		

1886		1926	
Cap Anson	.544	Hack Wilson	.539
King Kelly	.534	1927	
1887		Hack Wilson	.579
Cap Anson	.517	1928	
1888		Hack Wilson	.588
Jimmy Ryan	.515	Gabby Hartnett	.523

1889		1929	
Jimmy Ryan	.516	Rogers Hornsby	.681
		Hack Wilson	.618
1894		Riggs Stephenson	.562
Bill Dahlen	.569	Kiki Cuyler	.532
Cap Anson	.542	1930	

1895			
Bill Lange	.575	Hack Wilson	.723
		Gabby Hartnett	.630
1896		Kiki Cuyler	.547
Bill Dahlen	.561	Woody English	.511

.500 Sluggers in One Season (Continued)

1931		
Rogers Hornsby	.574	

1933		
Babe Herman	.502	

1934		
Chuck Klein	.510	
Gabby Hartnett	.502	

1935		
Gabby Hartnett	.545	

1937		
Gabby Hartnett	.548	

1939		
Hank Leiber	.556	

1940		
Bill Nicholson	.534	

1943		
Bill Nicholson	.531	

1944		
Bill Nicholson	.545	

1945		
Phil Cavarretta	.500	

1948		
Andy Pafko	.516	

1949		
Hank Sauer	.571	

1950		
Andy Pafko	.591	
Hank Sauer	.519	

1952		
Hank Sauer	.531	

1953		
Ralph Kiner	.529	

1954		
Hank Sauer	.563	

1955		
Ernie Banks	.596	

1956		
Ernie Banks	.530	

1957		
Ernie Banks	.579	

1958		
Ernie Banks	.614	

1959		
Ernie Banks	.596	

1960		
Ernie Banks	.554	

1961		
George Altman	.560	
Ernie Banks	.507	

1962		
George Altman	.511	
Ernie Banks	.503	

1964		
Ron Santo	.564	
Billy Williams	.532	

1965		
Billy Williams	.552	
Ron Santo	.510	

1966		
Ron Santo	.538	

1967		
Ron Santo	.512	

1968		
Billy Williams	.500	

1970		
Billy Williams	.586	
Jim Hickman	.582	

1971		
Billy Williams	.505	

1972		
Billy Williams	.606	

1975		
Andy Thornton	.516	

1976		
Rick Monday	.507	
Bill Madlock	.500	

1978		
Dave Kingman	.542	

1979		
Dave Kingman	.613	

Slugging by Position (Season)

Modern

1B	Jim Hickman	1970	.582
2B	Rogers Hornsby	1929	.681
SS	Ernie Banks	1958	.614
3B	Heinie Zimmerman	1912	.571
OF	Hack Wilson	1930	.723
OF	Dave Kingman	1979	.613
OF	Billy Williams	1972	.606
C	Gabby Hartnett	1930	.630

19th Century

1B	Cap Anson	1886	.544
2B	Ross Barnes	1876	.590
SS	Bill Dahlen	1894	.569
3B	Ed Williamson	1884	.554
OF	Bill Lange	1895	.575
OF	Jimmy Ryan	1889	.515
OF	Abner Dalrymple	1884	.505
C	King Kelly	1886	.534

All-Time

(Same as modern)

Hack Wilson's 190 RBI's in one season will probably never be equalled in major league baseball.

.400 Lifetime Sluggers (500-Game Minimum)

Player	Years	Average
Hack Wilson	(1926-1931)	.590
Hank Sauer	(1949-1955)	.512
Billy Williams	(1959-1974)	.503
Ernie Banks	(1953-1971)	.500
Gabby Hartnett	(1922-1940)	.490
Kiki Cuyler	(1928-1935)	.485
Ron Santo	(1960-1973)	.472
Bill Nicholson	(1939-1948)	.471
Riggs Stephenson	(1926-1934)	.469
Andy Pafko	(1943-1951)	.468
Jim Hickman	(1968-1973)	.467
Bill Lange	(1893-1899)	.459
George Altman	(1959-1962) (1965-1967)	.457
Rick Monday	(1972-1976)	.456
King Kelly	(1880-1886)	.453
Walt Moryn	(1956-1960)	.452
Bill Dahlen	(1891-1898)	.452
Cap Anson	(1876-1897)	.451
Jimmy Ryan	(1885-1900)	.448
Bill Serena	(1949-1954)	.446
Heinie Zimmerman	(1907-1916)	.444
Bill Buckner	(1977-)	.444
Walt Wilmot	(1890-1895)	.437
George Gore	(1879-1886)	.434
Frank Demaree	(1932-1938)	.433
Abner Dalrymple	(1879-1886)	.431
Randy Jackson	(1950-1955; 1959)	.430
Dee Fondy	(1951-1957)	.422
Jose Cardenal	(1972-1977)	.420
Billy Herman	(1931-1941)	.417
Stan Hack	(1932-1947)	.416
Phil Cavarretta	(1934-1953)	.416
Vic Saier	(1911-1917)	.414
Frank Schulte	(1904-1916)	.409
Augie Galan	(1934-1941)	.409
Jerry Morales	(1974-1977; 1981)	.409
Charlie Grimm	(1925-1936)	.405

TOTAL BASES

Year-by-Year Leaders in Total Bases

Year	Player	Total	Year	Player	Total
1876*	Ross Barnes	190	1918*	Charlie Hollocher	202
1877	Cal McVey	121	1919	Max Flack	184
1878*	Joe Start	125	1920	Dave Robertson	231
1879	Ed Williamson	143	1921	Ray Grimes	238
1880*	Abner Dalrymple	175	1922	Ray Grimes	291
1881*	Cap Anson	175	1923	Jigger Statz	288
1882	Cap Anson	174	1924	George Grantham	215
1883	George Gore	185	1925	Sparky Adams	231
1884*	Abner Dalrymple	263	1926	Hack Wilson	285
1885	Abner Dalrymple	219	1927	Hack Wilson	319
1886	Cap Anson	274	1928	Hack Wilson	306
1887	Cap Anson	244	1929*	Rogers Hornsby	410
1888*	Jimmy Ryan	283	1930	Hack Wilson	423
1889*	Jimmy Ryan	297	1931	Kiki Cuyler	290
1890	Walt Wilmot	240	1932	Billy Herman	265
1891	Cap Anson	221	1933	Babe Herman	255
1892	Bill Dahlen	245	1934	Kiki Cuyler	265
1893	Bill Dahlen	216	1935	Billy Herman	317
1894	Bill Dahlen	289	1936	Frank Demaree	300
1895	Bill Lange	275	1937	Frank Demaree	298
1896	Bill Dahlen	267	1938	Stan Hack	263
1897	Jimmy Ryan	238	1939	Billy Herman	282
1898	Jimmy Ryan	255	1940	Stan Hack	265
1899	Jimmy Ryan	207	1941	Stan Hack	250
1900	Sam Mertes	196	1942	Bill Nicholson	280
1901	Topsy Hartsel	265	1943	Bill Nicholson	323
1902	Jimmy Slagle	168	1944*	Bill Nicholson	317
1903	Johnny Kling	210	1945	Phil Cavarretta	249
1904	Frank Chance	194	1946	Phil Cavarretta	222
1905	Frank Schulte	207	1947	Andy Pafko	233
1906	Harry Steinfeldt	232	1948	Andy Pafko	283
1907	Harry Steinfeldt	182	1949	Andy Pafko	233
1908	Joe Tinker	217	1950	Andy Pafko	304
1909	Joe Tinker	192	1951	Hank Sauer	255
	Frank Schulte	192	1952	Hank Sauer	301
1910	Frank Schulte	257	1953	Dee Fondy	284
1911*	Frank Schulte	308	1954	Hank Sauer	293
1912*	Heinie Zimmerman	318	1955	Ernie Banks	355
1913	Vic Saier	247	1956	Ernie Banks	285
1914	Heinie Zimmerman	236	1957	Ernie Banks	344
1915	Vic Saier	221	1958*	Ernie Banks	379
1916	Cy Williams	186	1959	Ernie Banks	351
1917	Fred Merkle	205	1960	Ernie Banks	331

*Led League

Year-by-Year Leaders in Total Bases (Continued)

Year	Player	Total	Year	Player	Total
1961	George Altman	290	1972*	Billy Williams	348
1962	Ernie Banks	307	1973	Rick Monday	260
1963	Billy Williams	304	1974	Rick Monday	251
1964	Billy Williams	343	1975	Bill Madlock	246
1965	Billy Williams	356	1976	Rick Monday	271
1966	Ron Santo	302	1977	Bobby Murcer	252
1967	Billy Williams	305	1978	Ivan DeJesus	219
1968*	Billy Williams	321	1979	Dave Kingman	326
1969	Billy Williams	304	1980	Bill Buckner	264
1970*	Billy Williams	373	1981	Bill Buckner	202
1971	Billy Williams	300			

*Led League

Ivan DeJesus is known for his dazzling speed on the bases and making spectacular plays in the field.

300 Total Bases in a Season

1911			**1958**	
Frank Schulte	308	Ernie Banks		379
1912			**1959**	
Heinie Zimmerman	318	Ernie Banks		351
1927			**1960**	
Hack Wilson	319	Ernie Banks		331
1928			**1962**	
Hack Wilson	306	Ernie Banks		307
1929			**1963**	
Rogers Hornsby	410	Billy Williams		304
Hack Wilson	355	Ron Santo		303
1930			**1964**	
Hack Wilson	423	Billy Williams		343
Kiki Cuyler	351	Ron Santo		334
Woody English	326		**1965**	
Gabby Hartnett	320	Billy Williams		356
1935		Ron Santo		310
Billy Herman	317		**1966**	
Augie Galan	302	Ron Santo		302
1936			**1967**	
Frank Demaree	300	Billy Williams		305
1943		Ron Santo		300
Bill Nicholson	323		**1968**	
1944		Billy Williams		321
Bill Nicholson	317		**1969**	
1950		Billy Williams		304
Andy Pafko	304		**1970**	
1952		Billy Williams		373
Hank Sauer	301		**1971**	
1955		Billy Williams		300
Ernie Banks	355		**1972**	
1957		Billy Williams		348
Ernie Banks	344		**1979**	
		Dave Kingman		326

1,000-or-More Total Bases (Lifetime)

Player	Years	Total
Ernie Banks	(1953-1971)	4706
Billy Williams	(1959-1974)	4262
Cap Anson	(1876-1897)	4109
Ron Santo	(1960-1973)	3667
Gabby Hartnett	(1922-1940)	3079
Jimmy Ryan	(1885-1889; 1891-1900)	3026
Stan Hack	(1932-1947)	2889
Phil Cavarretta	(1934-1953)	2742
Frank Schulte	(1904-1916)	2377
Billy Herman	(1931-1941)	2305
Bill Nicholson	(1939-1948)	2209
Don Kessinger	(1964-1975)	1995
Charlie Grimm	(1925-1936)	1993
Joe Tinker	(1902-1912; 1916)	1929
Hack Wilson	(1926-1931)	1860
Tommy Burns	(1880-1891)	1804
Kiki Cuyler	(1928-1935)	1788
Bill Dahlen	(1891-1898)	1767
Glenn Beckert	(1965-1973)	1748
Frank Chance	(1898-1912)	1681
Johnny Evers	(1902-1913)	1677
Andy Pafko	(1943-1951)	1668
Woody English	(1927-1936)	1639
Riggs Stephenson	(1926-1934)	1631
Heinie Zimmerman	(1907-1916)	1623
Hank Sauer	(1949-1955)	1621
Ed Williamson	(1879-1889)	1604
Bill Lange	(1893-1899)	1446
Abner Dalrymple	(1879-1886)	1371
Augie Galan	(1934-1941)	1345
Jose Cardenal	(1972-1977)	1298
King Kelly	(1880-1886)	1289
Dee Fondy	(1951-1957)	1288
George Gore	(1879-1886)	1287
Johnny Kling	(1900-1911)	1267
Billy Jurges	(1931-1938) (1946-1947)	1232
Jimmy Sheckard	(1906-1912)	1219
Rick Monday	(1972-1976)	1174
Walt Wilmot	(1890-1895)	1169
Vic Saier	(1911-1917)	1153
Charlie Hollocher	(1918-1924)	1151
Frank Demaree	(1932-1938)	1150
Randy Hundley	(1966-1973) (1976-1977)	1133
Randy Jackson	(1950-1955; 1959)	1119
Max Flack	(1915-1922)	1102
Bill Buckner	(1977-)	1092
Jimmy Slagle	(1902-1908)	1062
Bill Everett	(1895-1900)	1057
Cliff Heathcote	(1922-1930)	1037
George Altman	(1959-1962) (1965-1967)	1009

700 to 1,000 Total Bases, Lifetime

Ivan DeJesus	(1977-)	975
Jerry Morales	(1974-1977)	973
	(1981-)	
P-Nuts Lowrey	(1942-1943)	957
	(1945-1949)	
Sparky Adams	(1922-1927)	950
Walt Moryn	(1956-1960)	949
Jim Hickman	(1968-1973)	931
Harry Steinfeldt	(1906-1910)	899
Jimmy Archer	(1909-1917)	887
Frankie Baumholtz	(1949; 1951-1955)	881
Frank Flint	(1879-1889)	880
Roy Smalley	(1948-1953)	794
Eddie Miksis	(1951-1956)	773
Bob O'Farrell	(1915-1925; 1934)	758
Clyde McCullough	(1940-1948)	757
	(1953-1956)	
Barry McCormick	(1896-1901)	728
Manny Trillo	(1975-1978)	726
Jigger Statz	(1922-1925)	706
Bill Madlock	(1974-1976)	703
Ray Grimes	(1921-1924)	701

Total Bases by Position (Season)

Modern

1B	Ernie Banks	1962	307
2B	Rogers Hornsby	1929	410
SS	Ernie Banks	1958	379
3B	Ron Santo	1964	334
OF	Hack Wilson	1930	423
OF	Billy Williams	1970	373
OF	Kiki Cuyler	1930	351
C	Gabby Hartnett	1930	320

19th Century

1B	Cap Anson	1886	274
2B	Fred Pfeffer	1884	240
SS	Bill Dahlen	1894	289
3B	Bill Everett	1895	242
OF	Jimmy Ryan	1889	297
OF	Walt Wilmot	1894	281
OF	Bill Lange	1895	278
C	King Kelly	1884	237

All-Time

(Same as modern team)

MISCELLANEOUS BATTING RECORDS

Cycle Hitters

Date	Player	Opponent
July 28, 1888	Jimmy Ryan	Detroit
July 1, 1891	Jimmy Ryan	Cleveland
September 16, 1894	George Decker	Brooklyn
June 13, 1904	Frank Chance	New York
July 20, 1911	Frank Schulte	Philadelphia
June 23, 1930	Hack Wilson	Philadelphia
September 30, 1933	Babe Herman	St. Louis
June 28, 1950	Roy Smalley	St. Louis
July 2, 1957	Lee Walls	Cincinnati
July 17, 1966	Billy Williams	St. Louis
August 11, 1966	Randy Hundley	Houston
April 22, 1980	Ivan DeJesus	St. Louis

(A player hits for the cycle when he collects a single, double, triple, and home run in the same game.)

Six Hits in a Game

Date	Player	AB	R	H	2B	3B	HR	
July 22, 1876	Cal McVey	7	4	6	1	0	0	
July 25, 1876	Cal McVey	7	4	6	1	0	0	
July 27, 1876	Ross Barnes	6	3	6	1	1	0	
May 7, 1880	George Gore	6	5	6	0	0	0	
June 29, 1897	Barry McCormick	8	5	6	0	1	1	
July 5, 1937	Frank Demaree	7	2	6	3	0	0	(1stG-14 in.)
June 17, 1971	Don Kessinger	6	3	6	1	0	0	(10 innings)
July 26, 1975	Bill Madlock	6	1	6	0	1	0	(10 innings)
May 2, 1976	Jose Cardenal	7	2	6	1	0	1	(14 innings)

Five Long Hits in a Game

Date	Player	2B	3B	HR	Total
July 9, 1885	George Gore	3	2	0	5

Four Long Hits in a Game

Date	Player	2B	3B	HR	Total
Sept. 16, 1923	Hack Miller	3	0	1	4
July 4, 1934	Kiki Cuyler	3	1	0	4
April 14, 1936	Billy Herman	3	0	1	4
June 25, 1950	Hank Sauer	2	0	2	4
April 9, 1969	Billy Williams	4	0	0	4

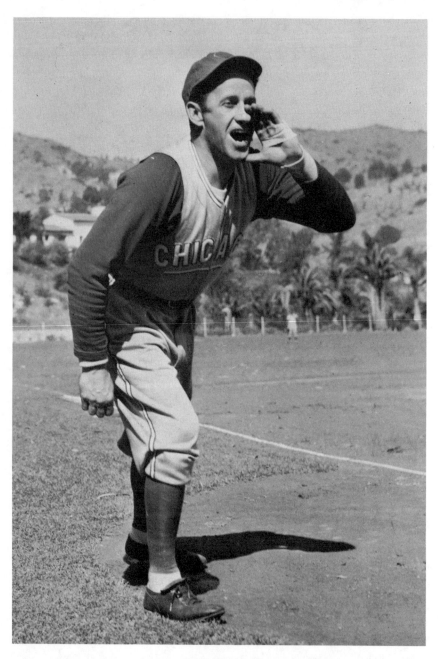

Hall-of Famer Kiki Cuyler pilfered 43 stolen bases in 1929. Here he is shown coaching third base for the Cubs in 1942 during spring training camp.

4
STEALS AND
HIGH SCORING

STOLEN BASE LEADERS

Year-by-Year Stolen Base Leaders

(Data prior to 1887 not available. Prior to 1898 a player was credited with a stolen base if he advanced from first to third on a single.)

Year	Player	Total	Year	Player	Total
1887	Fred Pfeffer	57	1907	Johnny Evers	46
1888	Fred Pfeffer	64	1908	Johnny Evers	36
1889	Hugh Duffy	52	1909	Frank Chance	29
1890	Walt Wilmot	76	1910	Frank Schulte	29
1891	Walt Wilmot	42	1911	Jimmy Sheckard	32
1892	Bill Dahlen	60	1912	Joe Tinker	25
1893	Bill Lange	47	1913	Victor Saier	26
1894	Walt Wilmot	74	1914	Wilbur Good	31
1895	Bill Lange	67	1915	Victor Saier	29
1896*	Bill Lange	84	1916	Max Flack	24
1897*	Bill Lange	73	1917	Max Flack	17
1898	Jimmy Ryan	29	1918	Charlie Hollocher	26
1899	Sam Mertes	45	1919	Fred Merkle	20
1900	Sam Mertes	38	1920	Charlie Hollocher	20
1901	Topsy Hartsel	41	1921	Max Flack	17
1902	Jimmy Slagle	41		George Maisel	17
1903*	Frank Chance	67	1922	Charlie Hollocher	19
1904	Frank Chance	42	1923	George Grantham	43
1905*	Billy Maloney	59	1924	Cliff Heathcote	26
1906*	Frank Chance	57	1925	Sparky Adams	26

Year-by-Year Stolen Base Leaders (Continued)

Year	Player	Total	Year	Player	Total
1926	Sparky Adams	27	1954	Dee Fondy	20
1927	Sparky Adams	26	1955	Ernie Banks	9
1928*	Kiki Cuyler	37		Gene Baker	9
1929*	Kiki Cuyler	43	1956	Dee Fondy	9
1930*	Kiki Cuyler	37	1957	Ernie Banks	8
1931	Kiki Cuyler	13	1958	Tony Taylor	21
1932	Billy Herman	14	1959	Tony Taylor	23
1933	Babe Herman	6	1960	Richie Ashburn	16
1934	Kiki Cuyler	15	1961	Richie Ashburn	7
1935*	Augie Galan	22	1962	George Altman	19
1936	Stan Hack	17	1963	Lou Brock	24
1937*	Augie Galan	23	1964	Billy Cowan	12
1938*	Stan Hack	16	1965	Jimmy Stewart	13
1939*	Stan Hack	17	1966	Adolfo Phillips	32
1940	Stan Hack	21	1967	Adolfo Phillips	25
1941	Stan Hack	10	1968	Don Kessinger	9
1942	Lennie Merullo	14	1969	Don Kessinger	11
1943	P-Nuts Lowrey	13	1970	Don Kessinger	12
1944	Roy Hughes	16	1971	Don Kessinger	15
1945	Stan Hack	12	1972	Jose Cardenal	25
1946	Peanuts Lowrey	10	1973	Jose Cardenal	19
1947	Lennie Merullo	4	1974	Jose Cardenal	23
	Andy Pafko	4	1975	Jose Cardenal	34
1948	Eddie Waitkus	11	1976	Jose Cardenal	23
1949	Hal Jeffcoat	12	1977	Ivan DeJesus	24
1950	Wayne Terwilliger	13	1978	Ivan DeJesus	41
1951	Ransom Jackson	14	1979	Ivan DeJesus	24
1952	Dee Fondy	13	1980	Ivan DeJesus	44
1953	Dee Fondy	10	1981	Bull Durham	25

*Led League

Tony Taylor led the Cubs in stolen bases in 1958 and 1959.

300-or-More Stolen Bases, Lifetime

Player	Years	Total
Bill Lange	1893-1899	399
Frank Chance	1898-1912	395
Jimmy Ryan	1885-1889; 1891-1900	359*
Joe Tinker	1902-1912; 1916	304

200-or-More Stolen Bases, Lifetime

Johnny Evers	1902-1913	291
Walt Wilmot	1890-1895	290
Bill Dahlen	1891-1898	285
Fred Pfeffer	1883-1889; 1891; 1896-1897	229*
Cap Anson	1876-1897	218*
Frank Schulte	1904-1916	215

150-or-More Stolen Bases, Lifetime

Jimmy Slagle	1902-1908	198
Bill Everett	1895-1900	179
Stan Hack	1932-1947	165
Jimmy Sheckard	1906-1912	163
Kiki Cuyler	1928-1935	161
Ivan DeJesus	1977-1981	154
Artie Hofman	1904-1912; 1916	153

100-or-More Stolen Bases, Lifetime

Tommy Burns	1880-1891	146*
Heinie Zimmerman	1907-1916	131
Jose Cardenal	1972-1977	125
Cliff Heathcote	1922-1930	121
Johnny Kling	1900-1908; 1910-1911	118
Vic Saier	1911-1917	116
Sparky Adams	1922-1927	114
Sam Mertes	1898-1900	110
Max Flack	1915-1922	108
Barry McCormick	1896-1901	102

90-or-More Stolen Bases, Lifetime

Charlie Hollocher	1918-1924	99
George Decker	1892-1897	96
Harry Steinfeldt	1906-1910	92
Augie Galan	1934-1941	90

80-or-More Stolen Bases, Lifetime

Danny Green	1898-1901	89
Billy Williams	1959-1974	86

70-or-More Stolen Bases, Lifetime

Ed Williamson	1879-1889	72*

60-or-More Stolen Bases, Lifetime

Jimmy Cooney	1890-1892	66
George Grantham	1922-1924	66
Dee Fondy	1951-1957	66
Adolfo Phillips	1966-1969	66
Hugh Duffy	1888-1889	65
Cliff Carroll	1890-1891	65
Jiggs Parrott	1892-1895	62
Arnold Statz	1922-1925	62
George Van Haltren	1887-1889	61
Phil Cavarretta	1934-1953	61

50-or-More Stolen Bases, Lifetime

Billy Maloney	1905	59
Wilbur Good	1911-1915	58
Les Mann	1916-1919	58
Fred Merkle	1917-1920	57
Tim Donahue	1895-1900	54
Doc Casey	1903-1905	54
Billy Herman	1931-1941	53
Woody English	1927-1936	51
Ernie Banks	1953-1971	50

*Incomplete because data prior to 1887 not available.

20-or-More Stolen Bases, Season

Year	Player	Total	Year	Player	Total
1887	Fred Pfeffer	57		Jimmy Cooney	45
	Jimmy Ryan	50		Tommy Burns	44
	Ed Williamson	45		Cliff Carroll	34
	Marty Sullivan	35		Bob Glenalvin	30
	Billy Sunday	34		Cap Anson	29
	Tommy Burns	32	1891	Walt Wilmot	42
	Tom Daly	29		Fred Pfeffer	40
	Cap Anson	27		Cliff Carroll	31
1888	Fred Pfeffer	64		Jimmy Ryan	27
	Jimmy Ryan	60		Jimmy Cooney	21
	Tommy Burns	34		Bill Dahlen	21
	Cap Anson	28	1892	Bill Dahlen	60
	Ed Williamson	25		Jim Canavan	33
	George Van Haltren	21		Walt Wilmot	31
1889	Hugh Duffy	52		Jimmy Ryan	27
	Fred Pfeffer	45	1893	Bill Lange	47
	Jimmy Ryan	45		Walt Wilmot	39
	George Van Haltren	28		Bill Dahlen	31
	Cap Anson	27		Jiggs Parrott	25
1890	Walt Wilmot	76		George Decker	22

20-or-More Stolen Bases, Season (Continued)

Year	Player	Total	Year	Player	Total
1894	Walt Wilmot	74		Johnny Evers	25
	Bill Lange	65		Doc Casey	21
	Bill Dahlen	42	1905	Billy Maloney	59
	Charlie Irwin	35		Frank Chance	38
	Jiggs Parrott	30		Joe Tinker	31
	George Decker	23		Jimmy Slagle	27
1895	Bill Lange	67		Doc Casey	22
	Bill Everett	47	1906	Frank Chance	57
	Bill Dahlen	38		Johnny Evers	49
	Walt Wilmot	28		Joe Tinker	30
1896	Bill Lange	84		Jimmy Sheckard	30
	Bill Dahlen	51		Harry Steinfeldt	29
	Bill Everett	46		Jimmy Slagle	25
	Jimmy Ryan	29		Frank Schulte	25
	Cap Anson	24	1907	Johnny Evers	46
	George Decker	20		Frank Chance	35
1897	Bill Lange	73		Jimmy Sheckard	31
	Barry McCormick	44		Artie Hofman	29
	Jimmy Ryan	27		Jimmy Slagle	28
	Bill Everett	26		Joe Tinker	20
1898	Jimmy Ryan	29	1908	Johnny Evers	36
	Bill Everett	28		Joe Tinker	30
	Bill Dahlen	27		Frank Chance	27
	Sam Mertes	27	1909	Frank Chance	29
	Bill Lange	22		Johnny Evers	28
1899	Sam Mertes	45		Joe Tinker	23
	Bill Lange	41		Frank Schulte	23
	Bill Everett	30		Harry Steinfeldt	22
1900	Sam Mertes	38		Artie Hofman	20
	Danny Green	28	1910	Artie Hofman	29
	Jack McCarthy	22		Johnny Evers	28
1901	Topsy Hartsel	41		Frank Schulte	22
	Danny Green	30		Jimmy Sheckard	22
	Frank Chance	27		Joe Tinker	20
	Charlie Dexter	22	1911	Jimmy Sheckard	32
1902	Jimmy Slagle	40		Artie Hofman	30
	Frank Chance	27		Joe Tinker	30
	Joe Tinker	27		Frank Schulte	23
	Johnny Kling	24		Heinie Zimmerman	23
1903	Frank Chance	67	1912	Joe Tinker	25
	Jimmy Slagle	33		Heinie Zimmerman	23
	Dick Harley	27	1913	Vic Saier	26
	Joe Tinker	27		Tommy Leach	21
	Johnny Evers	25		Frank Schulte	21
	Johnny Kling	23	1914	Wilbur Good	31
1904	Frank Chance	42	1915	Vic Saier	29
	Joe Tinker	41	1916	Max Flack	24
	Jimmy Slagle	28		Vic Saier	20

20-or-More Stolen Bases, Season (Continued)

Year	Player	Total	Year	Player	Total
1918	Charlie Hollocher	26	1937	Augie Galan	23
	Les Mann	21	1940	Stan Hack	21
	Fred Merkle	21	1954	Dee Fondy	20
	George Paskert	20	1958	Tony Taylor	21
1919	Fred Merkle	20	1959	Tony Taylor	23
1920	Charlie Hollocher	20	1963	Lou Brock	24
1923	George Grantham	43	1966	Adolfo Phillips	32
	Cliff Heathcote	32	1967	Adolfo Phillips	24
	Arnold Statz	29	1972	Jose Cardenal	25
	Sparky Adams	20	1974	Jose Cardenal	23
1924	Cliff Heathcote	26	1975	Jose Cardenal	34
	George Grantham	21	1976	Jose Cardenal	23
1925	Sparky Adams	26	1977	Ivan DeJesus	24
1926	Sparky Adams	27	1978	Ivan DeJesus	41
1927	Sparky Adams	26		Rodney Scott	27
1928	Kiki Cuyler	37	1979	Ivan DeJesus	24
1929	Kiki Cuyler	43	1980	Ivan DeJesus	44
1930	Kiki Cuyler	37	1981	Bull Durham	25
1935	Augie Galan	22		Ivan DeJesus	21

Base running expert Jose Cardenal slides into home plate as San Francisco Giants' catcher Chris Cannizzaro awaits throw.

Stolen Bases by Position (Season)

Modern

1B	Frank Chance	1903	67
2B	Johnny Evers	1906	49
SS	Ivan DeJesus	1980	44
3B	Harry Steinfeldt	1906	29
OF	Billy Maloney	1905	59
OF	Kiki Cuyler	1929	43
OF	Topsy Hartsel	1901	41
C	Johnny Kling	1902	24

19th Century

1B	Cap Anson	1890	29
2B	Fred Pfeffer	1888	64
SS	Bill Dahlen	1892	60
3B	Bill Everett	1895	47
OF	Bill Lange	1896	84
OF	Walt Wilmot	1890	76
OF	Jimmy Ryan	1888	60
C	Tom Daly	1887	29

All-Time

1B	Frank Chance	1903	67
2B	Fred Pfeffer	1888	64
SS	Bill Dahlen	1892	60
3B	Bill Everett	1895	47
OF	Bill Lange	1896	84
OF	Walt Wilmot	1890	76
OF	Jimmy Ryan	1888	60
C	Tom Daly	1887	29

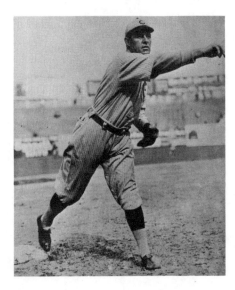

Harry Steinfeldt has the most stolen bases for a modern day Cubs' third baseman.

HIGH SCORING GAMES AND INNINGS

20-or-More Runs in a Game

July 22, 1876 — Cubs 30, Louisville 7
July 25, 1876 — Cubs 23, Cincinnati 3
August 26, 1876 — Cubs 23, St. Louis 3
August 7, 1877 — Cubs 21, Cincinnati 7
May 7, 1880 — Cubs 20, Providence 7
July 14, 1882 — Cubs 23, Detroit 4
July 24, 1882 — Cubs 35, Cleveland 4
September 9, 1882 — Cubs 24, Troy 1
May 30, 1883 — Cubs 22, Philadelphia 4
July 3, 1883 — Cubs 31, Buffalo 7
September 1, 1883 — Cubs 21, Cleveland 7
September 6, 1883 — Cubs 26, Detroit 6
July 4, 1884 — Cubs 22, Philadelphia 3
July 1, 1885 — Cubs 24, Boston 10
September 25, 1885 — Cubs 21, Providence 3
May 28, 1886 — Cubs 20, Washington 0
July 7, 1886 — Cubs 21, New York 9
July 20, 1886 — Cubs 20, St. Louis 4
July 28, 1888 — Cubs 21, Detroit 17
July 2, 1891 — Cubs 20, Cleveland 5
August 25, 1891 — Cubs 28, Brooklyn 5
July 25, 1894 — Cubs 24, Pittsburgh 6
August 1, 1894 — Cubs 26, St. Louis 8
September 20, 1894 — Cubs 20, Philadelphia 4
May 20, 1895 — Cubs 24, Philadelphia 6
June 29, 1897 — Cubs 36, Louisville 7
May 25, 1898 — Cubs 20, Baltimore 4
September 24, 1899 — Cubs 21, Cincinnati 5
June 11, 1911 — Cubs 20, Boston 2
August 25, 1922 — Cubs 26, Philadelphia 23
June 23, 1930 — Cubs 21, Philadelphia 8
August 13, 1937 — Cubs 22, Cincinnati 6
May 5, 1938 — Cubs 21, Philadelphia 2
July 3, 1945 — Cubs 24, Boston 2
August 15, 1945 — Cubs 20, Brooklyn 6
April 17, 1954 — Cubs 23, St. Louis 13
August 13, 1959 — Cubs 20, San Francisco 9
May 20, 1967 — Cubs 20, Los Angeles 3
May 17, 1977 — Cubs 23, San Diego 6
May 17, 1979 — Philadelphia 23, Cubs 22

10-or-More Runs in an Inning

July 22, 1876 — 10 in 1st inning vs. Louisville. Won 30-7
August 7, 1877 — 13 in 2nd inning vs. Cincinnati. Won 21-7
May 7, 1880 — 10 in 1st inning vs. Providence. Won 20-7
September 1, 1883 — 11 in 3rd inning vs. Cleveland. Won 21-7
September 6, 1883 — 18 in 7th inning vs. Detroit. Won 26-6
September 27, 1884 — 10 in 1st inning vs. Providence. Won 15-10
June 22, 1888 — 11 in 6th inning vs. Pittsburgh. Won 12-6
August 14, 1889 — 10 in 8th inning vs. Philadelphia. Won 19-7
May 8, 1890 — 12 in 6th inning vs. Cincinnati. Won 18-9
August 16, 1890 — 13 in 5th inning vs. Pittsburgh. Won 18-5
July 2, 1891 — 11 in 3rd inning vs. Cleveland. Won 20-5
September 20, 1894 — 10 in 1st inning vs. Philadelphia. Won 20-4
July 17, 1895 — 12 in 4th inning vs. Philadelphia. Won 12-7
April 17, 1896 — 10 in 1st inning vs. Louisville. Won 14-3
September 28, 1897 — 11 in 5th inning vs. Pittsburgh. Won 15-14
April 17, 1898 — 10 in 4th inning vs. St. Louis. Won 14-1
June 7, 1906 — 11 in 1st inning vs. New York. Won 19-0
August 25, 1922 — 10 in 2nd inning, 14 in 4th vs. Philadelphia. Won 26-23
May 28, 1925 — 12 in 7th inning vs. Cincinnati. Won 13-3
April 29, 1935 — 10 in 8th inning vs. Pittsburgh. Won 12-11
August 21, 1935 — 12 in 6th inning vs. Philadelphia. Won 19-5
June 13, 1937 — 10 in 5th inning vs. Philadelphia. Won 16-8
May 5, 1938 — 12 in 8th inning vs. Philadelphia. Won 21-2
May 5, 1946 — 11 in 7th inning vs. Philadelphia. Won 13-1
April 17, 1954 — 10 in 5th inning vs. St. Louis. Won 23-13
May 30, 1963 — 10 in 4th inning vs. New York. Won 12-0
May 1, 1964 — 10 in 1st inning vs. Houston. Won 11-3
May 31, 1973 — 10 in 1st inning vs. Houston. Won 16-8

Albert Spalding pitched the first game in Cubs' history on April 25, 1876. The game was also the first shutout in National League history, the Cubs won 4-0, at Louisville.

5
PITCHING RECORDS

WIN-LOSS RECORDS

Leading Pitchers, 1876 to Date
(Highest Won-Lost Percentage, 15 or More Decisions)

Year	Pitcher	W	L	Pct.
1876*	Al Spalding	46	12	.793
1877	George Bradley	18	23	.439
1878	Frank Larkin	29	26	.527
1879	Frank Hankinson	15	10	.600
1880*	Fred Goldsmith	21	3	.875
1881*	Larry Corcoran	31	14	.689
1882*	Larry Corcoran	27	13	.692
1883	Larry Corcoran	34	20	.630
1884	Larry Corcoran	35	23	.603
1885	Jim McCormick	20	4	.833
1886*	John Flynn	24	6	.800
1887	John Clarkson	38	21	.644
1888	Gus Krock	24	14	.641
1889	Frank Dwyer	16	13	.552
	Ad Gumbert	16	13	.552
1890	John Luby	20	9	.690
1891	Bill Hutchison	43	19	.698
1892	Ad Gumbert	22	19	.537
1893	Willie McGill	17	18	.486
1894	Clark Griffith	21	11	.656
1895	Clark Griffith	25	13	.650

Leading Pitchers, 1876 to Date (Continued)

Year	Pitcher	W	L	Pct.
1896	Clark Griffith	22	13	.629
1897	Jimmy Callahan	12	9	.571
1898	Clark Griffith	26	10	.722
1899	Jimmy Callahan	21	12	.636
1900	Clark Griffith	14	13	.519
1901	Rube Waddell	14	14	.500
1902	Jack Taylor	22	11	.667
1903	Jake Weimer	20	8	.714
1904	Bob Wicker	17	8	.680
1905	Carl Lundgren	13	5	.722
1906*	Ed Reulbach	19	4	.826
1907*	Ed Reulbach	17	4	.810
1908*	Ed Reulbach	24	7	.774
1909	Mordecai Brown	27	9	.750
1910*	Len Cole	20	4	.833
1911	Len Cole	18	7	.720
1912	Larry Cheney	26	10	.722
1913*	Bert Humpheries	16	4	.800
1914	Jim Vaughn	21	13	.618
1915	Jim Vaughn	20	12	.625
1916	Gene Packard	10	6	.625
1917	Jim Vaughn	23	13	.639
1918*	Claude Hendrix	20	7	.741
1919	Phil Douglas	10	6	.625
1920	Grover Alexander	27	14	.659
1921	Grover Alexander	15	13	.536
1922	Grover Alexander	16	13	.552
1923	Grover Alexander	22	12	.647
1924	Grover Alexander	12	5	.706
1925	Grover Alexander	15	11	.577
1926	Percy Jones	12	7	.632
1927	Charlie Root	26	15	.634
1928	Guy Bush	15	6	.714
1929*	Charlie Root	19	6	.760
1930*	Art Teachout	11	4	.733
1931	Guy Bush	16	8	.667
1932*	Lon Warneke	22	6	.786
1933*	Lyle Tinning	13	6	.684
1934	Lon Warneke	22	10	.688
1935*	Bill Lee	20	6	.769
1936	Larry French	18	9	.667
1937	Charlie Root	13	5	.722
1938*	Bill Lee	22	9	.710
1939	Larry French	15	8	.652
1940	Claude Passeau	20	13	.606
1941	Vern Olsen	10	8	.556
1942	Claude Passeau	19	14	.576
1943	Hiram Bithorn	18	12	.600
1944	Claude Passeau	15	9	.625

*Led League

Leading Pitchers, 1876 to Date (Continued)

Year	Pitcher	W	L	Pct.
1945	Hank Wyse	22	10	.688
1946	Paul Erickson	9	7	.563
1947	Doyle Lade	11	10	.526
1948	Johnny Schmitz	18	13	.581
1949	Bob Chipman	7	8	.467
1950	Frank Hiller	12	5	.706
1951	Dutch Leonard	10	6	.625
1952	Warren Hacker	15	9	.625
1953	Turk Lown	8	7	.533
1954	Jim Davis	11	7	.611
1955	Bob Rush	13	11	.542
1956	Bob Rush	13	10	.565
1957	Dick Drott	15	11	.577
1958	Glenn Hobbie	10	6	.625
1959	Don Elston	10	8	.556
1960	Don Elston	8	9	.471
1961	Don Cardwell	15	14	.517
1962	Cal Koonce	10	10	.500
1963	Dick Ellsworth	22	10	.688
1964	Larry Jackson	24	11	.686
1965	Bob Buhl	13	11	.542
1966	Ken Holtzman	11	16	.407
1967	Fergie Jenkins	20	13	.606
1968	Phil Regan	10	5	.667
1969	Phil Regan	12	6	.667
1970	Ken Holtzman	17	11	.607
1971	Fergie Jenkins	24	13	.649
1972	Milt Pappas	17	7	.708
1973	Bob Locker	10	6	.625
1974	Rick Reuschel	13	12	.520
1975	Ray Burris	15	10	.600
	Steve Stone	12	8	.600
1976	Rick Reuschel	14	12	.538
1977	Rick Reuschel	20	10	.667
1978	Donnie Moore	9	7	.563
1979	Dick Tidrow	11	5	.688
1980	Lynn McGlothen	12	14	.462
1981	Mike Krukow	9	9	.500

Most Victories by Pitcher, Season

Year	Pitcher	Record
1876	Al Spalding	46-12
1877	George Bradley	18-23
1878	Frank Larkin	29-26
1879	Frank Larkin	31-23

Most Victories by Pitcher, Season (Continued)

Year	Pitcher	Record
1880	Larry Corcoran	43-14
1881	Larry Corcoran	31-14
1882	Fred Goldsmith	28-17
1883	Larry Corcoran	34-20
1884	Larry Corcoran	35-23
1885	John Clarkson	53-16
1886	John Clarkson	36-17
1887	John Clarkson	38-21
1888	Gus Krock	24-14
1889	Frank Dwyer	16-13
	Ad Gumbert	16-13
	Bill Hutchison	16-17
1890	Bill Hutchison	42-25
1891	Bill Hutchison	44-19
1892	Bill Hutchison	37-34
1893	Willie McGill	17-18
1894	Clark Griffith	21-11
1895	Clark Griffith	25-13
1896	Clark Griffith	22-13
1897	Clark Griffith	21-18
1898	Clark Griffith	26-10
1899	Clark Griffith	21-13
	Jimmy Callahan	21-12
1900	Clark Griffith	14-13
1901	Rube Waddell	14-14
1902	Jack Taylor	22-11
1903	Jack Taylor	21-14
1904	Jake Weimer	20-14
1905	Mordecai Brown	18-10
	Ed Reulbach	18-14
	Jake Weimer	18-12
1906	Mordecai Brown	26-6
1907	Orval Overall	23-8
1908	Mordecai Brown	29-9
1909	Mordecai Brown	27-9
1910	Mordecai Brown	25-13
1911	Mordecai Brown	21-11
1912	Larry Cheney	26-10
1913	Larry Cheney	21-14
1914	Jim Vaughn	21-13
1915	Jim Vaughn	20-12
1916	Jim Vaughn	17-15
1917	Jim Vaughn	23-13
1918	Jim Vaughn	22-10
1919	Jim Vaughn	21-14
1920	Grover Alexander	27-14
1921	Grover Alexander	15-13
1922	Grover Alexander	16-13
	Vic Aldridge	16-15

Most Victories by Pitcher, Season (Continued)

Year	Pitcher	Record
1923	Grover Alexander	22-12
1924	Tony Kaufman	16-11
1925	Grover Alexander	15-11
1926	Charlie Root	18-17
1927	Charlie Root	26-15
1928	Pat Malone	18-13
1929	Pat Malone	22-10
1930	Pat Malone	20-9
1931	Charlie Root	17-14
1932	Lon Warneke	22-6
1933	Guy Bush	20-12
1934	Lon Warneke	22-10
1935	Bill Lee	20-6
	Lon Warneke	20-13
1936	Larry French	18-9
	Bill Lee	18-11
1937	Tex Carleton	16-8
	Larry French	16-10
1938	Bill Lee	22-9
1939	Bill Lee	19-15
1940	Claude Passeau	20-13
1941	Claude Passeau	14-14
1942	Claude Passeau	19-14
1943	Hiram Bithorn	18-12
1944	Hank Wyse	16-15
1945	Hank Wyse	22-10
1946	Hank Wyse	14-12
1947	Johnny Schmitz	13-18
1948	Johnny Schmitz	18-13
1949	Johnny Schmitz	11-13
1950	Bob Rush	13-20
1951	Bob Rush	11-12
1952	Bob Rush	17-13
1953	Paul Minner	12-15
	Warren Hacker	12-19
1954	Bob Rush	13-15
1955	Sam Jones	14-20
1956	Bob Rush	13-10
1957	Dick Drott	15-11
1958	Glen Hobbie	10-6
1959	Glen Hobbie	16-13
1960	Glen Hobbie	16-20
1961	Don Cardwell	15-14
1962	Bob Buhl	12-13
1963	Dick Ellsworth	22-10
1964	Larry Jackson	24-11
1965	Dick Ellsworth	14-15
	Larry Jackson	14-21
1966	Ken Holtzman	11-16

Most Victories by Pitcher, Season (Continued)

Year	Pitcher	Record
1967	Fergie Jenkins	20-13
1968	Fergie Jenkins	20-15
1969	Fergie Jenkins	21-15
1970	Fergie Jenkins	22-16
1971	Fergie Jenkins	24-13
1972	Fergie Jenkins	20-12
1973	Rick Reuschel	14-15
	Fergie Jenkins	14-16
	Burt Hooton	14-17
1974	Rick Reuschel	13-12
1975	Ray Burris	15-10
1976	Ray Burris	15-13
1977	Rick Reuschel	20-10
1978	Rick Reuschel	14-15
1979	Rick Reuschel	18-12
1980	Lynn McGlothen	12-14
1981	Mike Krukow	9-9

20-Game Winners

Year	Pitcher	Record
1876	Al Spalding	47-13
1878	Terry Larkin	29-26
1879	Terry Larkin	31-23
1880	Fred Goldsmith	22-3
	Larry Corcoran	43-14
1881	Fred Goldsmith	24-13
	Larry Corcoran	31-14
1882	Fred Goldsmith	28-16
	Larry Corcoran	27-13
1883	Fred Goldsmith	25-19
	Larry Corcoran	34-20
1884	Larry Corcoran	35-23
1885	John Clarkson	53-16
	Jim McCormick	20-4
1886	John Clarkson	36-17
	Jim McCormick	29-11
	John Flynn	24-6
1887	John Clarkson	38-21
1888	Gus Krock	25-14
1890	Bill Hutchison	42-25
	Pat Luby	20-9
1891	Bill Hutchison	43-19
1892	Bill Hutchison	37-33
	Ad Gumbert	23-18
1894	Clark Griffith	21-11
1895	Clark Griffith	25-14
	Bill Terry	21-14

20-Game Winners (Continued)

Year	Pitcher	Record
1896	Clark Griffith	23-12
1897	Clark Griffith	21-18
1898	Clark Griffith	25-12
	Jimmy Callahan	20-11
1899	Clark Griffith	21-13
	Jimmy Callahan	21-12
1902	Jack Taylor	22-11
1903	Jack Taylor	21-14
	Jake Weimer	20-8
	Bob Wicker	20-9
1904	Jake Weimer	20-13
1906	Mordecai Brown	26-6
	Jack Pfiester	20-9
1907	Orval Overall	23-8
	Mordecai Brown	20-6
1908	Mordecai Brown	29-9
	Ed Reulbach	24-7
1909	Mordecai Brown	27-9
	Orval Overall	20-11
1910	Mordecai Brown	25-14
	Len Cole	20-4
1911	Mordecai Brown	21-11
1912	Larry Cheney	26-10
1913	Larry Cheney	21-14
1914	Larry Cheney	20-18
	Jim Vaughn	21-13
1915	Jim Vaughn	20-12
1917	Jim Vaughn	23-13
1918	Jim Vaughn	22-10
	Claude Hendrix	20-7
1919	Jim Vaughn	21-14
1920	Grover Alexander	27-13
1923	Grover Alexander	22-12
1927	Charlie Root	26-15
1929	Pat Malone	22-10
1930	Pat Malone	20-9
1932	Lon Warneke	22-6
1933	Guy Bush	20-12
1934	Lon Warneke	22-10
1935	Bill Lee	20-6
	Lon Warneke	20-13
1938	Bill Lee	22-9
1940	Claude Passeau	20-13
1945	Hank Wyse	22-10
1963	Dick Ellsworth	22-10
1964	Larry Jackson	24-11
1967	Fergie Jenkins	20-13
1968	Fergie Jenkins	20-15

20-Game Winners (Continued)

Year	Pitcher	Record
1969	Fergie Jenkins	21-15
	Bill Hands	20-14
1970	Fergie Jenkins	22-16
1971	Fergie Jenkins	24-13
1972	Fergie Jenkins	20-12
1977	Rick Reuschel	20-10

100-or-More Wins, Pitcher

Pitcher	Years	Record
Charlie Root	1926-1941	201-156
Mordecai Brown	1904-1912; 1916	186-86
Bill Hutchison	1889-1895	181-154
Larry Corcoran	1880-1885	175-86
Clark Griffith	1893-1900	152-92
Guy Bush	1923-1934	152-101
Jim Vaughn	1913-1921	151-105
Fergie Jenkins	1966-1973	147-108
Bill Lee	1934-1943; 1947	139-123
Ed Reulbach	1905-1913	135-61
Rick Reuschel	1972-1981	129-121
Grover Alexander	1918-1926	128-83
Claude Passeau	1939-1947	124-94
Pat Malone	1928-1934	115-79
Bob Rush	1948-1957	110-140
Lon Warneke	1930-1936; 1942-1945	109-63
Fred Goldsmith	1880-1884	107-62
Jack Taylor	1898-1903; 1906-1907	107-90

80 to 99 Wins

Pitcher	Years	Record
Larry French	1935-1941	95-84
Bill Hands	1966-1972	92-86
Carl Lundgren	1902-1909	91-56
Dick Ellsworth	1958; 1960-1966	84-110
Sheriff Blake	1924-1931	81-92
Ken Holtzman	1965-1971; 1978-1979	80-81

Winningest Pitchers by Decades

1870's

Frank Larkin	60-49	.550
Albert Spalding	46-12	.793
George Bradley	18-23	.439
Frank Hankinson	15-11	.577
Cal McVey	10-10	.500
Larry Reis	4-4	.500

Winningest Pitchers by Decades (Continued)

1880's

Larry Corcoran	175-85	.673
Johnny Clarkson	137-57	.706
Fred Goldsmith	107-63	.629
Jim McCormick	49-15	.766
Mark Baldwin	31-32	.492
Gus Krock	27-17	.614
John Flynn	24-6	.241
George Van Haltren	24-20	.545
John Tener	22-20	.524
Frank Dwyer	20-14	.588

1890's

Bill Hutchison	166-141	.541
Clark Griffith	138-85	.619
Jimmy Callahan	53-31	.631
Bill Terry	41-39	.512
Ad Gumbert	39-30	.565
Pat Luby	38-37	.507
Dan Friend	32-29	.524
Kid McGill	24-37	.393
Walt Thornton	23-18	.561
Jack Taylor	23-21	.523

1900's

Mordecai Brown	135-50	.730
Ed Reulbach	97-39	.713
Carl Lundgren	91-56	.619
Jack Taylor	85-69	.552
Orval Overall	70-33	.680
Jack Pfiester	64-33	.660
Jake Weimer	58-34	.630
Bob Wicker	53-29	.646
John Menefee	37-36	.507
Herb Briggs	27-19	.587

1910's

Jim Vaughn	129-78	.623
Larry Cheney	76-51	.598
Jimmy Lavender	57-68	.456
Mordecai Brown	53-33	.616
Claude Hendrix	48-49	.495
Lew Richie	44-27	.620
Len Cole	39-13	.750
Ed Reulbach	39-26	.600
Phil Douglas	35-36	.493
George Pearce	34-26	.567
Bert Humpheries	34-27	.557

Winningest Pitchers by Decades (Continued)

1920's

Grover Alexander	110-71	.608
Charlie Root	77-56	.579
Sheriff Blake	71-74	.490
Guy Bush	64-50	.561
Tony Kaufman	63-57	.525
Vic Aldridge	47-36	.566
Percy Jones	46-41	.529
Pat Malone	40-23	.635
Vic Keen	30-33	.476
Hal Carlson	26-15	.634
Virgil Cheeves	26-27	.490

1930's

Charlie Root	114-90	.559
Bill Lee	106-70	.602
Lon Warneke	100-59	.629
Guy Bush	88-51	.633
Larry French	76-56	.576
Pat Malone	75-56	.572
Tex Carleton	51-35	.593
Clay Bryant	32-19	.627
Bud Tinning	22-15	.594
Roy Henshaw	21-11	.656
Curt Davis	21-14	.600

1940's

Claude Passeau	111-85	.566
Hank Wyse	69-54	.561
Johnny Schmitz	58-62	.483
Hank Borowy	36-34	.514
Bob Chipman	35-34	.507
Paul Erickson	35-48	.422
Hiram Bithorn	33-31	.516
Paul Derringer	33-38	.415
Bill Lee	33-35	.384
Vern Olsen	29-26	.527

1950's

Bob Rush	95-111	.461
Paul Minner	62-79	.440
Warren Hacker	47-70	.402
Johnny Klippstein	31-51	.378
Turk Lown	30-44	.405
Moe Drabowsky	29-40	.426
Glen Hobbie	26-19	.578
Don Elston	25-24	.510
Dick Drott	23-24	.489
Jim Davis	23-25	.479
Sam Jones	23-34	.403

Winningest Pitchers by Decades (Continued)

1960's

Dick Ellsworth	84-109	.435
Fergie Jenkins	67-51	.568
Larry Jackson	52-52	.500
Bill Hands	51-45	.531
Bob Buhl	51-52	.495
Ken Holtzman	48-43	.527
Glen Hobbie	35-60	.368
Don Cardwell	30-44	.405
Cal Koonce	29-32	.475
Joe Niekro	24-18	.571
Don Elston	24-30	.444

1970's

Rick Reuschel	114-101	.532
Fergie Jenkins	80-57	.583
Ray Burris	55-58	.486
Bill Bonham	53-70	.431
Milt Pappas	51-41	.554
Bill Hands	41-41	.500
Burt Hooton	34-44	.435
Ken Holtzman	32-38	.457
Bruce Sutter	27-22	.551
Mike Krukow	26-26	.500

1980-1

Mike Krukow	19-24	.442
Rick Reuschel	15-20	.429
Lynn McGlothen	12-14	.472
Dennis Lamp	10-14	.417
Dick Tidrow	9-15	.375
Randy Martz	6-9	.400
Lee Smith	5-6	.455
Bruce Sutter	5-8	.385
Bill Caudill	5-11	.313
Doug Bird	4-5	.444

Winning Streaks by Pitchers

Pitcher	Year	Total
John Luby	1890	17
Jim McCormick	1886	16
Jim McCormick	1885	14
John Flynn	1886	14
Ed Reulbach	1909	14
Larry Corcoran	1880	13
John Clarkson	1885	13
Ed Reulbach	1906	12
John Clarkson	1887	11

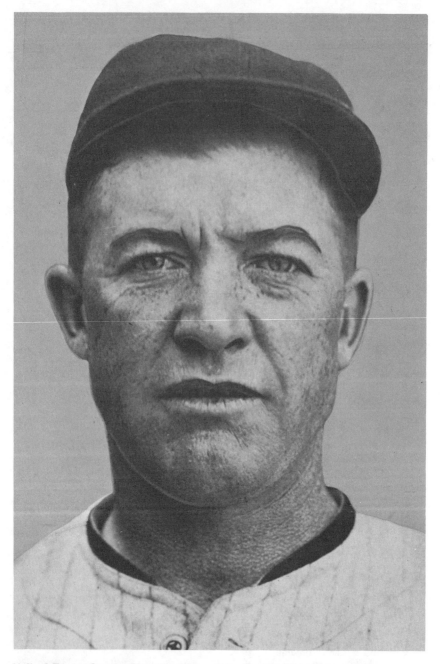

Hall-of-Famer Grover Cleveland Alexander had the lowest earned run average in the National League in five different years.

Winning Streaks (Continued)

Mordecai Brown	1906	11
Grover Alexander	1920	11
Guy Bush	1929	11
Milt Pappas	1972	11
Larry Corcoran	1882	10 (twice)
Mordecai Brown	1907	10

Losing Streaks

Dutch McCall	1948	13

ERA

Lowest Earned Run Average by Pitcher, Season
(Minimum 150 innings)

Year	Pitcher	ERA
1876	Al Spalding	1.75
1877	George Bradley	3.31
1878	Frank Larkin	2.24
1879	Frank Larkin	2.44
1880	Fred Goldsmith	1.75
1881	Larry Corcoran	2.31
1882*	Larry Corcoran	1.95
1883	Larry Corcoran	2.49
1884	Larry Corcoran	2.40
1885	John Clarkson	1.85
1886	John Flynn	2.24
1887	John Clarkson	3.08
1888	Gus Krock	2.44
1889	Bill Hutchison	3.54
1890	Bill Hutchison	2.75
1891	Bill Hutchison	2.81
1892	Bill Hutchison	2.74
1893	Willie McGill	4.61
1894	Clark Griffith	4.92
1895	Clark Griffith	3.93
1896	Clark Griffith	3.54
1897	Clark Griffith	3.72
1898*	Clark Griffith	1.88
1899	Clark Griffith	2.79
1900	Virgil Garvin	2.41

*Led League

Lowest Earned Run Average by Pitcher, Season (Continued)

Year	Pitcher	ERA
1901	Rube Waddell	2.81
1902*	Jack Taylor	1.33
1903	Jake Weimer	2.30
1904	Mordecai Brown	1.86
1905	Ed Reulbach	1.42
1906*	Mordecai Brown	1.04
1907*	Jack Pfiester	1.15
1908	Mordecai Brown	1.47
1909	Mordecai Brown	1.31
1910	Len Cole	1.80
1911	Lew Richie	2.31
1912	Larry Cheney	2.85
1913	George Pearce	2.31
1914	Jim Vaughn	2.05
1915	Bert Humpheries	2.31
1916	Jim Vaughn	2.20
1917	Jim Vaughn	2.01
1918*	Jim Vaughn	1.74
1919*	Grover Alexander	1.72
1920*	Grover Alexander	1.91
1921	Grover Alexander	3.39
1922	Victor Aldridge	3.52
1923	Victor Keen	3.00
1924	Grover Alexander	3.03
1925	Grover Alexander	3.39
1926	Charlie Root	2.82
1927	Guy Bush	3.03
1928	Sheriff Blake	2.47
1929	Charlie Root	3.47
1930	Pat Malone	3.94
1931	Bob Smith	3.22
1932*	Lon Warneke	2.37
1933	Lon Warneke	2.00
1934	Lon Warneke	3.21
1935	Bill Lee	2.96
	Larry French	2.96
1936	Curt Davis	3.00
1937	Tex Carleton	3.15
1938*	Bill Lee	2.66
1939	Claude Passeau	3.05
1940	Claude Passeau	2.50
1941	Vern Olsen	3.15
1942	Claude Passeau	2.68
1943	Hiram Bithorn	2.60
1944	Claude Passeau	2.89
1945	Ray Prim	2.40
1946	Johnny Schmitz	2.61
1947	Johnny Schmitz	3.22
1948	Johnny Schmitz	2.64

*Led League

Lowest Earned Run Average by Pitcher, Season (Continued)

Year	Pitcher	ERA
1949	Bob Rush	4.07
1950	Frank Hiller	3.53
1951	Paul Minner	3.79
1952	Warren Hacker	2.58
1953	Paul Minner	4.21
1954	Bob Rush	3.77
1955	Paul Minner	3.48
1956	Bob Rush	3.19
1957	Moe Drabowsky	3.53
1958	Glenn Hobbie	3.74
1959	Dave Hillman	3.53
1960	Dick Ellsworth	3.72
1961	Don Cardwell	3.82
1962	Bob Buhl	3.69
1963	Dick Ellsworth	2.11
1964	Larry Jackson	3.14
1965	Cal Koonce	3.69
1966	Fergie Jenkins	3.31
1967	Bill Hands	2.46
1968	Fergie Jenkins	2.63
1969	Bill Hands	2.49
1970	Ken Holtzman	3.38
1971	Fergie Jenkins	2.77
1972	Milt Pappas	2.77
1973	Rick Reuschel	3.00
1974	Bill Bonham	3.85
1975	Rick Reuschel	3.73
1976	Ray Burris	3.11
1977	Rick Reuschel	2.79
1978	Rick Reuschel	3.41
1979	Dennis Lamp	3.50
1980	Rick Reuschel	3.40
1981	Randy Martz	3.67

Ron Santo (#10) congratulating Ken Holtzman after his no-hitter (9-19-69).

NO-HITTERS

No-Hit Games

August 19, 1880 — Larry Corcoran vs. Boston, won 6-0
September 20, 1882 — Larry Corcoran vs. Worcester, won 5-0
June 27, 1884 — Larry Corcoran vs. Providence, won 6-0
July 27, 1885 — John Clarkson vs. Providence, won 4-0
* June 21, 1888 — George Van Haltren vs. Pittsburgh, won 2-0
August 21, 1898 — Walt Thornton vs. Brooklyn, won 2-0
** June 11, 1904 — Bob Wicker vs. New York, won 1-0
(12 innings)
*** July 31, 1910 — Len Cole vs. St. Louis, won 4-0 (2nd game)
August 31, 1915 — Jim Lavender vs. New York, won 2-0
(1st game)
**** May 2, 1917 — Jim Vaughn vs. Cincinnati, lost 1-0 (10 innings)
May 12, 1955 — Sam Jones vs. Pittsburgh, won 4-0
May 15, 1960 — Don Cardwell vs. St. Louis, won 4-0
August 19, 1969 — Ken Holtzman vs. Atlanta, won 3-0
June 3, 1971 — Ken Holtzman vs. Cincinnati, won 1-0
April 16, 1972 — Burt Hooton vs. Philadelphia, won 4-0
***** September 2, 1972 — Milt Pappas vs. San Diego, won 8-0

* Called after six innings because of rain.
** Allowed one hit in tenth inning; held New York hitless
thereafter.
*** Called after seven innings because both teams had to catch a
train.
**** Lost on two hits in tenth inning; Fred Toney of Cincinnati
pitched a no-hit ball game for the full ten innings.
***** One out short of perfect game; Pappas retired the first 26
batters, walked 27th before retiring 28th.

Burt Hooten on his way to a no-hitter (4-16-72).

Pitcher Milt Pappas, the last Cub to pitch a no-hitter (9-2-72), is asked his thoughts about the game by WGN announcer Lou Boudreau, a Hall-of-Famer, and Jim West.

No-Hit Games Pitched Against the Cubs

September 18, 1903 — Charles Fraser of Philadelphia, won 10-0

June 13, 1905 — Christy Mathewson of New York, won 1-0

May 2, 1917 — Fred Toney of Cincinnati, won 1-0 (10 innings)

June 19, 1952 — Carl Erskine of Brooklyn, won 5-0

August 19, 1965 — Jim Maloney of Cincinnati, won 1-0 (10 innings)

*September 9, 1965 — Sandy Koufax of Los Angeles, won 1-0

*Koufax pitched perfect game — no Cub batter reached first base

PITCHER LONGEVITY

Most Complete Games, Season

Year	Pitcher	CG	Year	Pitcher	CG
1876	Al Spalding	53	1920*	Grover Alexander	33
1877	George Bradley	35	1921	Grover Alexander	21
1878	Frank Larkin	56	1922	Grover Alexander	20
1879	Frank Larkin	57		Vic Aldridge	20
1880	Larry Corcoran	57	1923	Grover Alexander	26
1881	Larry Corcoran	43	1924	Vic Aldridge	20
1882	Fred Goldsmith	45	1925	Grover Alexander	20
1883	Larry Corcoran	51	1926	Charlie Root	21
1884	Larry Corcoran	57	1927	Charlie Root	21
1885*	John Clarkson	68	1928	Pat Malone	16
1886	John Clarkson	50		Sheriff Blake	16
1887*	John Clarkson	56	1929	Pat Malone	19
1888	Gus Krock	38		Charlie Root	19
1889	Bill Hutchison	33	1930*	Pat Malone	22
1890*	Bill Hutchison	65	1931	Charlie Root	19
1891*	Bill Hutchison	56	1932	Lon Warneke	25
1892*	Bill Hutchison	67	1933*	Lon Warneke	26
1893	Bill Hutchison	38	1934	Lon Warneke	23
1894	Bill Hutchison	28	1935	Lon Warneke	20
	Clark Griffith	28	1936	Bill Lee	20
1895	Clark Griffith	39	1937	Tex Carleton	18
1896	Clark Griffith	35	1938	Bill Lee	19
1897*	Clark Griffith	38	1939	Bill Lee	20
1898	Clark Griffith	36	1940	Claude Passeau	20
1899	Jack Taylor	39	1941	Claude Passeau	20
1900	Jimmy Callahan	32	1942	Claude Passeau	24
1901	Tom Hughes	32	1943	Hiram Bithorn	19
1902	Jack Taylor	33	1944	Claude Passeau	18
1903	Jack Taylor	33	1945	Hank Wyse	23
1904	Jake Weimer	31	1946	Johnny Schmitz	14
1905	Ed Reulbach	28	1947	Johnny Schmitz	10
1906	Mordecai Brown	27	1948	Johnny Schmitz	18
1907	Orval Overall	26	1949	Dutch Leonard	10
1908	Mordecai Brown	27	1950	Bob Rush	19
1909*	Mordecai Brown	32	1951	Paul Minner	14
1910*	Mordecai Brown	27	1952	Bob Rush	17
1911	Mordecai Brown	21	1953	Paul Minner	9
1912*	Larry Cheney	28		Warren Hacker	9
1913	Larry Cheney	25	1954	Paul Minner	12
1914	Jim Vaughn	23	1955	Bob Rush	14
1915	Jim Vaughn	18	1956	Bob Rush	13
1916	Jim Vaughn	21	1957	Moe Drabowsky	12
1917	Jim Vaughn	27	1958	Taylor Phillips	5
1918	Jim Vaughn	27	1959	Glen Hobbie	10
1919	Jim Vaughn	25	1960	Glen Hobbie	16

*Led League

Most Complete Games, Season (Continued)

Year	Pitcher	CG	Year	Pitcher	CG
1961	Don Cardwell	13	1972	Fergie Jenkins	23
1962	Bob Buhl	8	1973	Burt Hooton	9
1963	Dick Ellsworth	19	1974	Bill Bonham	10
1964	Larry Jackson	19	1975	Ray Burris	8
1965	Larry Jackson	12	1976	Ray Burris	10
1966	Dick Ellsworth	9	1977	Rick Reuschel	8
	Ken Holtzman	9	1978	Rick Reuschel	9
1967*	Fergie Jenkins	20	1979	Dennis Lamp	6
1968	Fergie Jenkins	20	1980	Rick Reuschel	6
1969	Fergie Jenkins	23	1981	Mike Krukow	2
1970*	Fergie Jenkins	24		Doug Bird	2
1971*	Fergie Jenkins	30			

*Led League

Pitcher Don Cardwell had the unique distinction of pitching a no-hitter in his major league debut for the Cubs on May 15, 1960.

Most Innings Pitched, Season

Year	Pitcher	IP	Year	Pitcher	IP
1876	Al Spalding	529	1925	Grover Alexander	236
1877	George Bradley	394	1926	Charlie Root	271
1878	Frank Larkin	506	1927*	Charlie Root	309
1879	Frank Larkin	513	1928	Pat Malone	251
1880	Larry Corcoran	536	1929	Charlie Root	272
1881	Larry Corcoran	397	1930	Pat Malone	272
1882	Fred Goldsmith	405	1931	Charlie Root	251
1883	Larry Corcoran	474	1932	Lon Warneke	277
1884	Larry Corcoran	517	1933	Lon Warneke	287
1885*	John Clarkson	623	1934	Lon Warneke	291
1886	John Clarkson	467	1935	Lon Warneke	262
1887*	John Clarkson	523	1936	Bill Lee	259
1888	Gus Krock	340	1937	Bill Lee	272
1889	Bill Hutchison	318	1938	Bill Lee	291
1890*	Bill Hutchison	603	1939	Bill Lee	282
1891*	Bill Hutchison	561	1940	Claude Passeau	281
1892*	Bill Hutchison	627	1941	Claude Passeau	231
1893	Bill Hutchison	348	1942	Claude Passeau	278
1894	Bill Hutchison	278	1943	Claude Passeau	257
1895	Clark Griffith	353	1944	Hank Wyse	257
1896	Clark Griffith	318	1945	Hank Wyse	278
1897	Clark Griffith	344	1946	Johnny Schmitz	224
1898	Clark Griffith	326	1947	Johnny Schmitz	207
1899	Jack Taylor	355	1948	Johnny Schmitz	242
1900	Jimmy Callahan	285	1949	Johnny Schmitz	207
1901	Tom Hughes	308	1950	Bob Rush	255
1902	Jack Taylor	325	1951	Bob Rush	211
1903	Jack Taylor	312	1952	Bob Rush	250
1904	Jake Weimer	307	1953	Warren Hacker	222
1905	Ed Reulbach	292	1954	Bob Rush	236
1906	Mordecai Brown	277	1955	Sam Jones	242
1907	Orval Overall	268	1956	Bob Rush	240
1908	Mordecai Brown	312	1957	Moe Drabowsky	240
1909*	Mordecai Brown	343	1958	Taylor Phillips	170
1910	Mordecai Brown	295	1959	Bob Anderson	235
1911	Mordecai Brown	270	1960	Glen Hobbie	259
1912	Larry Cheney	303	1961	Don Cardwell	259
1913	Larry Cheney	305	1962	Bob Buhl	212
1914	Larry Cheney	311	1963	Dick Ellsworth	291
1915	Jim Vaughn	270	1964	Larry Jackson	298
1916	Jim Vaughn	294	1965	Larry Jackson	257
1917	Jim Vaughn	296	1966	Dick Ellsworth	269
1918*	Jim Vaughn	290	1967	Fergie Jenkins	289
1919*	Jim Vaughn	307	1968	Fergie Jenkins	308
1920*	Grover Alexander	363	1969	Fergie Jenkins	311
1921	Grover Alexander	252	1970	Fergie Jenkins	313
1922	Vic Aldridge	258	1971*	Fergie Jenkins	325
1923	Grover Alexander	305	1972	Fergie Jenkins	289
1924	Vic Aldridge	244	1973	Fergie Jenkins	271

*Led League

Most Innings Pitched, Season (Continued)

Year	Pitcher	IP	Year	Pitcher	IP
1974	Bill Bonham	243	1978	Rick Reuschel	243
1975	Ray Burris	238	1979	Rick Reuschel	240
1976	Rick Reuschel	260	1980	Rick Reuschel	257
1977	Rick Reuschel	252	1981	Mike Krukow	144

300-or-More Innings Pitched, Season

Year	Pitcher	IP	Year	Pitcher	IP
1876	Al Spalding	529	1896	Clark Griffith	318
1877	George Bradley	394	1897	Clark Griffith	344
1878	Frank Larkin	506	1898	Clark Griffith	326
1879	Frank Larkin	513	1899	Jack Taylor	355
1880	Larry Corcoran	536		Clark Griffith	320
1881	Larry Corcoran	397	1901	Tom Hughes	308
	Fred Goldsmith	330	1902	Jack Taylor	325
1882	Fred Goldsmith	405	1903	Jack Taylor	312
	Larry Corcoran	356	1904	Jake Weimer	307
1883	Larry Corcoran	474	1908	Mordecai Brown	312
	Fred Goldsmith	383	1909	Mordecai Brown	343
1884	Larry Corcoran	517	1912	Larry Cheney	303
1885	John Clarkson	623	1913	Larry Cheney	305
1886	John Clarkson	467	1914	Larry Cheney	311
	Jim McCormick	348	1919	Jim Vaughn	307
1887	John Clarkson	523	1920	Grover Alexander	363
	Mark Baldwin	334		Jim Vaughn	301
1888	Gus Krock	340	1923	Grover Alexander	305
1889	Bill Hutchison	318	1927	Charlie Root	309
1890	Bill Hutchison	603	1968	Fergie Jenkins	308
1891	Bill Hutchison	561	1969	Fergie Jenkins	311
1892	Bill Hutchison	627		Bill Hands	300
	Ad Gumbert	383	1970	Fergie Jenkins	313
1893	Bill Hutchison	348	1971	Fergie Jenkins	325
	Willie McGill	303			
1895	Clark Griffith	353			
	Bill Terry	311			

2500-or-More Innings Pitched, Lifetime

Pitcher	IP
Charlie Root (1926-1941)	3168
Bill Hutchison (1889-1895)	3026

2000-or-More Innings Pitched, Lifetime

Larry Corcoran (1880-1885)	2330
Mordecai Brown (1904-1912; 1916)	2328
Fergie Jenkins (1966-1973)	2288
Bill Lee (1934-1943; 1947)	2270
Jim Vaughn (1913-1921)	2217
Guy Bush (1923-1934)	2201
Bob Rush (1948-1957)	2132
Rick Reuschel (1972-1981)	2093
Clark Griffith (1893-1900)	2090

1500-or-More Innings Pitched, Lifetime

Claude Passeau (1939-1947)	1914
Grover Alexander (1918-1926)	1884
Ed Reulbach (1905-1913)	1866
Jack Taylor (1898-1903; 1906-1907)	1801
John Clarkson (1884-1887)	1731
Pat Malone (1928-1934)	1632
Lon Warneke (1930-1936; 1942-1945)	1624
Dick Ellsworth (1958; 1960-1966)	1614
Bill Hands (1966-1972)	1564
Fred Goldsmith (1880-1884)	1518

1000-or-More Innings Pitched, Lifetime

Larry French (1935-1941)	1485
Sheriff Blake (1924-1931)	1455
Ken Holtzman (1965-1971; 1978-1979)	1448
Orval Overall (1906-1910; 1913)	1358
Carl Lundgren (1902-1909)	1322
Glenn Hobbie (1957-1964)	1219
Paul Minner (1950-1956)	1197
Johnny Schmitz (1941-1942; 1946-1951)	1181
Bill Bonham (1971-1977)	1153
Warren Hacker (1948-1956)	1092
Claude Hendrix (1916-1920)	1076
Ray Burris (1973-1979)	1069
Hank Wyse (1942-1947)	1062
Larry Cheney (1911-1915)	1061
Jimmy Callahan (1897-1900)	1043
Frank Larkin (1878-1879)	1019
Jack Pfiester (1906-1911)	1019

SHUTOUTS

Year-by-Year Leaders in Shutouts

Year	Pitcher	Shutouts
1876	Albert Spalding	8
1877	George Bradley	2
1878	Frank Larkin	1
1879	Frank Larkin	3
1880	Larry Corcoran	5
1881	Fred Goldsmith	5
1882	Fred Goldsmith	4
1883	Larry Corcoran	3
1884	Larry Corcoran	7
1885*	John Clarkson	10
1886	John Clarkson	3
1887	John Clarkson	2
1888	Gus Krock	4
	George Van Haltren	4
1889	Bill Hutchison	3
1890	Bill Hutchison	5
1891	Bill Hutchison	4
1892	Bill Hutchison	5
1893	Bill Hutchison	2
1894	None	
1895	Bill Hutchison	2
1896	Danny Friend	1
	Bill Terry	1
1897	Jimmy Callahan	1
	Clark Griffith	1
1898	Clark Griffith	4
1899	Virgil Garvin	4
1900*	Clark Griffith	4
1901	Mal Eason	1
	Tom Hughes	1
1902	Jack Taylor	7
1903	Jake Weimer	3
1904	Jake Weimer	5
1905	Buttons Briggs	5
	Ed Reulbach	5
1906*	Mordecai Brown	9
1907*	Orval Overall	8
1908	Mordecai Brown	9
1909*	Orval Overall	9
1910*	Mordecai Brown	7
1911	Lew Richie	4
1912	Lew Richie	4
	Larry Cheney	4
1913	George Pearce	3
1914	Larry Cheney	6

*Led League

Year-by-Year Leaders in Shutouts (Continued)

Year	Pitcher	Shutouts
1915	Jim Vaughn	4
	Bert Humpheries	4
1916	Jim Vaughn	4
	Jim Lavender	4
1917	Jim Vaughn	5
	Phil Douglas	5
1918*	Jim Vaughn	8
	George Tyler	8
1919*	Grover Alexander	9
1920	Grover Alexander	7
1921	Grover Alexander	3
1922	Victor Aldridge	2
	Percy Jones	2
1923	Grover Alexander	3
1924	Tony Kaufmann	3
1925	Tony Kaufmann	2
1926	Sheriff Blake	4
1927	Charlie Root	4
1928*	Sheriff Blake	4
1929*	Pat Malone	5
1930*	Charlie Root	4
1931	Charlie Root	3
1932*	Lon Warneke	4
1933	Lon Warneke	4
	Guy Bush	4
1934	Bill Lee	4
1935*	Larry French	4
1936*	Larry French	4
	Bill Lee	4
	Lon Warneke	4
	Tex Carleton	4
1937	Larry French	4
	Tex Carleton	4
1938*	Bill Lee	9
1939	Larry French	2
	Dizzy Dean	2
1940	Claude Passeau	4
	Vern Olsen	4
1941	Claude Passeau	3
1942	Claude Passeau	3
1943*	Hiram Bithorn	7
1944	Hank Wyse	3
	Paul Erickson	3
1945*	Claude Passeau	5
1946	Bob Chipman	3
1947	Johnny Schmitz	3
1948	Russ Meyer	3
1949	Johnny Schmitz	3
1950	Johnny Schmitz	3

*Led League

Year-by-Year Leaders in Shutouts (Continued)

Year	Pitcher	Shutouts
1951	Paul Minner	3
1952	Warren Hacker	5
1953	Paul Minner	2
1954	Howie Pollet	2
1955	Sam Jones	4
1956	Sam Jones	2
1957	Dick Drott	3
1958	John Briggs	1
	Moe Drabowsky	1
	Glen Hobbie	1
	Taylor Phillips	1
1959	Glen Hobbie	3
1960	Glen Hobbie	4
1961	Don Cardwell	3
1962	Don Cardwell	1
	Cal Koonce	1
	Bob Buhl	1
1963	Dick Ellsworth	4
	Larry Jackson	4
1964	Larry Jackson	3
	Bob Buhl	3
1965	Larry Jackson	4
1966	Fergie Jenkins	1
	Curt Simmons	1
1967	Fergie Jenkins	3
1968	Bill Hands	4
1969	Fergie Jenkins	7
1970	Fergie Jenkins	3
1971*	Milt Pappas	5
1972	Fergie Jenkins	5
1973	Rick Reuschel	3
1974	Rick Reuschel	2
	Bill Bonham	2
1975	Ray Burris	2
	Bill Bonham	2
1976	Ray Burris	4
1977	Rick Reuschel	4
1978	Rick Reuschel	3
1979	Ken Holtzman	2
1980	Lynn McGlothen	3
1981	None	

*Led League

Five-or-More Shutouts, Season

Year	Pitcher	Total
1876	Al Spalding	8
1880	Larry Corcoran	5
1881	Fred Goldsmith	5
1884	Larry Corcoran	7
1885	John Clarkson	10
1890	Bill Hutchison	5
1892	Bill Hutchison	5
1902	Jack Taylor	7
1904	Jake Weimer	5
1905	Herb Briggs	5
	Ed Reulbach	5
1906	Mordecai Brown	9
	Ed Reulbach	6
	Carl Lundgren	5
1907	Orval Overall	8
	Carl Lundgren	7
	Mordecai Brown	6
1908	Mordecai Brown	9
	Ed Reulbach	7
1909	Orval Overall	9
	Mordecai Brown	8
	Ed Reulbach	6
	Jack Pfiester	5
1910	Mordecai Brown	7
1914	Larry Cheney	6
1917	Jim Vaughn	5
	Phil Douglas	5
1918	Jim Vaughn	8
	George Tyler	8
1919	Grover Alexander	9
1920	Grover Alexander	7
1929	Pat Malone	5
1938	Bill Lee	9
1943	Hiram Bithorn	7
1945	Claude Passeau	5
1952	Warren Hacker	5
1969	Fergie Jenkins	7
1971	Milt Pappas	5
1972	Fergie Jenkins	5

For Rich Reuschel, the 1977 season was the turning point in his career. He not only became the Cub's 24th twenty-game winner (the first since Fergie Jenkins' even 20 in 1972), but his performance earned him a berth on the National League All-Star team.

Pitchers With 15-or-More Shutouts

Pitcher	Total
Mordecai Brown (1904-1912; 1916)	49
Jim Vaughn (1913-1921)	35
Ed Reulbach (1905-1913)	31
Fergie Jenkins (1966-1973)	27
Orval Overall (1906-1910; 1913)	26
Bill Lee (1934-1943; 1947)	25
Grover Alexander (1918-1926)	24
Larry Corcoran (1880-1885)	23
Claude Passeau (1939-1947)	22
Bill Hutchison (1889-1895)	21
Charlie Root (1926-1941)	21
Larry French (1935-1941)	21
Carl Lundgren (1902-1909)	19
Jack Pfiester (1906-1911)	17
Lon Warneke (1930-1936; 1942-1945)	17
Rick Reuschel (1972-1980)	17
Fred Goldsmith (1880-1884)	16
Pat Malone (1928-1934)	16
John Clarkson (1884-1887)	15

Shutout Records

Most Career Shutouts — 49, Mordecai Brown (1904-1912, 1916)

Most Shutouts, Season (50 foot pitching distance) —
9, Mordecai Brown, 1906
9, Mordecai Brown, 1908
9, Orval Overall, 1909
9, Grover Alexander, 1919
9, Bill Lee, 1938

Most Consecutive Shutouts — 4, Mordecai Brown, 1908
4, Ed Reulbach, 1908
4, Bill Lee, 1938

Most Shutouts, One Day — 2, Ed Reulbach vs. Brooklyn,
September 26, 1908 (5-0 and 3-0)

With a 24-13 record and a 2.77 earned run average in 1971, Fergie Jenkins became the first Cub pitcher to win a Cy Young Award. Chicago sportswriter Jim Enright (background) who later became The Cub's PA announcer, made the award presentation.

STRIKEOUTS

Most Strikeouts by Pitcher, Season

Year	Pitcher	Strikeouts
1876	Albert Spalding	39
1877	George Bradley	59
1878	Frank Larkin	163
1879	Frank Larkin	142
1880*	Larry Corcoran	268
1881	Larry Corcoran	150
1882	Larry Corcoran	170
1883	Larry Corcoran	216
1884	Larry Corcoran	272
1885*	John Clarkson	318
1886	John Clarkson	340
1887*	John Clarkson	237
1888	Gus Krock	161
1889	Bill Hutchison	136
1890	Bill Hutchison	289
1891	Bill Hutchison	261
1892*	Bill Hutchison	316
1893	Kid McGill	91
1894	Clark Griffith	71
1895	Billy Terry	88
1896	Danny Friend	86
1897	Clark Griffith	102
1898	Clark Griffith	97
1899	Jimmy Callahan	77
1900	Virgil Garvin	107
1901	Tom Hughes	225
1902	Pop Williams	94
1903	Jake Weimer	128
1904	Jake Weimer	177
1905	Ed Reulbach	152
1906	Jack Pfiester	153
1907	Orval Overall	141
1908	Orval Overall	167
1909*	Orval Overall	205
1910	Mordecai Brown	143
1911	Mordecai Brown	129
1912	Larry Cheney	140
1913	Larry Cheney	136
1914	Jim Vaughn	165
1915	Jim Vaughn	148
1916	Jim Vaughn	144
1917	Jim Vaughn	195
1918*	Jim Vaughn	148
1919*	Jim Vaughn	141
1920*	Grover Alexander	173

*Led League

223

Most Strikeouts by Pitcher, Season (Continued)

Year	Pitcher	Strikeouts
1921	Speed Martin	86
1922	Tiny Osborne	81
1923	Grover Alexander	72
	Tony Kaufmann	72
1924	Tony Kaufmann	79
1925	Sheriff Blake	93
1926	Charlie Root	127
1927	Charlie Root	145
1928	Pat Malone	155
1929*	Pat Malone	166
1930	Pat Malone	142
1931	Charlie Root	131
1932	Charlie Root	120
1933	Lon Warneke	133
1934	Lon Warneke	143
1935	Lon Warneke	120
1936	Lon Warneke	113
1937	Bill Lee	108
1938	Clay Bryant	135
1939	Claude Passeau	108
1940	Claude Passeau	124
1941	Paul Erickson	85
1942	Claude Passeau	89
1943	Claude Passeau	93
1944	Claude Passeau	89
1945	Claude Passeau	98
1946*	Johnny Schmitz	135
1947	Johnny Schmitz	97
1948	Johnny Schmitz	100
1949	Dutch Leonard	83
1950	Paul Minner	99
1951	Bob Rush	129
1952	Bob Rush	157
1953	Johnny Klippstein	113
1954	Bob Rush	124
1955*	Sam Jones	198
1956*	Sam Jones	176
1957	Dick Drott	170
	Moe Drabowsky	170
1958	Dick Drott	127
1959	Glen Hobbie	138
1960	Glen Hobbie	134
1961	Don Cardwell	156
1962	Dick Ellsworth	113
1963	Dick Ellsworth	185
1964	Larry Jackson	148
1965	Larry Jackson	131
1966	Ken Holtzman	171
1967	Fergie Jenkins	236

*Led League

Most Strikeouts by Pitcher, Season (Continued)

Year	Pitcher	Strikeouts
1968	Fergie Jenkins	260
1969*	Fergie Jenkins	273
1970	Fergie Jenkins	274
1971	Fergie Jenkins	263
1972	Fergie Jenkins	184
1973	Fergie Jenkins	170
1974	Bill Bonham	191
1975	Bill Bonham	165
1976	Rick Reuschel	146
1977	Rick Reuschel	166
1978	Rick Reuschel	115
1979	Lynn McGlothen	147
1980	Rick Reuschel	140
1981	Mike Krukow	101

*League Leader

200-or-More Strikeouts by Pitcher, Season

Year	Pitcher	Strikeouts
1880	Larry Corcoran	268
1883	Larry Corcoran	216
1884	Larry Corcoran	272
1885	John Clarkson	318
1886	John Clarkson	340
1887	John Clarkson	237
1890	Bill Hutchison	289
1891	Bill Hutchison	261
1892	Bill Hutchison	316
1901	Tom Hughes	225
1909	Orval Overall	205
1967	Fergie Jenkins	236
1968	Fergie Jenkins	260
1969	Fergie Jenkins	273
1970	Fergie Jenkins	274
	Ken Holtzman	202
1971	Fergie Jenkins	263

100-or-More Strikeouts by Pitcher, Season

Year	Pitcher	Strikeouts
1878	Frank Larkin	163
1879	Frank Larkin	142
1880	Larry Corcoran	268
1881	Larry Corcoran	150
1882	Larry Corcoran	170
	Fred Goldsmith	109
1883	Larry Corcoran	216

225

100-or-More Strikeouts by Pitcher, Season (Continued)

Year	Pitcher	Strikeouts
1884	Larry Corcoran	272
	John Clarkson	102
1885	John Clarkson	318
1886	John Clarkson	340
	Jim McCormick	172
	Jocko Flynn	146
1887	John Clarkson	237
	Mark Baldwin	164
1888	Gus Krock	161
	Mark Baldwin	157
	George Van Haltren	139
1889	Bill Hutchison	136
	John Tener	105
1890	Bill Hutchison	289
1891	Bill Hutchison	261
1892	Bill Hutchison	316
	Addison Gumbert	118
1897	Clark Griffith	102
1900	Virgil Garvin	107
1901	Tom Hughes	225
	Rube Waddell	168
1903	Jake Weimer	128
	Bob Wicker	110
1904	Jake Weimer	177
	Buttons Briggs	112
	Carl Lundgren	106
1905	Ed Reulbach	152
	Jake Weimer	107
1906	Jack Pfiester	153
	Mordecai Brown	144
	Carl Lundgren	103
1907	Orval Overall	141
	Mordecai Brown	107
1908	Orval Overall	167
	Ed Reulbach	133
	Mordecai Brown	123
	Jack Pfiester	117
1909	Orval Overall	205
	Mordecai Brown	172
	Ed Reulbach	105
1910	Mordecai Brown	143
	Len Cole	114
1911	Mordecai Brown	129
	Len Cole	101
1912	Larry Cheney	140
	Jimmy Lavender	109
1913	Larry Cheney	136
1914	Jim Vaughn	165
	Larry Cheney	157

100-or-More Strikeouts by Pitcher, Season (Continued)

Year	Pitcher	Strikeouts
1915	Jim Vaughn	148
	Jimmy Lavender	117
1916	Jim Vaughn	144
	Claude Hendrix	117
1917	Jim Vaughn	195
	Phil Douglas	151
1918	Jim Vaughn	148
	George Tyler	102
1919	Jim Vaughn	141
	Grover Alexander	121
1920	Grover Alexander	173
	Jim Vaughn	131
1926	Charlie Root	127
1927	Charlie Root	145
1928	Pat Malone	155
	Charlie Root	122
1929	Pat Malone	166
	Charlie Root	124
1930	Pat Malone	142
	Charlie Root	124
1931	Charlie Root	131
	Pat Malone	112
1932	Pat Malone	120
	Lon Warneke	106
1933	Lon Warneke	133
1934	Lon Warneke	143
	Pat Malone	111
	Bill Lee	104
1935	Lon Warneke	120
	Bill Lee	100
1936	Lon Warneke	113
	Larry French	104
	Bill Lee	102
1937	Bill Lee	108
	Tex Carleton	105
	Larry French	100
1938	Clay Bryant	135
	Bill Lee	121
1939	Claude Passeau	108
	Bill Lee	105
1940	Claude Passeau	124
	Larry French	107
1946	Johnny Schmitz	135
1948	Johnny Schmitz	100
1951	Bob Rush	129
1952	Bob Rush	157
	Johnny Klippstein	110
1953	Johnny Klippstein	113
	Warren Hacker	106

100-or-More Strikeouts by Pitcher, Season (Continued)

Year	Pitcher	Strikeouts
1954	Bob Rush	124
1955	Sam Jones	198
	Bob Rush	130
1956	Sam Jones	176
	Bob Rush	104
1957	Moe Drabowsky	170
	Dick Drott	170
	Bob Rush	103
	Don Elston	102
1958	Dick Drott	127
	Taylor Phillips	102
1959	Glen Hobbie	138
	Bill Henry	115
	Bob Anderson	113
1960	Glen Hobbie	134
	Don Cardwell	129
	Bob Anderson	115
1961	Don Cardwell	156
	Glen Hobbie	103
1962	Dick Ellsworth	113
	Bob Buhl	109
	Don Cardwell	104
1963	Dick Ellsworth	185
	Larry Jackson	153
	Bob Buhl	108
1964	Dick Ellsworth	148
	Larry Jackson	148
	Bob Buhl	107
1965	Larry Jackson	131
	Dick Ellsworth	130
	Ted Abernathy	104
1966	Ken Holtzman	171
	Fergie Jenkins	148
	Dick Ellsworth	144
1967	Fergie Jenkins	236
	Rich Nye	113
	Ray Culp	111
1968	Fergie Jenkins	260
	Ken Holtzman	151
	Bill Hands	148
1969	Fergie Jenkins	273
	Bill Hands	181
	Ken Holtzman	176
	Dick Selma	161
1970	Fergie Jenkins	274
	Ken Holtzman	202
	Bill Hands	170
1971	Fergie Jenkins	263
	Ken Holtzman	143
	Bill Hands	128

100-or-More Strikeouts by Pitcher, Season (Continued)

Year	Pitcher	Strikeouts
1972	Fergie Jenkins	184
	Burt Hooton	132
1973	Fergie Jenkins	170
	Rick Reuschel	168
	Burt Hooton	134
	Bill Bonham	121
1974	Bill Bonham	191
	Rick Reuschel	160
1975	Bill Bonham	165
	Rick Reuschel	155
	Steve Stone	139
	Ray Burris	108
1976	Rick Reuschel	146
	Ray Burris	112
	Steve Renko	112
	Bill Bonham	110
1977	Rick Reuschel	166
	Bill Bonham	134
	Bruce Sutter	129
	Mike Krukow	106
	Ray Burris	105
1978	Rick Reuschel	115
	Bruce Sutter	106
1979	Lynn McGlothen	147
	Rick Reuschel	125
	Mike Krukow	119
	Bruce Sutter	110
	Bill Caudill	104
1980	Rick Reuschel	140
	Mike Krukow	130
	Lynn McGlothen	119
	Bill Caudill	111
1981	Mike Krukow	101

500-or-More Strikeouts, Lifetime

Pitcher	Years	Total
Fergie Jenkins	(1966-1973)	1808
Charlie Root	(1926-1941)	1432
Rick Reuschel	(1972-1981)	1341
Bill Hutchison	(1889-1895)	1226
Jim Vaughn	(1913-1921)	1138
Larry Corcoran	(1880-1885)	1096
Bob Rush	(1948-1957)	1076
Mordecai Brown	(1904-1912; 1916)	1043
John Clarkson	(1884-1887)	997
Ken Holtzman	(1965-1971; 1978-1979)	988

500-or-More Strikeouts, Lifetime (Continued)

Pitcher	Years	Total
Dick Ellsworth	(1958; 1960-1966)	905
Bill Hands	(1966-1972)	900
Pat Malone	(1928-1934)	878
Bill Lee	(1934-1943; 1947)	874
Ed Reulbach	(1905-1913)	799
Claude Passeau	(1939-1947)	754
Orval Overall	(1906-1910; 1913)	727
Guy Bush	(1923-1934)	712
Lon Warneke	(1930-1936; 1942-1945)	706
Glen Hobbie	(1957-1964)	664
Larry French	(1935-1941)	642
Grover Alexander	(1918-1926)	614
Clark Griffith	(1893-1900)	573
Sheriff Blake	(1924-1931)	551
Johnny Schmitz	(1941-1942; 1946-1951)	550
Mike Krukow	(1976-	538
Carl Lundgren	(1902-1909)	535
Ray Burris	(1973-1979)	531
Don Elston	(1957-1964)	518
Larry Cheney	(1911-1915)	512

Most Strikeouts in a Game by Pitcher

Total	Pitcher	Date and Opponent	Place	Score
17	Jack Pfiester	May 30, 1906 vs. St. Louis	A	L 4-2 (15 inn.)
16	John Clarkson	Aug. 18, 1886 vs. Kansas City	H	W 7-2
15	Tom Hughes	July 31, 1901 vs. Cincinnati	A	L 5-4 (14 inn.)
15	Dick Drott	May 26, 1957 vs. Milwaukee	H	W 7-5
15	Burt Hooton	Sept. 15, 1971 vs. New York	A	W 3-2
14	Dick Drott	July 23, 1957 vs. New York	H	W 4-0
13	John Flynn	June 14, 1886 vs. Kansas City	H	W 6-1
13	Tom Hughes	Sept. 21, 1901 vs. Boston	H	W 1-0 (17 inn.)
13	Lon Warneke	April 17, 1934 vs. Cincinnati	A	W 6-0
13	Sam Jones	August 16, 1956 vs. Milwaukee	H	W 4-2

Fergie Jenkins delivers another strikeout pitch. His 1808 career total is the Cubs' all-time high.

Strikeout Records

Most Strikeouts, Lifetime — 1808, Fergie Jenkins (1966-1973)

Most Strikeouts, Season (50-Foot Pitching Distance) — 340, John Clarkson (1886)

Most Strikeouts, Season (60-Foot Pitching Distance) — 274, Fergie Jenkins (1970)

Most Strikeouts, Nine-Inning Game (50 Feet) — 16, John Clarkson, August 18, 1886

Most Strikeouts, Nine-Inning Game (60 Feet)
— 15, Dick Drott, May 26, 1957
— 15, Burt Hooton, September 15, 1971

Most Times, 200 Strikeouts Per Season — 5, Fergie Jenkins (1967-1971)

Most Times, 100 Strikeouts Per Season — 8, Fergie Jenkins (1966-1973)

Tickets to the 1945 World Series — the last one played in by the Cubs. Detroit won this world championship 4 games to 3.

6
FEATURES

THE CUBS IN
WORLD SERIES PLAY

To say that the Cubs have been outstanding in World Series competition would be an overstatement, since they have won only two series in modern times while losing eight, with a game record of 19 wins and 33 losses. Nevertheless, the fall classic has not been without its moments.

The first "subway series" took place in 1906 as the "Hitless Wonder" White Sox defeated the Cubs in six games, after the Cubs had won a record 116 games during the regular season. The main highlight for the Cubs came in the second game, October 10, when Ed Reulbach held the Sox to one hit, a single by Jiggs Donahue, in a 7-1 Cub victory.

The Cubs then rebounded by whipping the Detroit Tigers, 4 games to 0 (the first game was a tie called after 12 innings) in 1907 and 4 to 1 in '08, becoming the first team to win two consecutive series. In the 1907 series, the Cubs stole a record 18 bases, six by center-fielder Jimmy Slagle.

Unfortunately, things have not been the same since. In 1910, the Philadelphia A's mauled the Cubs, 4 games to 1, and eight years later the Boston Red Sox defeated them in six games, in a well-pitched series on both sides. Babe Ruth, who would haunt the Cubs later as a Yankee, beat them twice in this series as a Boston pitcher. Cub home games in the 1918 series, incidentally, were played at Comiskey Park becuse of its larger seating capacity.

Came 1929 as the Cubs won another pennant behind their "Murderer's Row" of Hack Wilson, Rogers Hornsby, Kiki Cuyler, and Riggs Stephenson. Despite their .303 team batting average and 140 homers in the regular season, the Cubs bowed to Connie Mack's Athletics in five games. Their worst humiliation came in game number four, October 12, when they went into the bottom of the seventh with an 8-0 lead, only to lose as the A's rallied for 10 runs and a 10-8 victory. The next day, Philadelphia won the series.

It was in the 1932 battle with the New York Yankees that the most celebrated play in Cub series history occurred. The scene was Wrigley Field in game number three, October 1, with the score tied at 4-4 in the top of the fifth and Charlie Root on the mound. Babe Ruth, after taking two strikes, pointed toward centerfield and supposedly "called his shot." Opinions are varied as to whether or not Ruth actually said he was going to hit Root's next offering into the bleachers. One thing is certain — Ruth did hit the home run as the Yankees won the game, 7-5, and the series in four straight.

The Yanks repeated the four-game sweep in 1938. In between drubbings by the Yankees, the Cubs lost to the Tigers in six games in 1935. Only Lon Warneke, who won both Cub victories, could tame them.

The last Cub world series to date was 1945, when the series went the full seven games before Detroit finally edged the Cubs. In the third game, October 5, Cub righthander Claude Passeau allowed the Tigers only one hit, a single by Rudy York in the second inning, as he shut them out, 3-0, at Detroit. But the Cubs' biggest thrill came in game six, October 8, at Wrigley Field. In the bottom of the 12th, Stan Hack's drive bounced over leftfielder Hank Greenberg's shoulder for a double to drive in the winning run, in an 8-7 Cub victory which tied up the series at three games apiece. But the Tigers clinched the title with a 9-3 win October 10, to finish the "most recent" chapter in Cub world series history.

Line Scores of World Series Games
1906
First game — October 9, at West Side Grounds

				R	H	E
Sox	000	011	000	2	4	1
Cubs	000	001	000	1	4	2

Second game — October 10, at South Side Grounds

				R	H	E
Cubs	031	001	020	7	10	2
Sox	000	010	000	1	1	2

Third game — October 11, at West Side Grounds

				R	H	E
Sox	000	003	000	3	4	1
Cubs	000	000	000	0	2	2

Fourth game — October 12, at South Side Grounds

				R	H	E
Cubs	000	000	100	1	7	1
Sox	000	000	000	0	2	1

Fifth game — October 13, at West Side Grounds

				R	H	E
Sox	102	401	000	8	12	6
Cubs	300	102	000	6	6	0

Sixth game — October 14, at South Side Grounds

				R	H	E
Cubs	100	010	001	3	7	0
Sox	340	000	01x	8	14	3

1907
First game — October 8, at Chicago

					R	H	E
Det.	000	000	030	000	3	9	3
Cubs	000	100	002	000	3	10	5

Line Scores of World Series Games (Continued)

Second game — October 9, at Chicago

Det.	010	000	000	1	9	1
Cubs	010	200	00x	3	9	1

Third game — October 10, at Chicago

Det.	000	001	000	1	6	1
Cubs	010	310	00x	5	10	1

Fourth game — October 11, at Detroit

Cubs	000	020	301	6	7	2
Det.	000	100	000	1	5	2

Fifth game — October 12, at Detroit

Cubs	110	000	000	2	7	1
Det.	000	000	000	0	7	2

1908

First game — October 10, at Detroit

Cubs	004	000	105	10	14	2
Det.	100	000	320	6	10	4

Second game — October 11, at Chicago

Det.	000	000	001	1	4	1
Cubs	000	000	06x	6	7	1

Third game — October 12, at Chicago

Det.	100	005	020	8	11	4
Cubs	000	300	000	3	7	2

Fourth game — October 13, at Detroit

Cubs	002	000	001	3	10	0
Det.	000	000	000	0	4	1

Fifth game — October 14, at Detroit

Cubs	100	010	000	2	10	0
Det.	000	000	000	0	3	0

1910

First game — October 17, at Philadelphia

Cubs	000	000	001	1	3	1
Phil.	021	000	01x	4	7	2

Second game — October 18, at Philadelphia

Cubs	100	000	101	3	8	3
Phil.	002	010	60x	9	14	4

Third game — October 20, at Chicago

Phil.	125	000	400	12	15	1
Cubs	120	000	020	5	6	1

Line Scores of World Series Games (Continued)

Fourth game — October 22, at Chicago

Phil.	001	200	000	0	3	11	3
Cubs	100	100	001	1	4	9	1

Fifth game — October 23, at Chicago

Phil.	100	010	050	7	9	1
Cubs	010	000	010	2	9	2

1918

First game — September 5, at Chicago

Bos.	000	100	000	1	5	0
Cubs	000	000	000	0	6	0

Second game — September 6, at Chicago

Bos.	000	000	001	1	6	1
Cubs	030	000	00x	3	7	1

Third game — September 7, at Chicago

Bos.	000	200	000	2	7	0
Cubs	000	010	000	7	1	1

Fourth game — September 9, at Boston

Cubs	000	000	020	2	7	1
Bos.	000	200	01x	3	4	0

Fifth game — September 10, at Boston

Cubs	001	000	020	3	7	0
Bos.	000	000	000	0	5	0

Sixth game — September 11, at Boston

Cubs	000	100	000	1	3	2
Bos.	002	000	00x	2	5	0

1929

First game — October 8, at Chicago

Phil.	000	000	102	3	6	1
Cubs	000	000	001	1	8	2

Second game — October 9, at Chicago

Phil.	003	300	120	9	12	0
Cubs	000	030	000	3	11	1

Third game — October 11, at Philadelphia

Cubs	000	003	000	3	6	1
Phil.	000	010	000	1	9	1

Fourth game — October 12, at Philadelphia

Cubs	000	205	100	8	10	2
Phil.	000	000	100	10	15	2

Line Scores of World Series Games (Continued)

Fifth game — October 14, at Philadelphia

Cubs	000	200	000	2	8	1
Phil.	000	000	003	3	6	0

1932

First game — September 28, at New York

Cubs	200	000	220	6	10	1
N.Y.	000	305	31x	12	8	2

Second game — September 29, at New York

Cubs	101	000	000	2	9	0
N.Y.	202	010	00x	5	10	1

Third game — October 1, at Chicago

N.Y.	301	020	001	7	8	1
Cubs	102	100	001	5	9	4

Fourth game — October 2, at Chicago

N.Y.	102	002	404	13	19	4
Cubs	400	001	001	6	9	1

1935

First game — October 2, at Detroit

Cubs	200	000	001	3	7	0
Det.	000	000	000	0	4	3

Second game — October 3, at Detroit

Cubs	000	010	200	3	6	1
Det.	400	300	10x	8	9	2

Third game — October 4, at Chicago

Det.	000	001	040	01	6	12	2
Cubs	020	010	002	00	5	10	3

Fourth game — October 5, at Chicago

Det.	001	001	000	2	7	0
Cubs	010	000	000	1	5	2

Fifth game — October 6, at Chicago

Det.	000	000	001	1	7	1
Cubs	002	000	10x	3	8	0

Sixth game — October 7, at Detroit

Cubs	001	020	000	3	12	0
Det.	100	101	001	4	12	1

1938

First game — October 5, at Chicago

N.Y.	020	000	100	3	12	1
Cubs	001	000	001	2	9	1

1945 WORLD SERIES CUBS' PLAYERS

Top Row: Lotshaw, Trainer - Wyse, P - Warneke, P - Starr, P - Erickson, P - Hanyzewski, P - R. Johnson, Coach - Signer, P - Sauer, OF - Hughes, IF - Schuster, IF - Stock, Coach

Middle Row: Passeau, P - Livingston, C - Derringer, P - Rice, C - Williams, C - Prim, P - Chipman, P - Vandenberg, P - Secory, OF - Becker, IF - Smith Coach.

Bottom Row: Hack, IF - Don Johnson, IF - Lowrey, OF - Cavarretta, IF - Pafko, OF - Grimm, Manager, Nicholson, OF - Gillispie, C - Merullo, IF - Borowy P.

Jimmie Chalikis, Bat Boy

Line Scores of World Series Games (Continued)

Second game — October 6, at Chicago

N.Y.	020	000	022	6	7	2
Cubs	102	000	000	3	11	0

Third game — October 8, at New York

Cubs	000	010	010	2	5	1
N.Y.	000	022	01x	5	7	2

Fourth game — October 9, at New York

Cubs	000	100	020	3	8	1
N.Y.	030	001	04x	8	11	1

1945

First game — October 3, at Detroit

Cubs	403	000	200	9	13	0
Det.	000	000	000	0	6	0

Second game — October 4, at Detroit

Cubs	000	100	000	1	7	0
Det.	000	040	00x	4	7	0

Third game — October 5, at Detroit

Cubs	000	200	100	3	8	0
Det.	000	000	000	0	1	2

Fourth game — October 6, at Chicago

Det.	000	400	000	4	7	1
Cubs	000	001	000	1	5	1

Fifth game — October 7, at Chicago

Det.	001	004	102	8	11	0
Cubs	001	000	201	4	7	2

Sixth game — October 8, at Chicago

Det.	010	000	240	000	7	13	1
Cubs	000	041	200	001	8	15	3

Seventh game — October 10, at Chicago

Det.	510	000	120	9	9	1
Cubs	100	100	010	3	10	0

World Series Batting Records

Player — Years	G	AB	R	H	2B	3B	HR	RBI	Pct.
Jimmy Archer (1910)	3	11	1	2	1	0	0	4	.143
Turner Barber (1918)	3	2	0	0	0	0	0	0	.000
Ginger Beaumont (1910)	3	2	1	0	0	0	0	0	.000
Heinz Becker (1945)	3	2	0	1	0	0	0	0	.500
Clarence Blair (1929)	1	1	0	0	0	0	0	0	.000

Mordecai "Three-Finger Brown — called that because he lost the first finger on his pitching hand below the second joint in a feed cutter when he was only five years old.

World Series Batting Records (Continued)

Player—Years	G	AB	R	H	2B	3B	HR	RBI	Pct.
Sheriff Blake (1929)	2	1	0	1	0	0	0	0	1.000
Hank Borowy (1945)	4	5	1	1	1	0	0	0	.200
Mordecai Brown									
(06-07-08-10)	9	20	0	2	0	0	0	0	.100
Clay Bryant (1938)	1	2	0	0	0	0	0	0	.000
Guy Bush (1929-32)	4	4	1	0	0	0	0	0	.000
Tex Carleton (1935-38)	2	1	0	0	0	0	0	0	.000
Hal Carlson (1929)	2	0	0	0	0	0	0	0	.000
Phil Cavarretta (1935-38-45)	17	63	9	20	3	0	1	5	.317
Frank Chance									
(1906-07-08-10)	20	71	11	22	3	1	0	6	.310
Bob Chipman (1945)	1	0	0	0	0	0	0	0	.000
King Cole (1910)	1	2	0	0	0	0	0	0	.000
Ripper Collins (1938)	4	15	1	2	0	0	0	0	.133
Kiki Cuyler (1929-32)	9	38	6	11	2	1	1	6	.289
Charlie Deal (1918)	6	17	0	3	0	0	0	0	.176
Dizzy Dean (1938)	2	3	0	2	0	0	0	0	.667
Frank Demaree (1932-35-38)	11	41	4	9	1	0	3	6	.219
Paul Derringer (1945)	3	0	0	0	0	0	0	0	.000
Phil Douglas (1918)	1	0	0	0	0	0	0	0	.000
Woody English (1929-32)	9	38	3	7	2	0	0	1	.184
Paul Erickson (1945)	4	0	0	0	0	0	0	0	.000
Johnny Evers									
(1906-07-08-10)	16	60	9	17	4	0	0	4	.283
Max Flack (1918)	6	19	2	5	0	0	0	1	.278
Larry French (1935-38)	5	4	1	1	0	0	0	0	.250
Augie Galan (1935-38)	8	27	2	4	1	0	0	2	.148
Paul Gillespie (1945)	3	6	0	0	0	0	0	0	.000
Mike Gonzalez (1929)	2	1	0	0	0	0	0	0	.000
Burleigh Grimes (1932)	2	1	0	0	0	0	0	0	.00
Charlie Grimm (1929-32)	9	33	4	12	2	0	1	5	.364
Marv Gudat (1932)	2	2	0	0	0	0	0	0	.000
Stan Hack (1932-35-38-45)	18	69	6	24	5	1	0	5	.348
Gabby Hartnett									
(1929-32-35-38)	16	54	3	13	2	1	2	3	.241
Cliff Heathcote (1929)	2	1	0	0	0	0	0	0	.000
Rollie Hemsley (1932)	3	3	0	0	0	0	0	0	.000
Claude Hendrix (1918)	2	1	0	1	0	0	0	0	1.000
Roy Henshaw (1935)	1	1	0	0	0	0	0	0	.000
Billy Herman (1932-35-38)	14	58	9	15	3	1	1	7	.259
Solly Hofman (1906-08-10)	16	57	7	17	1	1	0	8	.298
Charlie Hollocher (1918)	6	21	2	4	0	1	0	0	.190
Rogers Hornsby (1929)	5	21	4	5	1	1	0	1	.238
Del Howard (1907-08)	3	6	0	1	0	0	0	0	.167
Roy Hughes (1945)	6	17	1	5	1	0	0	3	.294
Don Johnson (1945)	7	29	4	5	2	1	0	0	.172
Billy Jurges (1932-35-38)	13	40	4	11	2	0	0	2	.275
John Kane (1910)	1	0	0	0	0	0	0	0	.000
Chuck Klein (1935)	5	12	2	4	0	0	1	2	.333

World Series Batting Records (Continued)

Player — Years	G	AB	R	H	2B	3B	HR	RBI	Pct.
Johnny Kling									
(1906-07-08-10)	21	65	6	12	2	0	0	3	.185
Mark Koenig (1932)	2	4	1	1	0	1	0	0	.250
Fabian Kowalik (1935)	1	2	1	1	0	0	0	0	.500
Tony Lazzeri (1938)	2	2	0	0	0	0	0	0	.000
Bill Lee (1935-38)	4	4	0	0	0	0	0	1	.000
Fred Lindstrom (1935)	4	15	0	3	1	0	0	1	.200
Mickey Livingston (1945)	6	22	3	8	3	0	0	4	.364
Peanuts Lowrey (1945)	7	29	4	9	1	0	0	0	.310
Pat Malone (1929-32)	4	4	0	1	1	0	0	0	.250
Les Mann (1918)	6	22	0	5	2	0	0	2	.227
Joe Marty (1938)	3	12	1	6	1	0	1	5	.500
Bill McCabe (1918)	3	1	1	0	0	0	0	0	.000
Clyde McCullough (1945)	1	1	0	0	0	0	0	0	.000
Harry McIntyre (1910)	2	1	0	0	0	0	0	0	.000
Norm McMillan (1929)	5	20	0	2	0	0	0	0	.091
Fred Merkle (1918)	6	18	1	5	0	0	0	1	.278
Lennie Merullo (1945)	3	2	0	0	0	0	0	0	.000
John Moore (1932)	2	7	1	0	0	0	0	0	.000
Pat Moran (1906-07)	3	2	0	0	0	0	0	0	.000
Tom Needham (1910)	1	1	0	0	0	0	0	0	.000
Art Nehf (1929)	2	0	0	0	0	0	0	0	.000
Bill Nicholson (1945)	7	28	1	6	1	1	0	8	.214
Ken O'Dea (1935-38)	4	6	1	2	0	0	1	2	.333
Bob O'Farrell (1918)	3	3	0	0	0	0	0	0	.000
Orval Overall									
(1906-07-08-10)	8	16	1	4	1	0	0	2	.250
Andy Pafko (1945)	7	28	5	6	2	1	0	2	.214
Vance Page (1938)	1	0	0	0	0	0	0	0	.000
Dode Paskert (1918)	6	21	0	4	1	0	0	2	.190
Claude Passeau (1945)	3	7	1	0	0	0	0	1	.000
John Pfeister (1906-07-08-10)	5	8	0	0	0	0	0	0	.000
Charlie Pick (1918)	6	18	2	7	1	0	0	0	.389
Ray Prim (1945)	2	0	0	0	0	0	0	0	.000
Ed Reulbach (1906-07-08-11)	7	11	0	1	0	0	0	2	.091
Carl Reynolds (1938)	4	12	0	0	0	0	0	0	.000
Lew Richie (1910)	1	0	0	0	0	0	0	0	.000
Charlie Root (1929-32-35-38)	6	7	0	0	0	0	0	0	.000
Eddie Sauer (1945)	2	2	0	0	0	0	0	0	.000
Frank Schulte									
(1906-07-08-10)	21	81	11	25	6	1	0	9	.309
Bill Schuster (1945)	2	1	1	0	0	0	0	0	.000
Frank Secory (1945)	5	5	0	2	0	0	0	0	.400
Jimmy Sheckard									
(1906-07-08-10)	21	77	7	14	6	0	0	5	.182
Jimmy Slagle (1907)	5	22	3	6	0	0	0	4	.273
Bob Smith (1932)	1	0	0	0	0	0	0	0	.000
Harry Steinfeldt									
(1906-07-08-10)	21	73	7	19	3	1	0	8	.260

World Series Batting Records (Continued)

Player—Years	G	AB	R	H	2B	3B	HR	RBI	Pct.
Riggs Stephenson (1929-32)	9	37	5	14	2	0	0	7	.378
Zack Taylor (1929)	5	17	0	3	0	0	0	3	.176
Joe Tinker (1906-07-08-10)	21	68	12	16	2	0	1	7	.235
Bud Tinning (1932)	2	0	0	0	0	0	0	0	.000
Chick Tolson (1929)	1	1	0	0	0	0	0	0	.000
Lefty Tyler (1918)	3	5	0	1	0	0	0	2	.200
Hy Vandenberg (1945)	3	1	0	0	0	0	0	0	.000
Hippo Vaughn (1918)	3	10	0	0	0	0	0	0	.000
Lon Warneke (1932-35)	5	9	0	1	0	0	0	0	.111
Dewey Williams (1945)	2	2	0	0	0	0	0	0	.000
Hack Wilson (1929)	5	17	2	8	0	1	0	0	.471
Bill Wortman (1918)	1	1	0	0	0	0	0	0	.000
Hank Wyse (1945)	3	3	0	0	0	0	0	0	.000
Rollie Zeider (1918)	2	0	0	0	0	0	0	0	.000
Heinie Zimmerman (1907-10)	6	18	0	4	1	0	0	4	.222
Totals		1,751	178	425	75	15	13	153	.243

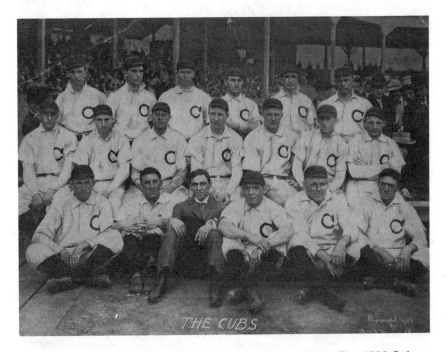

Winningest Team In History of Major League Baseball — The 1906 Cubs — These Chicagoans won 116 games while losing only 36 enroute to the Cubs' first pennant in the twentieth century.

In the 1945 World Series Claude Passeau pitched a one-hit masterpiece for a 3-0 victory.

World Series Pitching Records

Pitcher — Years	G	IP	CG	SH	H	R	ER	BB	SO	W	L	ERA
Sheriff Blake (1929)	2	1.1	0	0	4	2	2	0	1	0	1	13.50
Hank Borowy (1945)	4	18	1	1	21	8	8	6	8	2	2	4.00
Mordecai Brown (1906-07-08-10)	9	57.2	5	3	50	26	18	13	35	5	4	2.81
Guy Bush (1929-32)	4	16.2	1	0	17	12	10	8	6	1	1	5.40
Clay Bryant (1938)	1	5.1	0	0	6	4	4	5	3	0	1	6.75
Tex Carleton (1935-38)	2	7	1	0	7	4	3	11	6	0	1	3.86
Hal Carlson (1929)	2	4	0	0	7	3	3	1	3	0	0	6.75
Bob Chipman (1945)	1	.1	0	0	0	0	0	1	0	0	0	0.00
King Cole (1910)	1	8	0	0	10	3	3	3	5	0	0	3.38
Dizzy Dean (1938)	2	8.1	0	0	8	6	6	1	2	0	1	6.48
Paul Derringer (1945)	3	5.1	0	0	5	4	4	7	1	0	0	6.75
Phil Douglas (1918)	1	1	0	0	1	1	0	0	0	0	1	0.00
Larry French (1935-38)	5	14	1	0	16	6	5	3	10	0	2	3.21
Burleigh Grimes (1932)	2	2.2	0	0	7	7	7	2	0	0	0	23.63
Claude Hendrix (1918)	1	1	0	0	0	0	0	0	0	0	0	0.00
Roy Henshaw (1935)	1	3.2	0	0	2	3	3	5	2	0	0	7.36
Fabian Kowalik (1935)	1	4.1	0	0	3	1	1	1	1	0	0	2.08
Bill Lee (1935-38)	4	21.1	0	0	26	11	7	6	13	0	2	2.95
Pat Malone (1929-32)	4	15.2	1	0	13	9	6	11	15	0	2	3.45
Jakie May (1932)	2	4.2	0	0	9	7	6	3	4	0	1	11.57
Harry McIntire (1910)	2	5.1	0	0	4	5	4	3	3	0	1	6.75
Art Nehf (1929)	2	1	0	0	1	2	2	1	0	0	0	18.00
Orval Overall (1906-07-08-10)	8	51.1	3	1	37	11	9	15	35	3	1	1.58
Vance Page (1938)	1	1.1	0	0	2	2	2	0	0	0	0	13.50
Claude Passeau (1945)	3	16.2	1	1	7	5	5	8	3	1	0	2.70
Ray Prim (1945)	2	4	0	0	4	5	4	1	1	0	1	9.00
Ed Reulbach (06-07-08-10)	7	32.2	2	0	24	12	10	14	13	2	0	3.03
Lew Richie (1910)	1	1	0	0	1	0	0	0	0	0	0	0.00
Charlie Root (1929-32-35-38)	6	25.2	0	0	26	18	17	6	15	0	3	5.96
Jack Russell (1938)	2	1.2	0	0	1	0	0	1	0	0	0	0.00
Jack Pfiester (1906-07-08-10)	5	34	2	0	35	21	15	8	16	1	3	3.97
Bob Smith (1932)	1	1	0	0	2	1	1	0	1	0	0	9.00
Bud Tinning (1932)	2	2.1	0	0	0	0	0	0	3	0	0	0.00
Lefty Tyler (1918)	3	23	1	0	14	5	3	11	4	1	1	1.17
Hy Vandenberg (1945)	3	6	0	0	1	0	0	3	3	0	0	0.00
Hippo Vaughn (1918)	3	27	3	1	17	3	3	5	17	1	2	1.00
Lon Warneke (1932-35)	5	27.1	2	1	24	8	8	9	13	2	1	2.63
Hank Wyse (1945)	3	7.2	0	0	8	7	6	4	1	0	1	7.04
Totals		469.1	24	8	420	222	185	176	243	19	33	3.55

All-Star Hank Sauer (left) compares his bat with teammate Andy Pafko's.

THE CUBS
ALL-STAR STORY

In the 47-year history of the All-Star Game many members of the Chicago Cubs have played the hero's role. Such batters as Augie Galan, Hank Sauer, Ron Santo, Jim Hickman and Bill Madlock have delivered the winning blow for the National League in All-Star clashes. And Cub pitchers have been credited with four victories: Bob Rush, Larry Jackson and Bruce Sutter, with Sutter flashing his split-fingered fastball to gain back-to-back triumphs in 1978 and 1979.

Cub batsmen boast a lifetime batting average of .289 in All-Star competition with 58 base hits in 201 at bats, including five doubles, six triples and five homers.

Let's take a trip down memory lane and review the Cub exploits.

Back in 1936 the Cub quartet of Galan, Gabby Hartnett, Billy Herman and Frank Demaree collected five of the NL's nine hits in a 4-3 victory, a first for the senior circuit after three failures.

Hartnett produced a run-scoring triple and Galan, a two-run homer. The winning manager? A Cub — Charlie Grimm.

In the 1940 classic, Herman added three hits and Stan Hack had three more in 1943. And in the 1944 renewal Phil Cavarretta and Bill Nicholson supplied the one-two punch in a 7-1 NL rout.

Nicholson, in a pinch-hitting role, doubled off the rightfield wall and drove in the tying run to ignite a four-run fifth inning. "Cavy," meanwhile, set an All-Star record by reaching base five times on a triple, two singles and two walks.

Cub bats remained silent until 1952 when the contest moved to Philadelphia's Connie Mack Stadium. Thunder clouds were forming as the tobacco-chewing Sauer strode to the plate with the NL trailing 2-1 in the fourth inning.

Sauer then supplied some thunder of his own by unloading a two-run homer into the leftfield seats. Sauer's clout must have shook a few clouds as the game was called after five innings. The winning pitcher on that rain-soaked afternoon was another Cub, Bob Rush.

Three years later, Randy Jackson's clutch-RBI single to right sparked a three-run rally that enabled the NL to tie the score 5-5. St. Louis' Stan Musial's first pitch-hit homer, leading off the bottom of the 12th inning, gave the NL a 6-5 triumph.

Cub pitcher Larry Jackson had a brief stint in the 1963 game, but gained the victory as the NL prevailed 5-3. And Santo's single in the seventh inning drove in the deciding run as the NL edged the AL 6-5 in 1965.

When baseball historians review the 1970 All-Star clash, they'll always picture Pete Rose bowling over catcher Ray Fosse at home plate to score the winning run in the 12th inning. But who was the lanky batter who delivered the clutch hit in the 5-4 NL triumph? It was Jim Hickman of the Cubs.

In 1975 a chunky little swatter named Bill Madlock got his opportunity in the ninth inning. The bases were loaded and Rich Gossage of the crosstown White Sox was on the mound.

The Goose wound up and zipped a fastball plateward. Madlock uncoiled his short stroke, and the Goose was cooked. Billy singled down the leftfield line to snap a 3-3 tie and help the NL to a 6-3 victory.

And then Bruce Sutter and his split-fingered fastball entered the All-Star scene. In 1978, Sutter retired all five batters he faced, striking out AL homer king Jim Rice, and gained credit for a 7-3 victory.

Sutter fanned three batters in a 1979 encore and again was the winning pitcher as the NL prevailed 7-6.

Cubs All-Star Batting Averages

Player	G	AB	R	H	2B	3B	HR	RBI	Avg.
George Altman	3	3	1	1	0	0	1	1	.333
Gene Baker	1	1	0	0	0	0	0	0	.000
Ernie Banks	13	33	4	10	3	1	1	3	.303
Glenn Beckert	4	7	0	0	0	0	0	0	.000
Bill Buckner	1	1	0	0	0	0	0	0	.000
Phil Cavarretta	3	4	1	2	0	1	0	0	.500
Rip Collins	2	3	0	1	0	0	0	0	.333
Kiki Cuyler	1	2	0	0	0	0	0	0	.000
Curt Davis	1	0	0	0	0	0	0	0	.000
Frank Demaree	2	8	1	2	0	0	0	0	.250
Don Elston	1	0	0	0	0	0	0	0	.000
Woody English	1	1	0	0	0	0	0	0	.000
Larry French	1	0	0	0	0	0	0	0	.000
Augie Galan	1	5	1	2	0	0	1	2	.400
Stan Hack	4	15	2	6	0	0	0	0	.400
Gabby Hartnett	5	10	2	2	0	1	0	1	.200
Billy Herman	8	22	3	9	1	1	0	0	.405
Jim Hickman	1	4	0	1	0	0	0	1	.250
Randy Hundley	1	1	0	0	0	0	0	0	.000
Larry Jackson	1	1	0	0	0	0	0	0	.000
Randy Jackson	2	5	1	1	0	0	0	1	.200
Fergie Jenkins	2	1	0	0	0	0	0	0	.000
Sam Jones	1	0	0	0	0	0	0	0	.000
Don Kessinger	6	12	1	3	0	1	0	1	.250
Ralph Kiner	1	1	0	0	0	0	0	0	.000
Chuck Klein	1	3	0	1	0	0	0	1	.333
Bill Lee	2	1	0	0	0	0	0	0	.000
P-Nuts Lowrey	1	2	0	1	0	0	0	0	.500
Bill Madlock	1	2	0	1	0	0	0	2	.500
Jerry Morales	1	0	1	0	0	0	0	0	.000
Bill Nicholson	4	6	1	1	1	0	0	1	.167
Andy Pafko	4	10	0	4	0	0	0	0	.400
Claude Passeau	3	2	0	0	0	0	0	0	.000
Rick Reuschel	1	0	0	0	0	0	0	0	.000
Bob Rush	1	1	0	0	0	0	0	0	.000
Ron Santo	8	15	1	5	0	0	0	3	.333
Hank Sauer	2	4	1	1	0	0	1	3	.250
Johnny Schmitz	1	0	0	0	0	0	0	0	.000
Bruce Sutter	3	0	0	0	0	0	0	0	.000
Manny Trillo	1	1	0	0	0	0	0	0	.000
Eddie Waitkus	1	0	0	0	0	0	0	0	.000
Lee Walls	1	1	0	0	0	0	0	0	.000
Lon Warneke	3	2	1	1	0	1	0	0	.500
Billy Williams	6	11	2	3	0	0	1	2	.273
Don Zimmer	1	1	0	0	0	0	0	0	.000
Totals		202	24	58	5	6	5	22	.287

Cubs All-Star Pitching Averages (Continued)

Player	G	IP	H	R	BB	SO	W	L	ERA
Curt Davis	1	2/3	4	3	1	0	0	0	54.00
Don Elston	1	1	1	0	0	1	0	0	0.00
Larry French	1	2	1	0	0	2	0	0	0.00
Larry Jackson	1	2	4	2	0	3	1	0	9.00
Fergie Jenkins	2	4	6	3	0	6	0	0	6.75
Sam Jones	1	2/3	0	0	2	1	0	0	0.00
Bill Lee	2	6	4	3	4	6	0	1	4.50
Claude Passeau	3	7-2/3	9	7	3	4	0	2	7.88
Rick Reuschel	1	1	1	0	0	0	0	0	0.00
Bob Rush	1	2	4	1	1	1	1	0	4.50
Johnny Schmitz	1	1/3	3	3	1	0	0	1	81.00
Bruce Sutter	2	3-2/3	2	0	1	5	2	0	0.00
Lon Warneke	3	7-1/3	10	5	6	5	0	0	6.42
Totals		37-1/3	40	27	19	34	4	4	6.51

All-Star Bruce Sutter delivers the pitch he made famous—the split-fingered fastball.

AWARDS
(First Year of Award in Parenthesis)

MOST VALUABLE PLAYER (1911)
1911 Frank Schulte (Chalmers Award)
1929 Rogers Hornsby (League Award)
1935 Gabby Hartnett
1945 Phil Cavarretta
1952 Hank Sauer
1958 Ernie Banks
1959 Ernie Banks

CY YOUNG (1956)
1971 Fergie Jenkins
1979 Bruce Sutter

ROOKIE OF THE YEAR (1947)
1961 Billy Williams
1962 Ken Hubbs

FIREMAN OF THE YEAR (1960)
1963 Lindy McDaniel
1965 Ted Abernathy
1968 Phil Regan
1979 Bruce Sutter

SPORTING NEWS PLAYER OF THE YEAR (1948)
1952 Hank Sauer
1958 Ernie Banks
1959 Ernie Banks
1972 Billy Williams

SPORTING NEWS PITCHER OF THE YEAR (1948)
1971 Fergie Jenkins

Billy Williams was named The National League's Rookie of the Year in 1961 and the Sporting News' Player of the Year in 1972.

NICKNAMES

How the Cubs got Their Name

Can you imagine Ernie Banks as "Mr. Spud?"

The Spuds are just one of the many nicknames the Cubs have sported in their 106-year history in the National League. Over the years the ballclub was known as the White Stockings, Black Stockings, Colts, Rainmakers, Orphans, Cowboys, Rough Riders, Desert Rangers, Remnants, Panamas, Zephyrs, Nationals, Spuds, Trojans, and finally, Cubs.

When the NL was organized in 1876, the Chicago franchise adopted the name White Stockings because the team uniform included white hose. Under the leadership of manager-pitcher Albert Spalding and captain Cap Anson, the White Stockings won the first NL pennant.

Spalding soon was elevated to the presidency and Anson was appointed manager. During Anson's reign the White Stockings created baseball's first dynasty, winning five pennants from 1880 through 1886.

In 1888, a new uniform was adopted: white jerseys and knickers, blue lettering, blue caps and black socks. Accordingly, the White Stockings became the Black Stockings. But that name was shortlived.

Two seasons later a player union was formed, calling itself the Brotherhood of Professional Base Ball Players. Among its grievances were the salary limit and the reserve clause. Nearly all of Anson's players jumped to the newly formed Players League.

Anson had to rebuild his team that was composed of a lot of half-broken "Colts." The newspapers soon adopted the name Colts and Cap Anson became Pop Anson.

In mockery of sports writers who were suggesting that he was too old to play at age 40, Anson donned a false white beard for one game. He went 0-for-3 with one walk, but the frisky Colts defeated the Boston Beaneaters (Braves), 5-3.

After becoming the first player to reach the 3,000-hit plateau and the oldest to hit a home run at age 40, Anson was fired in 1897. Without Anson the Colts became the Orphans.

The Orphans stuck for a brief, wet interlude. In 1898 a number of early season games were rained out and the ballclub became the Rainmakers.

The following season the team held spring training at a ranch in New Mexico and newspapermen were sending daily dispatches about the Cowboys and Rough Riders. One account even referred to them as the Desert Rangers. Then it was back to Orphans again.

The new century brought new problems. The American League was formed in 1901 and declared itself a major league. On the South Side of town, owner-manager Charles Comiskey not only stole the Orphans' star pitcher, Clark Griffith, but he took the storied name, White Stockings, for his ballclub.

Almost immediately, the newspapers began shortening the name to White Sox and, in 1904 the abbreviated version was officially adopted as the club nickname.

Meanwhile, the Orphans with their ranks depleted, were quickly relabeled the Remnants. But that name was too demeaning and it was dropped the following season. That's when the first mention of Cubs appeared.

The Chicago Daily News of March 27, 1902, in an unsigned sports column, noted that "manager Frank Selee will devote his strongest efforts on the team work of the new Cubs this year."

The name has been credited to sports reporter George Rice, and at other times to headline writer Chris Sinsabaugh. Anyway, Daily News sports editor Fred Rayner took a liking to the name and that paper used it exclusively.

Other nicknames were appearing with regularity. Following a trip to Panama, several players returned with straw hats and the team was commonly referred to as the Panamas.

The Interocean and Journal then joined the Daily News and began using the Cubs on a fulltime basis. But the Tribune, after failing to revive the Colts, substituted Zephyrs and Nationals. That paper called the team the Third Nationals or Fourth Nationals, depending on its standings in the pennant race.

During the winter of 1905, the club was purchased by Charles A. Murphy, giving rise to a new nickname, the Spuds. The name was more of a tongue-in-cheek Irish joke, but the Tribune stayed with the Spuds.

Frank Chance replaced Selee as manager late in the 1905 season and he preferred the name Cubs. This was the Chance of Tinker-to-Evers-to-Chance fame, and under his leadership the team won four pennants in five seasons.

By 1907, even the Tribune recognized them as the Cubs, and in 1908 a Cub emblem was put on the uniform — a large C enclosing a bear cub carrying a baseball bat.

In 1913, Johnny Evers succeeded Chance as Cub manager and Tribune writer Ring Lardner called the team the Trojans after Evers' hometown, Troy, N.Y. It's a good thing Evers wasn't a native of Shamokin, Pa.

But the Trojans never caught on, and they remained the beloved Cubbies down through the eras of Grover Alexander, Hack Wilson, Charlie Grimm, Gabby Hartnett, and Ernie Banks, "Mr. Cub."

Nicknames Used by the Chicago National League Baseball Club Inc.

White Stockings, 1876-1894
Colts, 1887-1906
Black Stockings, 1888-1889
Ex-Colts, 1898
Rainmakers, 1898
Orphans, 1898-1902
Cowboys, 1899
Rough Riders, 1899-1900
Remnants, 1901-1902
Cubs, 1902 to date
Recruits, 1902
Panamas, 1903
Zephyrs, 1905
Nationals, 1905-1907
Spuds, 1906
Trojans, 1913

Names Most Frequently Used

White Stockings, 1876-1889
Colts, 1890-1897
Orphans, 1898-1901
Colts, 1902-1904
Cubs, 1905 to date

Player Nicknames

ADONIS
Bill Terry

ANTELOPE
Emil Verban

**ARKANSAS
HUMMING BIRD**
Lon Warneke

AVAILABLE
Sheldon Jones

BABE
Floyd Herman
Clarence Twombly
Ellsworth Dahlgren

BAD BILL
Bill Dahlen
Bill Eagan

BALD EAGLE
Frank Isbell

BARNEY
Gustaf Friberg
George Schultz

BARON
George Mitterwald

BEAR
Frank Baumann

BEAR TRACKS
Johnny Schmitz

BEAST
Jimmy Foxx

BIG BIRD
Dave Kingman

BINGO
Ernie Banks

BIRD EYE
Harry Truby

BILLY BUCK
Bill Buckner

BLACKIE
Gus Mancuso

BOOTS
Charles Day
George Grantham

BRAT
Eddie Stanky

BROADWAY
Billy Schuster

BOBO
Norman Newsom

BUB
Norm McMillan

BUBBA
Emory Church

BUBBLES
Eugene Hargrave

BUCK
Bill Buckner
William Congalton
Alex Freeman
Charles Herzog
Norman Newsom

BUCKSHOT
Tommy Brown

BUD
Lyle Tinning

BUDDY
Shelton Napier
Charles Schultz

BULL
Leon Durham

BUNIONS
Rollie Zeider

BUTTONS
Herb Briggs

CAP
Adrian Anson

CASEY
Kendall Wise

CATFISH
George Metkovich

CHEROKEE
Bill Fisher

CHEWING GUM
John O'Brien

CHIEF
Virgil Cheeves
Vallie Eaves

CHICK
Art Ceccarelli
Charles Fraser
Charles Pedroes
Chester Tolson

CHICO
Sal Hernandez

CHINSKI
Charlie Root

CHIPPY
George Gaw

CHOPPY
Jimmy Adair

CHRIS
Everett Krug

CHUCK
Kevin Connors
Charles Klein
Bill Wortman

CIRCUS SOLLY
Art Hofman

CLAY
Claiborne Bryant

COLDWATER
Jim Hughey

COZY
Pat Dolan

COONSKIN
Curt Davis

COWBOY
Ray Harrell

CRAB
Johnny Evers

CUNO
Facundo Barragan

CUPID
Clarence Childs

CY
Seymour Block
Fred Williams

Player Nicknames (Continued)

DAD
William Clarke

DEACON
Jim White

DEERFOOT
Thomas Needham

DILLY
Steve Dillard

DIM DOM
Dominic Dallessandro

DING DONG
Dave Kingman

DIRT
Dick Tidrow

DIZZY
Jay Dean

DOC
James Casey
Walter Curley
Edward Farrell
Roy Miller
Harley Parker

DODE
George Paskert

DOUBLE X
Jimmy Foxx

DUKE
Herb Brett
Paul Derringer
Charles Farrell
Gordon Massa
Tom Simpson

DUKE OF TRALEE
Roger Bresnahan

DUMMY
Danny Lynch

DUSTY
Bob Rhoades

DUTCH
Heinz Becker
Jim Bolger
Herman Bronkie
Emil Leonard
Bob McCall

DUTCH (Continued)
Lambert Meyer
John Rudolph
Walter Reuther
Art Schult
Art Wilson
Ed Zwilling

EGYPTIAN
John Healy

EVERYDAY
Don Elston

FIDDLER
Frank Corridon

FIDGETY PHIL
Phil Collins

FOOTSIE
Clarence Blair

FORDHAM FLASH
Frankie Frisch

FRITZ
Fred Mollwitz

FUZZY
Fred Richards

GABBY
Charles Hartnett

GABE
Bill Gabler

GEE GEE
Jim Gleeson

GERMANY
Herman Schaefer

GIG
Norm Gigon

GILLY
William Campbell

GINGER
Clarence Beaumont

GINK
Harvey Hendrick

GRANDMOTHER
Phil Powers

GREEK
Charles George

GUS
August Mancuso

HACK
Lawrence Miller
Lewis Wilson

HANDSOME HARRY
Harry Taylor

HANDSOME RANSOM
Ransom Jackson

HANK
Henry Borowy
Henry Aguirre
Henry Edwards
Henry Leiber
Henry Sauer
Henry Schenz
Henry Schreiber
Henry Gornicki
Henry Wyse

HANDY ANDY
Andy Pafko

HARDROCK
Roy Johnson
Clyde Shoun

HARRY THE HAT
Harry Walker

HEAT
George Riley

HEINIE
Henry Zimmerman

HEITY
Hector Cruz

HIGHPOCKETS
George Kelly

HIPPO
Jim Vaughn

HORN
Ed Sauer

HOOKS
Henry Wyse

HOOT
Hal Rice

HUSK
Frank Chance

Player Nicknames (Continued)

HY
Harold Vandenberg

IKE
Charles Van Zandt

JACK THE GIANT KILLER
John Pfiester

JAKE
Merwyn Jacobson
Paul Jaeckel
J.T. Mooty

JAKIE
Frank May

JELLY
Frank Jelincich

JERRY
Julio Morales

JIGGER
Arnold Statz

JIGGS
Walter Parrott

JITTERY JOE
Joe Berry

JOCKO
John Flynn
John Menefee

JOLLY CHOLLY
Charlie Grimm

JOSH
Charles Reilly

JUG
Dave Gerard

JUMBO
Bob Barrett
Walter Brown

KANGAROO
Davey Jones

KEWPIE
Dick Barrett

KID
Winfield Camp
Blaine Durbin
Mal Eason

KID (Continued)
Roy Henshaw
Willie McGill

KIKI
Hazen Cuyler

KING
Len Cole
Mike Kelly
Fred Lear

KITTY
William Bransfield

KONG
Dave Kingman

LEFTY
Fred Baczewski
Howie Fitzgerald
Wilbur Good
Al Leifield
Paul Minner
George Tyler

LIL ABNER
Paul Erickson

LINE DRIVE
Lynn Nelson

LINK
Bobby Lowe

LIP
Leo Durocher

LITTLE EVA
Bill Lange

LONG TOM
Tom Hughes

MAD MONK
Russ Meyer

MAD RUSSIAN
Lou Novikoff

MAGNET
Bob Addy

MANDY
Jonathon Brooks

MICK
Michael Kelleher

MICKEY
Art Kreitner
Thompson Livingston
Arnold Owen

MINER
Mordecai Brown

MISSISSIPPI MUDCAT
Guy Bush

MISTER CHIPS
Bob Chipman

MISTER CUB
Ernie Banks

MOE
Myron Drabowsky
Meredith Morhardt
Morris Thacker
Seth Morehead

MONK
Walt Dubiel

MOOSE
Gordon Massa
Walt Moryn

MOONLIGHT ACE
Fred Fussell

MUNCKY
Mick Kelleher

NED
Ed Williamson
Virgil Garvin

NICK
Paul Carter
Bill Nicholson

NIXEY
Jimmy Callahan

NOISY
Johnny Kling

OLD FOX
Clark Griffith

OLD HOSS
Riggs Stephenson

OLD RELIABLE
Joe Start

Player Nicknames (Continued)

OL' STUBBLEBEARD
Burleigh Grimes

OX
John Miller

PANCHO
Jorge Comellas

PARD
Al Epperly

PATCHEYE
Johnny Gill

PATSY
Oliver Tebeau

PEACHES
George Graham

PEERLESS LEADER
Frank Chance

PEP
Don Johnson

PETE
Grover Alexander
Milo Allison
Floyd Scott

PHILLIBUCK
Phil Cavarretta

PIANO LEGS
George Gore

PICKLES
Bill Dillhoefer

PINKY
Charles Pittenger

P-NUTS
Harry Lowrey

POLLY
Howard McLarry

POOSH EM UP
Tony Lazzeri

POP
Adrian Anson
Roy Joiner
Ed Lytle
Bill Schriver
Ray Prim

PORKY
Doyle Lade

POSS
Eul Eubanks

PROFESSOR
Jim Brosnan

PRUNES
George Moolic

PRUSHKA
Andy Pafko

PUD
William McChesney

RABBIT
Cecil Garriott
George Maranville
Jimmy Slagle

RAJAH
Rogers Hornsby

REBEL
Karl Adams
Randy Hundley

RED
Charles Adams
John Corridon
Jerome Downs
Japhet Lynn
Benn Mann
Robert Thomas

REINDEER BILL
Bill Killefer

RICK
Robert Monday

RIP
Zeriah Hagerman
Glen Russell

RIPPER
James Collins

ROB
Richard Gardner

ROCKS
Harry McIntyre

ROLLIE
Ralston Hemsley

ROLY POLY
Ron Northey

ROWDY RICHARD
Dick Bartell

RUBE
Ralph Novotney
George Waddell
Al Walker

SAD SAM
Sam Jones

SAGE
Roy Hughes

SANDOW
Sam Mertes

SCOOPS
Jimmy Cooney

SCRAPPY
Cliff Carroll

SHAD
John Barry

SHADOW
Harry Pyle

SHERIFF
John Blake
Charlie Gassaway

SHORTY
Jimmy Slagle
Bob Raudman

SHUFFLIN' PHIL
Phil Douglas

SILVER
Frank Flint

SKIP
Gene Mauch

SLIM
Grover Lowdermilk

SMOKY
Forrest Burgess

SNAPPER
Sherman Kennedy

SOLDIER
Alex Carson

Player Nicknames (Continued)

SPARKY Earl Adams	**THREE STAR** George Hennessey	**TWITCH** Marv Rickert
STATEN ISLAND SCOT Bobby Thomson	**TIDO** Tom Daly	**UNZER FRITZ** Fred Pfeffer
SPEED Elwood Martin	**TOBY** Maurice Atwell	**VULTURE** Phil Regan
SUGAR Les Sweetland	**TOOTHPICK** Sam Jones	**WEE** Tommy Leach
SWATS Carl Sawatski	**TOPSY** Tullos Hartsel	**WHITEY** Carroll Lockman
SWEETBREADS Abraham Bailey	George Magoon	**WILD BILL** Bill Hutchison
SWISH Bill Nicholson Steve Swisher	**TORNADO JAKE** Jake Weimer **TOT** Forest Pressnell	**WILDFIRE** Frank Schulte **WILLIE THE KNUCK** Willard Ramsdell
SY Elmer Sutcliffe	**TRADER** Berlyn Horne	**WIMPY** Wellington Quinn
TALL PAUL Paul Minner	**TROJAN** Johnny Evers	**WOODY** Elwood English
TARZAN Roy Parmelee Walter Stephenson Joe Wallis	**TROLLEY LINE** Johnny Butler **TURK** Omar Lown	**ZACK** James Taylor **ZAZA** Erwin Harvey
T-BONE Taylor Phillips	**TWIG** Wayne Terwilliger	**ZEKE** Henry Bonura
TEX James Carleton	**TWIGGY** Chuck Hartenstein	**ZIP** George Zabel
THREE FINGER Mordecai Brown		

BALLPARKS

Ballparks Where the Cubs Have Played

23rd Street Grounds, 1876-1877
Location: 23rd and State Streets
First game: May 10, 1876 — Chicago 6, Cincinnati 0

Lakefront Park, 1878-1884
Location: South of Randolph Street between Michigan Avenue and the Illinois Central
    Railroad tracks
First game: May 14, 1878 — Indianapolis 5, Chicago 3

Wrigley Field scoreboard construction 1937.

Wrigley Field construction 1937.

Wrigley Field, 1938.

The corner of Addison and Sheffield Avenues.

Ballparks Where the Cubs Have Played (Continued)

West Side Park, 1885-1892
Location: Congress and Throop Streets
First game: June 6, 1885 — Chicago 9, St. Louis 2

West Side Grounds, 1893-1915
Location: Polk and Lincoln (Wolcott) Streets
First game: May 14, 1893 — Cincinnati 13, Chicago 12

Wrigley Field, 1916 to present
Location: Addison and Clark Streets
First game: April 20, 1916 — Chicago 7, Cincinnati 6

Note: In the seasons of 1891 and 1892, the Cubs occasionally played home games at the 35th Street Grounds, 35th Street and Wentworth Avenue, which had been the home of the Chicago Players League team in 1890. The Cubs again used this park briefly in 1894, after the West Side Grounds had been partially destroyed by fire.

HALL OF FAME

Cubs in the Hall of Fame
(Year elected in parenthesis)

Grover Alexander (1938)   Mordecai Brown (1949)
Albert Spalding (1939)   Gabby Hartnett (1955)
Cap Anson (1939)   Joe McCarthy (1957)
Rogers Hornsby (1942)   John Clarkson (1963)
King Kelly (1945)   Kiki Cuyler (1968)
Joe Tinker (1946)   Billy Herman (1975)
Johnny Evers (1946)   Ernie Banks (1977)
Frank Chance (1946)   Hack Wilson (1979)
Clark Griffith (1946)

Others Who Have Worn Cub Uniforms That Are Enshrined
(Year elected in parenthesis)

Roger Bresnahan (1945)   Burleigh Grimes (1964)
Hugh Duffy (1945)   Lou Boudreau (1970)
Rube Waddell (1946)   George Kelly (1973)
Frankie Frisch (1947)   Ralph Kiner (1975)
Jimmy Foxx (1951)   Fred Lindstrom (1976)
Dizzy Dean (1953)   Chuck Klein (1980)
Rabbit Maranville (1954)

Selected Cubs in National Baseball Hall Of Fame

GROVER CLEVELAND ALEXANDER
GREAT NATIONAL LEAGUE PITCHER
FOR TWO DECADES WITH PHILLIES,
CUBS AND CARDINALS STARTING
IN 1911. WON 1926 WORLD CHAMPIONSHIP
FOR CARDINALS BY STRIKING OUT
LAZZERI WITH BASES FULL IN
FINAL CRISIS AT YANKEE STADIUM.

ADRIAN CONSTANTINE ANSON
"CAP"
GREATEST HITTER AND GREATEST
NATIONAL LEAGUE PLAYER-MANAGER
OF 19TH CENTURY. STARTED WITH
CHICAGO IN NATIONAL LEAGUE'S
FIRST YEAR 1876. CHICAGO MANAGER
FROM 1879 TO 1897, WINNING 5 PENNANTS.
WAS .300 CLASS HITTER 20 YEARS,
BATTING CHAMPION 4 TIMES.

MORDECAI PETER BROWN
(THREE-FINGERED AND MINER)
MEMBER OF CHICAGO N.L. CHAMPIONSHIP
TEAM OF 1906,'07,'08,'10. A RIGHT HANDED
PITCHER. WON 239 GAMES DURING MAJOR
LEAGUE CAREER THAT ALSO INCLUDED
ST. LOUIS AND CINCINNATI N.L. AND CLUBS
IN F.L. FIRST MAJOR LEAGUER TO PITCH
FOUR CONSECUTIVE SHUTOUTS, ACHIEVING
THIS FEAT ON JUNE 13, JUNE 25, JULY 2
AND JULY 4 IN 1908.

FRANK LEROY CHANCE
FAMOUS LEADER OF CHICAGO CUBS. WON
PENNANT WITH CUBS IN FIRST FULL SEASON
AS MANAGER IN 1906. THAT TEAM COMPILED
116 VICTORIES UNEQUALLED IN MAJOR
LEAGUE HISTORY. ALSO WON PENNANTS
IN 1907, 08 AND 1910 WORLD SERIES
WINNER IN 07 AND 08. STARTED WITH
CHICAGO IN 1898. ALSO MANAGER
NEW YORK A.L. AND BOSTON A.L.

JOHN GIBSON CLARKSON
WORCESTER, N.L. 1882
CHICAGO, N.L. 1884-87
BOSTON, N.L. 1888-92
CLEVELAND, N.L. 1892-94
PITCHED 4 TO 0 NO-HIT GAME AGAINST
PROVIDENCE IN 1885. WON 328 LOST 173
PCT. 652 LED LEAGUE WITH 53 VICTORIES
IN 1885 (INCLUDING 10 SHUTOUTS) 36 IN
1887, 49 IN 1888 AND 49 IN 1889. HAD
2013 STRIKEOUTS IN 4514 INNINGS.

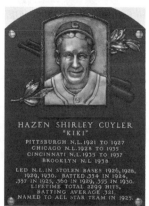

HAZEN SHIRLEY CUYLER
"KIKI"
PITTSBURGH N.L. 1921 TO 1927
CHICAGO N.L. 1928 TO 1935
CINCINNATI N.L. 1935 TO 1937
BROOKLYN N.L. 1938
LED N.L. IN STOLEN BASES 1926, 1928,
1929, 1930. BATTED .354 IN 1924,
.357 IN 1925, .360 IN 1929, .355 IN 1930.
LIFETIME TOTAL 2299 HITS,
BATTING AVERAGE .321.
NAMED TO ALL STAR TEAM IN 1925.

JOHN JOSEPH EVERS
"THE TROJAN"
MIDDLE-MAN OF THE FAMOUS DOUBLE PLAY COMBINATION OF TINKER TO EVERS TO CHANCE. WITH THE PENNANT WINNING CHICAGO CUBS OF 1906,'07-08-10 AND WITH THE BOSTON BRAVES' MIRACLE TEAM OF 1914, VOTED MOST VALUABLE PLAYER IN N.L. IN 1914. SERVED AS PLAYER, COACH AND MANAGER IN BIG LEAGUES AND AS A SCOUT FROM 1902 THROUGH 1934. SHARES RECORD FOR MAKING MOST SINGLES IN FOUR GAME WORLD SERIES.

CHARLES LEO (GABBY) HARTNETT
CHICAGO N.L. 1922 TO 1940
NEW YORK N.L. 1941
CAUGHT 100 OR MORE GAMES PER SEASON FOR 12 YEARS, EIGHT IN SUCCESSION, 1930 TO 1937 FOR LEAGUE RECORD. SET MARK FOR CONSECUTIVE CHANCES FOR CATCHER WITHOUT ERROR, 452 IN 1933-34. HIGHEST FIELDING AVERAGE FOR CATCHER IN 100 OR MORE GAMES IN 7 SEASONS; MOST PUTOUTS N.L. 7292; MOST CHANCES ACCEPTED N.L. 8546. LIFETIME BATTING AVERAGE .297.

WILLIAM JENNINGS HERMAN
CHICAGO, N.L.   BROOKLYN, N.L.
BOSTON, N.L.   PITTSBURGH, N.L.
1931 - 1947
MASTER OF HIT-AND-RUN PLAY OWNED .304 LIFETIME BATTING AVERAGE. MADE 200 OR MORE HITS IN SEASON THREE TIMES. LED LEAGUE IN HITS (227) AND DOUBLES (57) IN 1935. SET MAJOR LEAGUE RECORD FOR SECOND BASEMEN WITH FIVE SEASONS OF HANDLING 900 OR MORE CHANCES AND N.L. MARK OF 466 PUTOUTS IN 1933. LED LOOP KEYSTONERS IN PUTOUTS SEVEN TIMES.

ROGERS HORNSBY
NATIONAL LEAGUE BATTING CHAMPION 7 YEARS - 1920 TO 1925;1928. LIFETIME BATTING AVERAGE .358 HIGHEST IN NATIONAL LEAGUE HISTORY. HIT .424 IN 1924, 20TH CENTURY MAJOR LEAGUE RECORD. MANAGER 1926 WORLD CHAMPION ST. LOUIS CARDINALS. MOST-VALUABLE-PLAYER 1925 AND 1929.

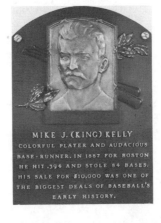

MIKE J. (KING) KELLY
COLORFUL PLAYER AND AUDACIOUS BASE-RUNNER. IN 1887 FOR BOSTON HE HIT .394 AND STOLE 84 BASES. HIS SALE FOR $10,000 WAS ONE OF THE BIGGEST DEALS OF BASEBALL'S EARLY HISTORY.

JOSEPH VINCENT McCARTHY
CHICAGO N.L. 1926 - 1930
NEW YORK A.L. 1931 - 1946
BOSTON A.L. 1948 - 1950
OUTSTANDING MANAGER WHO NEVER PLAYED IN MAJOR LEAGUES. THE MAJOR LEAGUE TEAMS MANAGED BY HIM DURING 24 YEARS NEVER FINISHED OUT OF FIRST DIVISION. WON PENNANTS CHICAGO N.L. 1929, NEW YORK A.L. 1932-6-7-8-9-41-2-3. WON SEVEN WORLD'S CHAMPIONSHIPS WITH NEW YORK YANKEES - FOUR OF THEM CONSECUTIVELY 1936-7-8-9.

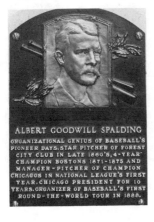

ALBERT GOODWILL SPALDING
ORGANIZATIONAL GENIUS OF BASEBALL'S PIONEER DAYS. STAR PITCHER OF FOREST CITY CLUB IN LATE 1860'S, 4-YEAR' CHAMPION BOSTONS 1871-1875 AND MANAGER - PITCHER OF CHAMPION CHICAGOS IN NATIONAL LEAGUE'S FIRST YEAR. CHICAGO PRESIDENT FOR 10 YEARS. ORGANIZER OF BASEBALL'S FIRST ROUND-THE-WORLD TOUR IN 1888.

JOSEPH B. TINKER
FAMOUS AS A MEMBER OF ONE OF BASEBALL'S GREATEST DOUBLE PLAY COMBINATIONS - FROM TINKER TO EVERS TO CHANCE. A BIG LEAGUER FROM 1902 THROUGH 1916 WITH THE CHICAGO CUBS AND CINCINNATI REDS AND THE CHICAGO FEDS. MANAGER CINCINNATI 1913 AND CHICAGO N.L. 1916. SHORTSTOP ON CUBS' TEAM THAT WON PENNANTS IN 1906,'07 '08 AND 1910.

Hack Wilson, the Cubs' great home run hitter, chats with his American League counterpart—Babe Ruth.

Tinker to Evers to Chance

This poem was written by Franklin P. Adams, a columnist for the New York World. Adams' verse helped immortalize the Cubs' double play combination of shortstop Joe Tinker, second baseman Johnny Evers and first baseman Frank Chance.

These are the saddest of possible words —
    Tinker to Evers to Chance.
A trio of bear Cubs and fleeter than birds —
    Tinker to Evers to Chance.
Ruthlessly pricking our gonfalon bubble —
Making a Giant hit into a double —
Words that are weighty with nothing but trouble —
    Tinker to Evers to Chance.

Joe Tinker, Johnny Evers, Frank Chance.

Don Kessinger spears a high liner.

7
ALL-TIME ROSTER INDEX (1876-1981)

A

Abbey, Albert	1893-95
Abernathy, Ted	1965-66, 1969-70
Aberson, Clifford	1947-49
Adair, James	1931
Adams, Bobby	1957-59
Adams, Charles ("Red")	1946
Adams, Earl ("Sparky")	1922-27
Adams, Karl	1915
Adams, Robert ("Mike")	1976-77
Addis, Robert	1952-53
Addy, Robert	1876
Adkins, Dewey	1949
Aguirre, Henry ("Hank")	1969-70
Aker, Jack	1972-73
Alderson, Dale	1943-44
Aldridge, Vic	1917-18
	1922-24
Alexander, Grover Cleveland	1918-26
Alexander, Matt	1973-74
Allen, Artemus ("Nick")	1916
Allen, Ethan	1936
Allison, Milo	1913-14
Altman, George	1959-62
	1965-67
Amalfitano, Joseph	1964-67
Amor, Vincente	1955
Anderson, Bob	1957-62
Andre, John	1955

Andrews, James	1890
Andrus, Fred	1876, 1884
Angley, Thomas	1929
Anson, Adrian ("Cap")	1876-97
Archer, James	1909-17
Arcia, Jose	1968
Asbell, James	1938
Ashburn, Richie	1960-61
Aspromonte, Kenneth	1963
Atwell, Maurice ("Toby")	1952-53
Averill, Earl	1959-60

B

Baczewski, Fred	1953
Badcock, Tom	
Baecht, Edward	1932-32
Bailey, Abraham ("Sweetbreads")	1919-21
Bailey, Edgar	1965
Baker, Gene	1953-57
Baker, Thomas	1963
Baldwin, Mark	1887-88
Balsamo, Anthony	1962
Banks, Ernie	1953-71
Barber, Turner	1917-22
Barber, Stephen	1970
Barnes, Ross	1876-77
Barragan, Facundo ("Cuno")	1961-63

267

Callison, Johnny	1969-71	Clines, Gene	1977-79
Calmus, Richard	1967	Clingman, William	1900
Camilli, Adolph	1933-34	Clymer, Otis	1913
Camp, Llewellyn	1893-94	Coakley, Andrew	1908-09
Camp, Winfield	1894	Cogan, Richard	1899
Campbell, Arthur ("Vin")	1908	Coggins, Frank	1972
Campbell, Gilly	1933	Cohen, Hyman	1955
Campbell, Joseph	1967	Colborn, James	1969-71
Campbell, Ronald	1964-66	Cole, David	1954
Canava, James	1892	Cole, Leonard	1909-12
Cannizzaro, Chris	1971	Coleman, Joe	1976
Capilla, Doug	1979-81	Collins, James ("Rip")	1937-38
Cardenal, Jose	1972-77	Collins, Philip	1923
Cardwell, Don	1960-62	Collins, Robert	1940
Carleton, James ("Tex")	1935-38	Collins, William	1911
Carlsen, Donald	1948	Collum, Jack	1957
Carlson, Harold	1927-30	Comellas, Jorge	1945
Carney, William	1904	Compton, Clint	1972
Carpenter, Robert	1947	Congalton, William	1902
Carroll, Samuel ("Cliff")	1890-91	Connor, James	1892, 1897-99
Carson, Alexander	1910	Connors, Bill	1966
Carter, Paul	1916-20	Connors, Kevin ("Chuck")	1951
Carty, Rico	1973	Cook, James	1903
Caruthers, Robert	1893	Cooney, James	1926-27
Casey, Hugh	1935	Cooper, Wilbur ("Arlie")	1925-26
Casey, James ("Doc")	1903-05	Cooper, Mort	1949
Cassidy, John	1878	Cooper, Walker	1954-55
Caudill, Bill	1979-81	Corcoran, Lawrence	1880-85
Cavarretta, Phil	1934-53	Corcoran, Mike	1884
Ceccarelli, Arthur	1959-60	Corriden, John ("Red")	1913-15
Chambers, Clifford	1948	Corridon, Frank	1904
Chance, Frank	1898-1912	Cosman, James	1970
Chapman, Harry	1912	Cotter, Harvey	1922, 1924
Cheeves, Virgil	1920-23	Cotter, Richard	1912
Cheney, Lawrence	1911-15	Cottrell, Ensign	1912
Childs, Clarence	1900-01	Coughlin, Roscoe ("William")	1890
Childs, George ("Pete")	1901	Covington, Wes	1966
Chipman, Robert	1944-49	Cowan, Billy	1963-64
Chiti, Harry	1950-56	Cox, Larry	1978
Christopher, Lloyd	1945	Croft, Henry	1901
Church, Emory ("Bubba")	1953-55	Crosby, George	1884
Church, Leonard	1966	Crosby, Ken	1975-76
Churry, John	1924-27	Cross, Joffre	1948
Clark, Frederick	1902	Cruz, Hector	1978, 1981
Clarke, Henry	1898	Culler, Richard	1948
Clarke, Sumpter	1920	Culp, Ray	1967
Clarke, Tommy	1918	Cunningham, Bert	1900-01
Clarkson, John	1884-87	Curley, Walter ("Doc")	1899
Clausen, Frederick	1893-94	Currie, Clarence	1903
Clemmons, Clement	1916	Curtis, Jack	1961-62
Clemmons, Douglas	1964-65	Cusick, John	1951
Cline, Ty	1966	Cuyler, Hazen ("Kiki")	1928-35

Graham, George	1903, 1911	Hartenstein, Charles	1965-68
Grammas, Alex	1962-63	Hartnett, Leo ("Gabby")	1922-40
Grampp, Henry	1927, 1929	Hartsel, Tullos ("Topsy")	1902
Grantham, George	1922-24	Harvey, Erwin	1900
Graves, Joseph	1926	Hatten, Joseph	1951-52
Green, Edward ("Danny")	1898-1902	Hatton, Grady	1960
Gregory, Leroy	1964	Hayes, Bill	1980-81
Griffin, John ("Hank")	1911	Hayden, John	1908
Griffin, Mike	1981	Healey, John	1889
Griffith, Clarke	1893-1900	Heath, William	1969
Griffith, Edward	1892	Heathcote, Clifton	1922-30
Griffith, Thomas	1925	Hechinger, Michael	1912-13
Grigsby, Denver	1923-25	Hegan, James	1960
Grimes, Burleigh	1932-33	Heist, Alfred	1960-61
Grimes, Oscar ("Ray")	1921-24	Hemsley, Ralston ("Rollie")	1931-32
Grimm, Charles	1925-36	Henderson, Ken	1979-80
Gross, Greg	1977-78	Henderson, Steve	1981
Groth, Edward	1904	Hendley, Robert	1965-67
Gudat, Marv	1932	Hendrick, Harvey	1933
Gumbert, Addison	1888-89, 1891-92	Hendricks, Elrod	1972
Gura, Larry	1970-73	Hendricks, John	1902
Gustine, Frank	1949	Hendrix, Claude	1916-20
Guth, Emil ("Charlie")	1880	Hennessey, George	1945
		Henry, William	1958-59
H		Henshaw, Roy	1933, 1935-36
		Herman, Floyd ("Babe")	1933-34
Haas, Eddie	1957	Herman, William	1931-41
Hack, Stan	1932-47	Hermanski, Eugene	1951-53
Hacker, Warren	1948-57	Hernandez, Guillermo ("Wilie")	1977-81
Hageman, Kurt ("Casey")	1914	Hernandez, Salvador ("Chico")	1942-43
Hagerman, Zeriah	1909	Hernon, Thomas	1897
Hairston, Johnny	1969	Herrmann, LeRoy	1932-33
Hall, Jimmie	1969-70	Herrnstein, John	1966
Hall, Mel	1981	Herzog, Charles ("Buck")	1919-20
Hallinan, James	1877-78	Hiatt, Jack	1970
Hamner, Ralph	1947-49	Hibbard, John	1884
Hands, Bill	1966-72	Hickey, Mikew	1901
Haney, Frederick	1927	Hickman, Jim	1968-73
Hankinson, Frank	1878-79	Higbe, Kirby	1937-39
Hamilton, Steve	1972	Higginbotham, Irving	1909
Hanlon, William	1903	Hildebrand, R.E.	1902
Hanson, Earl	1921	Hiller, Frank	1950-51
Hanyzewski, Edward	1942-46	Hillman, Dave	1955-59
Harbidge, William	1878-79	Hines, Paul	1876-77
Hardie, Lewis	1886	Hiser, Gene	1971-75
Hardin, William	1952	Hoak, Donald	1956
Hardy, Alex	1902-03	Hobbie, Glen	1957-64
Hardy, John	1907	Hoeft, Billy	1965-66
Hargrove, Eugene	1913-15	Hoffman, Lawrence	1901
Harley, Richard	1903	Hofman, Arthur ("Solly")	1904-12, 1916
Harper, Charles	1906	Hogg, Brad	1915
Harrell, Raymond	1939	Holley, Edward	1928
Harris, Vic	1974-75		

Hollison, John	1892
Hollocher, Charles	1918-24
Holm, Billy	1943-44
Holmes, Frederick	1904
Holtzman, Ken	1965-71, 1978-79
Honan, Martin	1890-91
Hooton, Burt	1971-75
Horne, Berlyn	1929
Hornsby, Rogers	1929-32
Hosley, Tim	1975-76
Houseman, John	1894
Howard, George	1907-09
Howe, Calvin	1952
Howell, Jay	1981
Hubbs, Ken	1961-63
Hudson, Johnny	1941
Hughes, Edward	1902
Hughes, James	1956
Hughes, Roy	1944-45
Hughes, Terry	1970
Hughes, Thomas	1900-01
Hughey, James	1893
Humphreys, Robert	1965
Humphries, Bert	1913-15
Hundley, Randy	1966-73, 1976-77
Hunter, Herbert	1916-17
Huntzinger, Walter	1926
Hurst, Don	1934
Hutchinson, Edward	1890
Hutchison, William	1889-95
Hutson, Herb	1974

I

Irvin, Monford ("Monte")	1956
Irwin, Charles	1893-95
Isbell, Frank	1898

J

Jackson, Larry	1963-66
Jackson, Louis	1958-59
Jackson, Ransom	1950-55
Jacobs, Tony	1948
Jacobs, Elmer	1924-25
Jacobs, Morris	1902
Jacobs, Raymond	1928
Jacobson, Merwin	1916
Jaeckel, Paul	1964
Jaegar, Joseph	1920
Jahn, Arthur	1925
James, Cleo	1970-71, 1973
James, Richard	1967
Jeffcoat, Harold	1948-55

Jelincich, Frank	1941
Jenkins, Ferguson	1966-73
Jimenez, Manuel	1969
Johnson, Abraham	1893
Johnson, Benjamin	1959-60
Johnson, Cliff	1980
Johnson, David	1978
Johnson, Donald	1943-48
Johnson, Kenneth	1969
Johnson, Louis	1960, 1968
Johnson, Richard	1958
Johnston, James	1914
Joiner, Ray	1934-35
Jones, Charles	1877
Jones, Clarence	1967-68
Jones, Davey	1902-04
Jones, Percy	1920-22, 1925-28
Jones, Samuel ("Sad Sam")	1955-56
Jones, Sheldon	1953
Jonnard, Claude	1929
Jurges, William	1931-38, 1946-47

K

Kahoe, Michael	1901-02, 1907
Kaiser, Al	1911
Kaiser, Donald	1955-57
Kane, John	1909-10
Katoll, John	1898-99
Kaufman, Anthony	1921-27
Kearns, Edward ("Ted")	1924-25
Keating, Walter	1913-15
Keen, Howard	1921-25
Kelleher, John	1921-23
Kelleher, Mick	1976-80
Kellert, Frank	1956
Kelly, George	1930
Kelly, Joseph	1916
Kelly, Joseph	1926, 1928
Kelly, Michael ("King")	1880-86
Kelly, Robert	1951-53
Kennedy, Sherman	1902
Kennedy, Theodore	1885
Kenzie, Walter	1884
Keough, Marty	1966
Kerr, John ("Mel")	1925
Kessinger, Don	1964-75
Kilduff, Peter	1917-19
Killefer, William	1918-21
Killen, Frank	1900
Kilroy, Matthew	1898
Kimball, Newel	1937-38
Kimm, Bruce	1979

Z

8
CHRONOLOGICAL INDEX

Bottle throwing incident,
   in Brooklyn 7/8/07, 5/20/27
   at Wrigley Field 9/16/23
BOUDREAU, Lou, radio announcer;
   and, Grimm, Charlie, manager; switch
   positions 5/4/60
BOURQUE, Pat 6/10/73
BOWA, Larry 5/17/79
Boy's Benefit Game 7/11/49, 8/14/72
BRADLEY, George 5/5/1876, 5/8/1877
BRECHEEN, Harry 4/20/46, 4/23/48
BRESNAHAN, Roger 5/1/14
BREWER, Jim 8/4/60
BRICKHOUSE, Jack 4/16/48
BRIGGS, Herb "Buttons" 9/18/04
BROCK, Lou 5/13/62, 5/20/62, 6/17/62, 5/4/63,
                                              6/15/64, 8/13/79
BROGLIO, Ernie 6/15/64
BROSNAN, Jim 4/24/57
BROWN, Mordecai 12/12/03, 6/13/04, 6/13/05, 7/4/06,
                                              8/7/06, 9/1/06, 9/13/06, 10/9/06,
                                              10/1/06, 10/12/06, 6/21/07, 7/8/07,
                                              9/23/07, 10/12/07, 7/4/08, 7/17/08,
                                              10/1/08, 10/4/08, 10/10/08, 10/13/08,
                                              6/25/09, 9/16/09, 10/15/09, 5/30/10,
                                              6/28/10, 10/22/10, 8/7/11, 9/22/38,
                                              9/8/72
BRUSH, John 8/7/06
BRYANT, Clay 8/28/37
BUCKNER, Bill 1/11/77, 5/17/79, 4/19/80
BUHL, Bob 5/20/62, 4/21/66
BURNS, Tommy 7/24/1882, 9/9/1882, 5/30/1883,
                                              9/6/1883, 7/4/1884, 9/27/1884,
                                              7/1/1885, 7/28/1888, 8/16/1890
BURRIS, Ray 7/13/77
BURTON, Ellis 8/1/63, 9/7/64
BUSH, Guy 5/14/27, 6/18/29, 8/9/29, 10/11/29,
                                              6/23/30, 6/27/30, 9/13/31, 9/20/32,
                                              9/30/33, 9/22/34, 11/22/34, 4/29/35
BYRON, Bill 9/13/13

C

CALLAGHAN, Marty 5/4/23
CALLAHAN, Jimmy 6/29/1897, 4/30/1899
CALLISON, Johnny 8/19/70
CAMILLI, Dolf 5/11/34
CANAVAN, James 4/4/1892
CARDENAL, Jose 5/1/73, 5/2/76
CARDWELL, Don 5/15/60
CARLETON, Tex 6/25/37
CARLSON, Hal 6/16/27, 8/3/29

D

E

five in a game, Cap Anson	8/26/1876
20 in a game by Cub opponent	9/25/1885
Errorless chances, 418 in a row by	
Ken Hubbs	9/5/62
Errorless games, 54 in a row by	
Stan Hack	7/4/42
78 in a row by Ken Hubbs	9/5/62
ERSKINE, Carl	6/19/52
EVERETT, Bill	7/17/1895, 4/17/1898, 5/25/1898,
	6/6/1898, 6/5/1899
EVERS, Johnny	9/15/02, 6/11/04, 9/14/05, 4/16/06,
	9/3/08, 8/27/10, 7/18/12, 12/12/13
EWING, Bob	4/19/02
Ex-Cubs whip former club as Dodgers	7/14/42
Extra-base hits; five (three doubles	
& two triples) in one game; George	
Gore	7/9/1885
43 in a doubleheader	7/12/31
Extra-inning games	
22 innings, Cubs 4 at Boston 3	5/17/27
21 innings, Cubs 2 at Philadelphia 1	7/17/18
20 innings, Cubs 7 vs. Cincinnati 7	6/30/1892
Cubs 2 at Philadelphia 1	8/24/05
19 innings, Cubs 3 vs. Pittsburgh 2	6/22/02
18 innings, Cubs 2 at St. Louis 1	6/24/05
Cubs 7 at Boston 2	5/14/27
Cubs 10 at Cincinnati 8	8/9/42
. Cubs 9 vs. Cincinnati 8	5/10-7/23/79
17 innings, Cubs 2 vs. Cincinnati 1	9/18/04
Cubs 3 vs. St. Louis 2	10/1/20
14 innings, longest game in history	
to date	7/4/1882
most runs scored in an inning,	
nine in 12th	7/23/23

F

FABER, Red	10/5/33
FARRELL, Charles	8/14/1889
Dick	4/18/62
FAUL, Bill	7/14/65, 7/25/65, 10/3/65
FAUTZ, Dave	10/21/1886
Fight between	
Joe Tinker & fan	4/16/06
Joe Tinker & Johnny Evers	9/14/05
Rabbit Maranville & taxi driver	7/6/25
Hack Wilson & milkman in stands	6/21/28
Hack Wilson & Red pitcher at	
train station	7/4/29
Fire in grandstand at West Side	
Grounds	8/5/1894
at Bridgeport, Conn	8/18/07
FLACK, Max	7/17/18, 5/30/22
Flag, U.S. National Ensign, rescued	
by Rick Monday	4/25/76

RANEW, Merritt 7/21/63
RADER, Dave 6/26/78
RAYMER, Fred 6/14/01
REINHART, Wit 4/20/26
REUSCHEL, Paul 8/21/75
        Rick 6/26/72, 6/20/74, 8/21/75
REULBACH, Ed 6/24/05, 8/24/05, 8/7/06, 9/19/06,
        10/1/06, 10/10/06, 9/23/07, 10/10/07,
        7/4/08, 9/26/08, 10/1/08, 10/10/08,
        8/10/09, 9/22/38
REYNOLDS, Carl 10/6/30
        Ken 9/26/71
Rhubarb between Cubs & Dodgers
  at Ebbets Field 5/22/46
RICE, Jim 7/11/78
RICHARD, Gene 6/9/78
RICHIE, Lou 8/13/13
RICKERT, Marv 6/23/46, 7/29/47
"Rifleman" TV series star in later
  years, Chuck Connors, hits second
  & final homer 8/26/51
RIGLER, Cy 7/4/29
Riot at Polo Grounds 5/21/07
ROBERTS, Robin 7/29/51, 6/9/54, 6/9/57
ROBERTSON, Charlie 5/14/27
ROBINSON, Hank 5/1/14
        Jackie 5/18/47
RODGERS, Andre 6/6/62, 9/30/62, 7/21/63, 4/21/64
RODRIGUEZ, Roberto 7/5/70
ROE, Preacher 8/30/45
ROOT, Charlie 9/29/26, 5/1/27, 5/19/28, 9/2/32,
        10/1/32, 8/28/37, 10/1/38, 8/27/41
ROSE, Pete 7/14/70
ROSELLO, Davey 5/17/77, 7/28/77
RUCKER, Nap 8/2/11
RUSH, Bob 6/25/49, 7/8/52, 8/2/55
RUSIE, Amos 10/31/1890
RUSSELL, "Rip" 9/6/39
RUTH, Babe
  1-0 World Series duel with Jim Vaughn . 9/5/18
  "calls his shot" at Wrigley Field 10/1/32
  other subjects 6/17/62
Runs, team (also see "High scoring
  games")
    18 in an inning (7th) 9/6/1883
    14 in an inning (4th) 8/25/22
    13 in an inning (5th) 8/16/1890
    12 in an inning (6th) 5/8/1890
      (4th) 7/17/1895
      (7th) 5/28/25
      (8th) 5/5/38

U

V

THE AUTHORS

Gold (left), Ahrens (right)

Autobiographical Sketch by Edward Alan Gold

On May 10, 1932, Lou Warneke pitched a five-hitter, Billy Jurges drove in three runs, the Cubs beat the Giants 9-2 — and I was born in Green Bay, Wis. I attended my first game on Aug. 1, 1939 and saw Bill (Swish) Nicholson hit his first big league homer in his Cub debut. For the past 31 years I've been a member of the Sun-Times sports department, with time out for the Korean War (I was on our side, I think). Over the years I've covered Black Hawks' hockey, horse racing and harness racing. I've authored **Eddie Gold's White Sox and Cubs Trivia Book,** am a member of the Society for American Baseball Research, am married, reside on Chicago's Northwest Side, have two sons, two cats and a dog named "Cubby."

Autobiographical Sketch by Arthur Ronald Ahrens

I was born in Chicago, March 12, 1949, and have lived in the area all my life, both in the city and the suburbs. The year I was born the Cubs finished in last place, although I hope there was no cause and effect relationship involved. I have been a Cub fan since 1956, and went to my first game on September 26, 1959. I have studied baseball history since I was ten years old, and have been contributing free lance articles since 1972. My writings have appeared in **Baseball Digest, Baseball Research Journal, Chicago History, Chicago Sport Scene, Sports Scoop, The Diamond Report,** and **National Pastime.** I have a Bachelor of Arts Degree from University of Illinois, where I majored in speech and minored in history. I am a member of Society for American Baseball Research and Catholic Alumni Club. I presently live on Chicago's Northwest Side, and for the benefit (?) of any female reader, I am an eligible bachelor.